The Presidents of American Fiction

T0244203

The Presidents of American Fiction

Fashioning the U.S. Political Imagination

Michael J. Blouin

BLOOMSBURY ACADEMIC
NEW YORK · LONDON · OXFORD · NEW DELHI · SYDNEY

BLOOMSBURY ACADEMIC
Bloomsbury Publishing Inc
1385 Broadway, New York, NY 10018, USA
50 Bedford Square, London, WC1B 3DP, UK
29 Earlsfort Terrace, Dublin 2, Ireland

BLOOMSBURY, BLOOMSBURY ACADEMIC and the Diana logo are trademarks of
Bloomsbury Publishing Plc

First published in the United States of America 2023

Cover design: Eleanor Rose
Cover images: Lincoln Memorial © Brendan Wahl / EyeEm / Getty Images; American flag
© CSA-Printstock / Getty Images; Kennedy for President, poster circa 1960 © Alamy

A catalogue record for this book is available from the British Library.

A catalog record for this book is available from the Library of Congress.

ISBN: HB: 978-1-5013-8170-6
PB: 978-1-5013-8169-0
ePDF: 978-1-5013-8172-0
eBook: 978-1-5013-8171-3

Typeset by Deanta Global Publishing Services, Chennai, India
Printed and bound in the United States of America

To find out more about our authors and books visit www.bloomsbury.com and sign up for
our newsletters.

Dedicated to My Brothers:
Jesse, Ethan, and Josh

CONTENTS

Acknowledgments viii

Introduction: Moving Portraits of the President 1

1   James Fenimore Cooper's Exceptional Presidents 19

2   George Lippard and the Gothic President 41

3   William Wells Brown and the Disembodied President 61

4   The President in Books for Boys 81

5   The President in Books for Girls 101

6   Hamlin Garland, Ulysses S. Grant, and the Tortured Heart of American Realism 121

7   Gore Vidal and the Performative Presidency 139

8   The Imperial Presidents of American Literature 159

Epilogue: George Saunders and Presidential Melancholia 185

References 197
Index 209

ACKNOWLEDGMENTS

This book was written during a pandemic—a time during which the importance of my community was dramatically heightened. My partner, Kate, supported me in every way imaginable, my two daughters, Emerson and Willow, reminded me on a daily basis why the future matters, and my mother offered ceaseless encouragement. My colleagues and students at Milligan University gave me the fertile space in which to cultivate the germs of ideas that now fill the pages of this book.

Beyond the incredibly perceptive comments that I received from the editors and reviewers at Bloomsbury, I have benefited from the keen insights of a number of friends and colleagues during the composition of this book: Dana Nelson, who helped me to understand why literature matters in these conversations; Dale Townshend, who led me to rethink the importance of the king with two bodies; Sean McCann, who prompted me to refine my reading of Roth's *Plot Against America*; Sarah Turner, who encouraged me to dig even deeper into William Wells Brown's unique political context; Jay Parini, who graciously shared his wisdom concerning the life and works of Gore Vidal; Ann Larabee, who provided keen editorial insights; and special thanks to Todd McGowan, who read most of the chapters and, as always, challenged me to exceed my own limitations. The strengths of this book can be traced back to the generous feedback of these individuals; the book's weaknesses remain my own.

Introduction

Moving Portraits of the President

Among other things, the presidency is a fiction. While most contemporary readers are accustomed to consuming images of America's commander in chief as a lightning rod on cable news, a titanic figure on the silver screen, or a series of semi-disjointed soundbites filtered through social media, generations of citizens first familiarized themselves with POTUS in the pages of American prose.[1] Since the medium remains the message, readers ought to contemplate how this particular medium frames the presidency.[2] Readers might, in turn, recognize literature as an indispensable medium for maintaining the complexities of this prominent American symbol. It is not just that one *could* interpret the president as a fiction—one *must*.

To be clear, this book does not merely survey the presidents featured in American fiction, nor does it simply index the accuracy of renditions of chief magistrates. Instead, it investigates the presidency as "a publicly sanctioned shorthand," "a constant point of reference in political discussion and popular culture, in which we are all implicated," and "a system of signs which settles deep in the symbolic foundations of a society" (Fielding et al. 2020: 1–3).[3] Audiences have read the presidency as a myth, an organizing principle, and a disciplinary strategy. When Americans contemplate the president, a topic to which many of them dedicate a tremendous amount of their daily time and energy, they contemplate much more than an elected official. In oft-

---

[1]For the sake of variety, I interchangeably employ a handful of terms to describe the president, including commander in chief, POTUS, executive, and chief magistrate. The term "POTUS" is a relatively recent invention, and the term "commander in chief" undoubtedly carries with it the baggage of the military-industrial complex. In other words, each of these designations contains, within itself, its own complexities—a point that only further enhances my thesis.

[2]See McLuhan (1964).

[3]A recent study of Winston Churchill by Fielding et. al. offers an interesting site for further study. How do popular representations of the British prime minister compare to popular representations of the American president? That is, just how "American" is the phenomenon outlined in this book?

unexpected ways, the executives of American fiction help shape (*mise en forme*) as well as stage (*mise-en-scène*) a democratic consciousness.

Countless writers and readers continue to be drawn to the President of the United States (POTUS), not only due to the omnipresence of this character in America's political imagination, but because the office itself has been so loosely defined and, therefore, leaves plenty of room for creative license. Outlined in Article II of the Constitution, the presidency serves as a source of frustrating—but, as we shall see, essential—uncertainty.[4] Crystallized in the Helvidius-Pacificus debates between Alexander Hamilton and James Madison, as well as the passionate parleys that took place during the Constitutional Convention of 1787, American thinkers have long investigated the makeup of the presidency. Is the commander in chief a fulfillment of democracy's promise, or its antithesis? What, if anything, could be done to curb presidential excesses should occupants of the office wield their authority in a problematic fashion? For scholars of the presidency, these questions remain rich reservoirs of philosophical, political, and cultural concern. However, with several important exceptions, literary critics have not yet participated in the larger debates. And our silence is confounding, since many of the threads woven into these inquiries remain part and parcel of literary analysis: genre and its attendant complexities; power and symbolic representation; and the belief that reading with care remains a democratic imperative. Fictional POTUS trains citizens to construct and deconstruct national plotlines by offering sites of recognition as well as resistance. If readers accept the premise that the chief magistrate is at least partially a fiction, it behooves them to pursue more insightful readings of the presidency.

Still, a significant percentage of readers hesitate to treat the presidency as a fiction. Many American intellectuals have been reluctant to consider politics as aesthetics, or to recognize aesthetics as politics. For his part, Hamilton doubted the validity of attempts to render the commander in chief in a fictional guise, rather churlishly deploring the "regions of fiction" for working "to disfigure or . . . to metamorphose the (presidential) object" through "devices" that "pervert the public opinion" (Hamilton 1987: 389–90). Jeff Smith summarizes Hamilton's position: "A president who was fully represented in the literary sense would be less representative in the way a republic needed him to be" (Smith 2009: 42). Because novels deal with the interiority of subjects, which is to say, because literary characters prove all-too-human over the course of a given narrative, readers might worry that fiction could seriously damage the honorable standing of an executive. Fiction either overly dramatizes the presidency, and thus depicts the chief magistrate as akin to a monarch, or, by exposing the reality of the man beneath the pomp, fiction

---

[4]E. S. Corwin describes Article II as the "most loosely drawn chapter of the Constitution" (Corwin 1948: 2).

diminishes the larger-than-life persona needed to embody—and effectively rule over—a nation. Ironically, even as Hamilton criticized "scurrilous" antifederalist attacks on the proposed presidency, he busily constructed his counter-fiction (particularly in Federalist 72), fantasizing about the narrative underpinnings of future presidencies. It remains preposterous, then, to think that writers and readers would not gravitate incessantly toward POTUS. Furthermore, to separate the president from the collective imaginary of the young republic is to uphold an illusion that politics and literature are not always and everywhere co-constitutive. As Smith counters, "Rulership of any kind is an essentially metaphorical act . . . The presidency could not exist without first being imagined" (Smith 2009: 7, 19).

Of course, one could reasonably worry that by dwelling on the presidency authors spread a highly noxious fiction. Dana Nelson confronts the negative aspects of presidentialism (or, America's unsavory reliance upon the president as a symbolic catchall). She argues that presidentialism endangers democracy by making "the unpleasantness of political disagreement go away" and teaching "citizens to abjure political disagreement, and—importantly—to feel most democratic in the moment that we cede our self-governing agency to the president" (Nelson 2008: 16–17). Subsequently, one might assume that twenty-first century audiences remain placated by the presidential fetishes that crop up in American letters. One could presume that the fictionalized commander in chief unswervingly functions as a coercive tool for generating or reinforcing consensus among a coalition of readers. Without a doubt, some fictionalized executives do promote the illusion of consensus, or they are clearly intended to do so. Nevertheless, when a given author erects such a figure, she never guarantees anything like unanimity. By its nature as a textual medium, literature can never present the presidency in strictly monolithic terms. In truth, fictional presidents remind readers of the inherent slipperiness of all texts: neighbors interpret a given executive through starkly different prisms; one reader's perspective on a given chief magistrate will evolve from moment to moment; and what individuals consciously or unconsciously seek to get out of these presidential encounters diverges from what they receive.

As heavily constructed texts, presidents sustain disagreement—a point that critics of presidentialism miss if they overlook the crucial part that literature plays in sustaining the office. For his part, Pierre Rosanvallon describes presidentialism as a "pathology of representation," as "a sort of national disease for which a cure (will) have to be found," and he encourages his readers to demand a panacea for ills caused by demagogues (Rosanvallon 2018: 10, 5). However, to rush for a cure to presidentialism is to ignore what truly drives readers in their readerly encounters with POTUS: not absolute satisfaction, but its constant deferral. Fictionalized presidents do not foreclose political disagreement; they problematize static representations of the office and induce skirmishes among interpreters. While authoritarian regimes attempt to limit possible interpretations of their supreme leaders, democracy demands that fictional presidents be read through more than one lens. To re-read the chief magistrate as a literary text therefore complicates the presumed homogeneity of a presidential fetish. That is, to approach the presidency as a fiction empowers readers to appreciate inconsistencies within America's political as well as aesthetic imaginaries.

There is no doubt that presidentialism currently holds sway through constructions of POTUS in pre-packaged political speeches and via blind consumerism. Presidentialism lacks precious few signs of subtlety in venues like cable news. The vice-like grip of presidentialism may be partially a byproduct of a cultural shift away from literature in the twentieth and twenty-first centuries—a cultural shift in which the executive appears predominantly as a flattened icon, marketed by merchants accustomed to shorter attention spans and devoured by individuals accustomed to easily digested propaganda. Consumed increasingly through the spoken word, the figure of the president starts to lose a good deal of its potential, which is to say, when consumers encounter the presidency exclusively through snippets from his speeches as well as the televised commentary of politicos, they fall into the trap of *logocentrism* (an over-investment in the spoken word that misses the richness of written texts). Just what is it about literature in particular that challenges increasingly narrow perspectives on POTUS? The chapters to follow take this question as an invitation for sustained inquiry. But let us gesture at a possible answer at the start: for one, literature wrestles with its own metaphorical nature. It provides textual stand-ins for the person and/or principle, only to circle back on itself and interrogate its nature *as a text* (a tendency that endures in American writers from Herman Melville to modernist poets to Joseph McElroy).[5] Every fictional president retains within itself a resistance to its own permanence, coherence, and even legibility. This intrinsic reflexivity explains the usefulness of literature as a vehicle for taking stock of the American presidency. Readers that confront POTUS as a fiction might break away from the rut of presidentialism to ruminate on the office, its contested conciliation within the public sphere, and the dramatic revisions that will be demanded in the days ahead.

A Concise History of Presidents in American Fiction

The omnipresent commander in chief is hardly a niche icon. So, where should one establish boundaries for this sort of study, to avoid becoming unwieldy?

---

[5]Shoshana Felman refers to "the textual dynamic as a field of clashing and heterogeneous forces (with) a never quite predictable potential for *surprise*" (Felman 1993: 6, author's emphasis).

I could commence with a discussion of Phillis Wheatley, one of the country's first published African American poets, who composed a devotional poem to George Washington and then sent it to the man himself. According to Sean McCann, poetic renderings of the presidency are of the utmost significance. In recent years, both modernists and modern presidents have periodically posed as elixirs, able, "through the exercise of imagination and oratory, to cure the major ailments of liberal society and government" (McCann 2008: 20). Self-defined truth-givers, "poet and president are analogs and rivals" (21). But as McCann's analysis proves, poetry possesses its own complicated relationship to political power. The chapters that follow consequently stick to prose, omitting analysis of the poetic presidents portrayed by Wheatley, Henry Wadsworth Longfellow, William Cullen Bryant, Walt Whitman, or Carl Sandburg.

Maybe one ought to initiate this conversation, then, with the nation's first professional novelist, Charles Brockden Brown, who dedicated his 1798 novel *Wieland; Or, The Transformation: An American Tale* to Thomas Jefferson and, like Wheatley, went so far as to send a copy directly to the future president. Although the novel wrestles with the assumptions of an impending Jefferson administration, such as its emphasis on an inherently rational subject, it cannot be said to be a text singularly focused upon the chief magistrate—unless one presupposes that the novel's patriarchal madman, who kills his family because a disembodied voice tells him to do so, represents the folly of putting too much trust in a solitary leader (a bit of an interpretive stretch, given the fact that the novel was published in 1798). The earliest American literature engages with POTUS, certainly, but not typically in an overt or sustained manner.

Substantive presidents only start to surface in American fiction in the 1820s and 1830s. Infused with renewed political intrigue, the Jacksonian moment spurred greater—albeit thornier—literary engagement with the presidency. The Era of Good Feelings that preceded the presidency of Andrew Jackson, in which presidents were, in a sense, anointed rather than elected, produced few captivating portrayals of the executive. Admittedly, one could discuss how Washington Irving's arch-Federalist burlesques eventually culminated in an unusual pseudo-biography of Washington at the end of Irving's life (a text I have analyzed in depth elsewhere),[6] and one cannot bypass completely the presidential interjections of Hugh Henry Brackenridge's *Modern Chivalry* (c. 1815). Still, the commander in chief did not occupy a prominent place in the fiction of the day.[7] This reality changed

---

[6]See Blouin (2021).
[7]The satirical *Modern Chivalry* devotes an inordinate amount of attention to the chief magistrate, but predominantly as a foil to hapless rubes who think that democracy means genuine equality for everyone. At the beginning of the novel, the protagonist admits, "The lowest citizen may become chief magistrate." But, faced with a feckless crowd and unworthy

thanks to Jackson's populist push to democratize the presidency and posit the chief magistrate as an agent of that other timeless fiction, the people.[8] Writers like Edgar Allan Poe and James Fenimore Cooper, the subject of Chapter 1, subsequently turned their creative gazes upon the president. For his part, Poe scrutinized POTUS in stories like "Four Beasts in One—the Homo-Camelopard." In this oft-overlooked tale, Poe took aim at Jackson, ridiculing painted personas that "shout and gesticulate to the rabble" (Poe 1984: 183). Poe's "Four Beasts" casts doubt upon the wave of Jacksonian politics by illuminating a society that prostrates itself before an ape-like man: "The whole town is topsy-turvy ... what a Babel of languages! What a screaming of beasts!" (188). In a later story, "The Man that was Used Up," Poe once again critiqued the Jacksonian moment, this time by undercutting blowhard Brevet Brigadier General John A. B. C. Smith, whose name evokes his abject commonness. Poe's former military man—fueled by "blood and thunder, and all that!"—rises to political prominence thanks to his inflated record as a soldier (Poe 1984: 309). A fairly overt stand-in for Jackson, Smith reveals himself to be a mere assortment of slogans and, in the end, nothing more than a bundle of garments. When it comes to the presidency, Poe's tales imply that the emperor has no clothes, or, perhaps, that the emperor is nothing *but* clothes. Some of the elements in these tales resurface in the chapters that follow: later fiction about the nation's leading executive lambasts the electorate as a mindless mob—an ironically anti-democratic sentiment, given the nature of the office in question; some fiction attacks the presidency as performance in order to demonstrate the innate vacuity of the position (see, for instance, my readings of Vidal, Sinclair Lewis, John Dos Passos, and Stephen King). Although Poe's stories contemplate the presidency, they are texts designed to sabotage America's burgeoning Cult of Personality. While they make for entertaining satire, these stories are the equivalent of editorial cartoons. This book dwells instead on authors with an ambition to do more than deride or glorify a particular administration.

By considering authors like Poe and Cooper, I resist a tendency to rush ahead to twentieth-century presidents. Unlike a number of other analysts who have tackled this subject, I do not dismiss nineteenth-century texts concerned with the chief magistrate as basic *agitprop*, or hagiography. Gesturing at the

---

candidates, he quickly adds: "You are surely carrying the matter too far" (Brackenridge 2020: 21). Later, the protagonist's lowly servant, with a laughable amount of confidence, goes to visit the president in search of an appointment. Brackenridge said almost nothing about the president himself, instead using the occasion to ridicule the groveling masses as having "weak minds" and being mostly "gaping haubucks" (86–87).

[8]Daniel Walker Howe records, "Ultimate authority, that is, sovereignty, became the subject of explicit and bitter debate during Jackson's administrations ... (Jackson) believed in the sovereignty of the American people and in himself as the embodiment of that sovereignty" (Howe 2007: 367).

political machinery of pre–Civil War US politics, analysts tend to maintain that writers from this period depicted the executive as only one governmental actor among many others. Overwhelmed by unfavorable checks and balances, and enslaved to a partisan system, these analysts complain that presidents throughout the 1800s were simply too dull to occupy America's literary imagination. James Bryce asks: "Who now knows or cares to know anything about ... Franklin Pierce?" (qtd. in McCann 2008: 14). But the Pierce example is a revealing one because no less a literary giant than Nathaniel Hawthorne cared—and very deeply, in fact—about Pierce's presidency, going so far as to compose the man's campaign biography and, in the process, Hawthorne effectively destroyed his reputation among his peers.[9] Readers should not too hastily discount nineteenth-century works concerning POTUS; many of these works prove to be considerably more complex in their handling of the chief magistrate than denigrators have hitherto allowed.

Following in the wake of the Jacksonian turn, the president habitually materialized in canonical fiction composed during the American Renaissance. In his monumental *Moby Dick* (1851), Herman Melville emphasized the metaphysical underpinnings of democracy by rendering POTUS in a manner not dissimilar from his treatment of that most slippery of signifiers, the white whale: "Bear me out in it, thou great democratic God! . . . Thou who didst pick up Andrew Jackson from the pebbles; who didst hurl him upon a war-horse; who didst thunder him higher than a throne" (Melville 1973: 112).[10] Like the mighty Leviathan, Melville's Jackson grants temporary form to an otherwise formless energy—the proverbial will of the people. At the same time, the whale is only ever a whale, to be caught and dissected, and likewise, the president only ever proves to be a mortal being, destined to be cast back into the teeming sea from which he was first reeled. Another popular writer during the Renaissance, Ralph Waldo Emerson similarly unpacked the slippery position of a president caught in the web of a democratic society:

Our delight in reason degenerates into idolatry of the herald . . . we touch and go, and sip the foam of many lives. Rotation is the law of nature . . . no man, in all the procession of famous men, is reason or illumination, or the essence we were looking for; but is an exhibition, in some quarter, of new possibilities. Could we one day complete the immense figure which these flagrant points compose! (Emerson 1983a: 623, 630)

---

[9]For more on the intersection of American literature and campaign biographies, especially on the topic of Hawthorne and Pierce, see Blouin (2021).

[10]Like Poe, the younger Melville was drawn into presidential mimicry with his "Authentic Anecdotes of 'Old Zack,'" a collection of satirical letters aimed at would-be president Zackary Taylor. The letters poke fun at the indignities that often accompany a run for the highest office in the land: "Think General, of yourself reclining on the poop of the Chinese junk, receiving the visits of your friends; adopt this course and you must be elected president" (Melville 1973: n.p.).

Akin to Melville's Leviathan, Emerson's "great man" may be elevated to the level of chief magistrate, but a chief magistrate can never provide the last word of a democratic order because there will always be another immense figure to replace the previous one (and thus recommence a steady rotation of representatives). Like Emerson and Melville, Hawthorne repeatedly ruminated on the role of the president. His 1850 short story "The Great Stone Face," for example, tracks a restless people in search of a president to match their pre-existing ideals; by the close of the story, however, the protagonist has realized that he can achieve true wisdom only by recognizing the futility of his quest for a perfect commander in chief.

In this sense, literature from the American Renaissance foregrounds presidential figures to navigate uneven terrain between the One and the Many, which is to say, literature from this era consolidates the Many into the One while, at the same time, dissolving the One into the Many. Social formation in America remains an acutely restless sort of thing, specifically as it tarries around the nodal point of POTUS: "Failing to conserve difference . . . is not acceptable in America . . . (America remains) endlessly open" (Harris 2005: 36). The works of Melville, Emerson, and Hawthorne present a literary presidency that does not re-enforce societal norms but instead serves a vital function within any democratic order: opening, foreclosing, and then opening once more a nation's vision of itself, in a Sisyphean process of self-actualization. Just as the white whale embodies the universal in a singular guise, and, by so doing, says something significant about the inner mechanisms of American life, a fictionalized president encourages readers to envision the totality of their community—even as it asks them to deconstruct false idols. With their fictionalized executives, American writers sought to represent the essence of their nation in tension with a latent knowledge that this sort of representation could never fully capture the thing itself. And this failure to capture the imagined thing itself—the so-called national spirit—can be seen as merciful, since to capture it could signal an end to America's constitutive search for a City on the Hill. A literary failing of this sort could nudge modern democracy toward authoritarian designs.

The tensions that characterize fictionalized presidents endure well beyond the metaphysical heights of the American Renaissance. They continue to inform American realism in the second half of the nineteenth century, a point further developed in the chapter concerning noted realist Hamlin Garland and his book on Ulysses S. Grant. Published in 1880, during the heyday of literary realism in the United States, Henry Adams's *Democracy: An American Novel* tracks the amorphous shape of democracy through a reassessment of prior lionizations of POTUS. Adams's protagonist visits the Capitol to seek the heart of democratic society and quickly finds herself enchanted by the executive. Adams manifested his wariness with this enchantment by detailing a bust of Andrew Jackson, that super-charged example. Adams's heroine slowly realizes that she has wasted her leisure hours "reading in succession the lives and letters of the American presidents . . . what a melancholy spectacle it was, from George Washington down to the last incumbent . . . what did they amount to, after all?" (Adams 2008: 49). When she finally meets the man himself, her disappointment is palpable: the "great man" proves to be a pale substitution for his nation's assumed greatness. Adams combined this disquiet with concerns attendant to American realism: a literary mode that attempts to convey an authentic Truth and, at the same time, challenges the very notion of authenticity. Yet, while Adams sought to undermine the false pretense of the elected sovereign, thereby holding firm in his commitment to the realer-than-thou mentality of American realists in their fight against the inflated rhetoric of the Gilded Age, there is something else going on here as well, something that echoes the dialectical maneuvers of earlier writers like Melville, Emerson, and Hawthorne. Even as Adams mocked the chief magistrate for aping the monarchy, he understood well the push and pull of the presidency within the American imagination. Adams' text forces the president to fail because in Adams' estimation any plebiscitary figurehead within a democratic society must fail; nevertheless, this failure does not stop the next president from arriving with a renewed sense of optimism, "determined to be the Father of his country; to gain a proud immortality" (92). The yearning of American readers for a communitarian avatar abides. Although immersed in America's realist moment, Adams' portrait of democracy struggles with its own overly romantic proclivities, which is to say, its compulsion to erect a new, unimpeachable idol.

Nineteenth-century stories involving presidents are not exclusively concerned with POTUS as a tool meant to enforce consensus among audiences; rather, they expose an incommensurability between romanticized godheads and a democratic wrangling driven by difference—or, different interpretations held by different readers. In other words, fictional treatments of the president in the nineteenth century gave form to an ever-elusive national essence, even as they acknowledged that the Leviathan can only be glimpsed and never wrestled into submission. Dwelling on the slipperiness of executives, George Lippard, the subject of Chapter 2, wanted to endow his Founding Fathers with weighty bodies. He longed to transpose his country's word into flesh, and his final product was far from orthodox. Elsewhere, William Wells Brown, one of America's earliest African American novelists (and the subject of Chapter 3), highlighted a profound chasm that separated the fabled presidency from its real-world inheritors, including the daughter of Sally Hemings and Thomas Jefferson. Fictional presidencies do not merely affirm the status quo, or convince readers to follow the leader; they reflect the inability of an author to inscribe a single presidential narrative into the ledger of a reader's life. This rift would be further expanded in the decades to come.

POTUS and the Drive to Difference

To probe into the gap between presidential ideal and the lived realities of American readers, and thus open the doorway into twentieth-century renditions of POTUS, let us consider Americo Paredes's novel from the

1930s, *George Washington Gomez*. This seminal text follows a young man born at the border of Texas and Mexico, whose Mexican parents endow him with Washington's name in hopes that he will one day fulfill the dreams of his people. Consequently, the boy grows up with delusions of presidential grandeur at odds with his family's oppression at the hands of the abusive Texas Rangers (*rinches*). When his school selects him to memorize and recited a speech about Washington, George Washington Gomez experiences a surge of pride in his name; but when the *rinches* attack his community, he becomes estranged from what can only be described, in a superegoic sense, as the presidential part of himself: "(He) looked up eagerly at the portrait of his namesake. What a disappointment! . . . What a man to be named after" (Paredes 1990: 109). This self-divided young man occupies a liminal space as he must confront his presumed alignment with the president, an embodiment of the law. In effect, the boy's namesake provides a set of normative assumptions that establishes the horizons of his expectations and against which he must define his own hyphenated identity (as both Mexican and American). One particularly compelling scene inverts a long-standing George Washington myth composed by biographer Parson Weems: the boy witnesses the murder of his neighbor as the neighbor chops down a tree, and when law enforcement arrives, the young man flees in a panic. While Weems' mythologized Washington chops down a cherry tree to unveil his unimpeachable character and his innate connection to the law, Paredes's boy does precisely the opposite, distancing himself from the legislated reality of (white) America—an apparatus that actively undermines the interests of his community. In *George Washington Gomez*, the American presidency trains the boy, organizes his thoughts, places pressure upon his identity formation, and spurs self-discipline through internalized mandates. That is, the notion of the presidency erects a figurative border within the young man, between the mutually informed concepts of law and lawlessness. By the novel's end, the young man has become a border security officer engaged in espionage on behalf of the nation-state.

However, to read the president as a relatively straightforward component of a vast disciplinary apparatus is to overlook the ways that desire and difference actually function. In reality, the boy's split self affirms a boundary between the imagined presidency and that which eludes it—the young man's "Mexicanness"; his status as criminalized Other. A painful schism prevails.[11] Parades' text mirrors a boy from the Mexican American border with the nation's foremost Founding Father and, in so doing, explores not

---

[11]Gloria Anzaldua would describe this phenomenon as a "border culture," established "to define the places that are safe and unsafe, to distinguish *us* from *them*." As a result of this "border culture," she continues, "Not only was the brain split into two functions but so was reality. Thus people who inhabit both realities are forced to live in the interface between the two, forced to become adept at switching modes" (Anzaldua 2012: 25, 59, author's emphasis).

only significant distinctions between the confused boy and the president but also significant similarities. For instance, the historical Washington and the Mexican American adolescent play dual roles: fixed in place by the status quo yet evasive; good yet capable of evil; a reliable embodiment of the establishment yet mercifully unpredictable. Fictional POTUS undoubtedly doubles as a placeholder for an all-encompassing national ideology, or, an organizational principle of the highest order. However, POTUS also serves as a vital reminder of exteriors, antagonisms, and differences.

Indeed, Paredes's doubling of a Mexican American boy with Washington aids his audience in reassessing how the presidency functions—or, more interestingly, *fails* to function—in fashioning a cohesive political imagination for readers in the United States (the fact that such a monolithic political imaginary remains fundamentally impossible because of the slipperiness of a pluralist population remains part and parcel of my argument). Thanks to perforations like the ones on display in *George Washington Gomez*, presidents remain signs of neither wholeness nor total accord, but of something invaluable that is missing: a glorified Founding Father to inspire reverence for vanishing national origins; a Messianic redeemer for whom the citizenry must wait with bated breath. The polychromatic presence of the executive marks not a fixed point of identification, then, but an absence, or a ceaseless deferral. It advances a democratic belief that the reader's fulfillment must remain tantalizingly out of reach because if the icon of the president did, in fact, capture a national essence that binds every citizen, the open-endedness of democracy would have reached its terminus and it would be replaced by authoritarian certitude. As I discuss in Chapter 5, the pursuit of pleasure never fully subsides from these representations. Far from ready-made objects made for effortless adoration, the presidents of American fiction prove to be indispensable catalysts for disaffection.

Twentieth-century examples abound of fictional works structured around a missing commander in chief. In 1934, Rex Stout, a popular detective and mystery writer, published *The President Vanishes*, a novel in which the president fakes his kidnapping. Stout's president instigates his own absence to fuel pining in the populace—specifically, a desire for Americans to stay out of the war in Europe and, just as powerfully, the "correct" cravings in an all-too-modern girl for her hardboiled boyfriend: "They wanted their president back, and they intended to find him" (Stout 1934: 57). Stout's acknowledgment that the presidency acts not as a realization of the people's will but as a lacuna appears to reverse itself when, in the novel's *denouement*, the president acts like a stand-in for Santa Claus and rewards his faithful helpers with whatever their heart desires. But this repression only stimulates a longing in the reader for the president to go missing once more.

On a closely related note, one ought to consider the evolution of fictional genres—including the thriller, the detective story, the mystery, and the popular romance—alongside ongoing constructions of the presidency (a topic considered at length in Chapters 4, 5, and 6). The fantasies produced by writers like Stout depend upon the promise of consummation in tandem with its necessary impediment: the delayed gratification, for example, of a detective in frustrated pursuit of answers, or the romantic union that cannot be consummated until the novel's close. Of course, the plot need not feature a president who literally goes missing since, in a figurative sense, even the most visceral president is always already missing. The president serves as the marker of a democratic fantasy that, by its very nature, can never be totally realized: the coherence of America's body politic, made visible in a singular figure. Along similar lines, Henry Milton's thriller *The President is Missing!* (1967) places its executive in mortal danger at the hands of American radicals. POTUS is once again kidnapped and a male and female character must find each other by first finding him. The text interlocks personal and political desires. Repeatedly referencing the collective trauma of John F. Kennedy's assassination, *The President is Missing!* confirms my thesis that a fictional POTUS, instead of exclusively offering a *whole* vision of a nation's essence, maintains a *hole* in the political as well as aesthetic imaginary. And champions of American democracy should rejoice, because instead of promoting the coherence required by authoritarianism—a definitive representative of the nation that maintains an illusion of permanence— fictional POTUS sustains the dissatisfaction required to keep a democratic order alive and well. Of note, this template retains a good deal of cultural currency: in 2018, former president Bill Clinton coauthored another novel entitled *The President is Missing*. Presidential thrillers thus demonstrate that "fantasies are not, as is sometimes thought, wish-fulfilling linear narratives of mastery and control leading to closure and the attainment of desire. They are marked, rather, by the prolongation of desire, and by the lack of fixed position with respect to the objects and events fantasized" (Williams 2009: 612).

In the aftermath of Franklin Delano Roosevelt's so-called imperial presidency, writers and readers consistently imagined POTUS as a fiction that privileged the bald pursuit of power, and they responded by carving out methods for evading the totalizing tendencies of the state. Readers can truthfully trace this tendency back to Abraham Lincoln's suspension of *habeas corpus* during the Civil War, or to the consolidations of Martin van Buren, or even as far back as Washington's militant standing as the original Founding Father. What most differentiates modern representations of the office from earlier efforts, though, is the erosion of faith in large-scale government programs, accompanied by a rampant mistrust in mastery of any kind. In the second half of the twentieth century, POTUS became yet another shorthand for the postmodern condition. Depictions of the president signaled a nefarious cabal of hidden interests attempting to consolidate control; at the same time, the fictional president reminded readers of a growing schism between official metanarratives—the chief magistrate as the face of the nation, carved into a mountainside—and the revelation that real life is far from orderly. In sum, late twentieth-century fiction concerning the commander in chief focused on fragmentation, randomness, and the dismantlement of metanarratives. President Ryan, the protagonist of Tom Clancy's 1997 novel, *Executive Orders*, repeatedly describes the presidency as "a prison" (Clancy 1997: 33). Clancy's text portrays POTUS as a "soap opera," in which a flesh-and-blood actor (Ryan) must pantomime his role (556). By design, Clancy's presidency abhors innovation: "The system is only ready for itself" (751). On the other hand, *Executive Orders* advocates for unrestrained invention, albeit exclusively by white males with military training: "The Constitution and the law cannot anticipate every eventuality" (1078). Through his presidential fictions, Clancy's readers experience a creeping sense of paranoia as well as the thrill of deconstruction—staples of the postmodern turn.

Let us highlight a particular example of this postmodern turn as it manifests in other presidents of American fiction. Late twentieth-century prose treats POTUS as a device with which to undermine the temporal logic that characterized the so-called era of Big Government under Presidents Roosevelt, Lyndon B. Johnson, and most infamously Nixon. "It is the presidency that stands out as the chief point of reference for evaluating the polity *as it moves through time*" (Skowronek 1997: 20, emphasis mine). It nearly goes without saying that the oversized presidency provides major signposts in the nation's collective timeline, such as birthdays and deaths; every four years the election of an executive punctuates the (re) construction of the country's joint story. A number of contemporary works challenge this presidential timeline by installing in its place a distinctive temporality. *Executive Orders*, for one, presents presidential historians as convenient foils because they prefer to dwell upon what-if scenarios and pontificate upon hypotheticals; Clancy's heroic executive, in contrast, rejects intellectualism in favor of "manly" action. Eternally under siege, President Ryan thrives in the here and now. Clancy's work therefore reflects a drift away from the impetus of the imperial presidency, with its emphasis upon social planning, toward a kind of anti-presidency that embraces the intrinsic merits of randomness. Elsewhere, Stephen King's 2011 novel *11/22/63* tells the tale of a time-traveling writer that learns through his engagement with the tragic timeline of Kennedy to write "more freely." By reimagining the presidential storyline, King's protagonist realizes the power of prose *sans* plotting, and he comes to privilege spontaneity over the predictability on display in Johnson's Great Society. Finally, Philip Baruth's 2003 novel *The X-President* charts an alternative history in which an aging Clinton, referred to as BC, must go back to adjust a doomed timeline that began under his administration. *The X-President* radically revises a prevailing sense of being-in-time (linear, chronological, and orderly) by disturbing a widely held belief in the presidency as an anchor, a fixture that preserves a definitive chronology.

Baruth's novel contemplates a world in which a citizen biographer can remake her own private universe without the coordinates imposed upon her by an all-powerful executive. Spanning the political spectrum—Clancy on the right, Baruth on the left, and King somewhere in-between—these popular authors employ the metaphorical presidency to declare the triumph of atemporality, which is to say, to valorize an immersive present, detached from the pressing demands of a shared past as well as future. Fictionalized presidents of the late twentieth century inspired readers to react against oppressive orderliness and to imagine an American experience driven by disruption instead of docility. Crucially, the atemporal shift of these works is not a straightforward pivot away from the presumably hagiographic depictions that came before them; instead, this atemporality unveils how fictional presidencies have—since the nation's inception—goaded audiences into desiring something other than the status quo.

Though it may seem commonsensical to assume that depictions of the president trend toward the propagandistic, a study of prominent examples opens American audiences to distinctive possibilities. As we shall see, fictionalized chief magistrates have long marked a deep-seated disconnect between American readers and the presumed legibility of their political practices. These prominent figures remain sites of rupture. Whether reckoning with the exceptionalism of the commander in chief, a schism between governing ideals and embodied experience, or the drive to dissatisfaction required in a modern democracy, American fiction has incessantly emphasized the unplanned nature of the presidency. And without the refusal of a static national essence enacted by these texts, what precisely would stop American audiences from relying upon fetishized leaders, authoritarians in everything but name?

Democracy's Flesh

In short, fictional POTUS signifies a nation's complicated relationship to its own democratic promise. This literary figure offers a meditation on the openness of a democratic model in which every citizen theoretically counts as much as every other citizen. Hardly an uncritical transmission of authoritative imperatives, this messy character actually complicates the relationship between what American writers and readers might assume that they want—the fully formed embodiment of a national essence, in the form of an exceptional president—and the imperfect iconography that they ultimately receive. From the Jacksonian white whale to a breakdown of the mythical totalities that once marshaled Johnson's Great Society, the presidents of American literature maintain *a requisite unrealizability*. That is to say, because the imagined president is always already missing, and because literary works wrestle with metaphors instead of submitting to the thing itself, textual encounters with imaginary executives re-enforce the anti-foundationalist impulse of democracy: a social order that must maintain a plurality of perspectives, foster healthy antagonisms, and reject the supremacy of any solitary, power-hungry regime.

Still, it has become common of late to imbibe images of the presidency through mediums designed to limit self-reflexivity and reduce the poetic interplay between a word and the thing itself. To paraphrase Theodor Adorno and Max Horkheimer, new technologies for communication have empowered leaders to simulate the voice of God; in turn, powerful purveyors of disinformation have depicted the commander in chief as a corporate CEO, elevated above the proverbial fray. To be fair, Americans have confronted an increasingly vast global order, and so one might appreciate the widespread longing for a singular entity that could be held accountable for societal ills. Accordingly, purveyors of disinformation ask contemporary readers to consume POTUS via fixed imagery that has been prefabricated for a target demographic, tied to a one-way dissemination of knowledge and passed down from monied stakeholders to compliant consumers. In response to this relatively narrow mode of spectatorship, I wish to advocate for a deeper understanding of the literariness of the presidency, and thereby invoke a mode of interpretation that privileges democratic engagement over the docility of authoritarianism.[12] Simply put, literary engagement assists readers in resisting the inertia of presidentialism.

But before I turn my attention to salient texts in the chapters that follow, the question of fictionalized presidencies warrants a bit more theorizing. To begin, one might ask why countless Americans prostrate themselves before imperfect, even incompetent, chief magistrates. Even more importantly, how do readers reconcile an infantile investment in presidential father figures with the nation's professed goals of personal independence? In her discussion of the presidency, Joan Copjec argues that television's "imbecilic devotion to the referent" obscures the real reason why innumerable Americans succumb to presidentialism (Copjec 1996: 143). She contends that naysayers of America's slavish devotion to its executives simplify what is, in truth, a rather unruly relationship. Most Americans are hung up on neither the policies nor the promises of a president; in contrast, to avoid falling prey to delusions of absolute harmony, most Americans unconsciously yearn for a master who remains "demonstrably fallible" (149). Copjec conjectures that it is these slippages, these *imperfections*, that genuinely drive the phenomenon of presidentialism. In other words, thanks to what the presidential symbol lacks—the constitutional fissure between a word and the thing itself—readers of the presidency continue to crave incompleteness, or the absence

---

[12]Lewis Lapham contends, "The television camera demands prophetic certainty . . . and over the course of the last thirty years the amplification of images increasingly has shifted the weight of magical personality against the play of ideas" (Lapham 1993: 159).

of any final representation, be it political and/or literary (an absence that empowers them to persist as subjects with variegated desires). "The very vanity of our hopes (. . .) sustains them," Copjec writes. "Democracy seems designed, if not to brew up more dissatisfaction, at least to acknowledge the impossibility of its alleviation" (150, 161). When one employs Copjec's logic, even the most elemental presidents in American fiction reveal themselves to be much more than mere black-and-white devices for elementary coercion.

Said another way, the complexity of fictional presidents reveals the latent complexity of a democratic consciousness striving to achieve adequate expression. The ever-slippery presidential signifier alerts readers to "the unavoidable—and no doubt ontological—difficulty democracy has in reading its own story" (Lefort 2006: 187). Without a doubt, the fictional president offers an important nodal point for conveying national identity; as I discuss in Chapter 3, William Wells Brown used POTUS to argue for a Federalist solution to the pressing problem of citizenship for recently freed slaves. But because American democracy presumably necessitates division in lieu of conformity and consensus, this convenient avatar is always already accompanied by a sense of dislocation. Authors do not merely deposit democracy in the content of their narratives, as if the truth of democracy could be extracted from the imaginary executives themselves; no, democracy is made possible by the restless form through which authors deliver their presidential figurations, and the ways in which authors consequently compel readers to make meaning for themselves.

Although audiences may harbor an urge to conceptualize the president as offering unmediated access to something real—the fantasy of a homogeneous nation-state—or, as a site of straightforward conformity—one that was meant to be worshiped by followers or utterly eradicated by opponents—it is due to the president's position as a symbol that the figure proves so intriguing, and so invaluable. The image of the president imparts upon readers a feeling of discontentment that remains indispensable to recurrent (re)formulations of the national storyline. Indeed, the fiction of a modern democracy ought to represent "power in such a way as to show that power is an *empty place* and (to maintain) a gap between the symbolic and the real . . . (to show that) those who exercise power do not possess it" (Lefort 2006: 159, author's emphasis). In Claude Lefort's terms, fiction within a modern democratic society should not construe the story of that society in a positivist fashion, or present it as a source of unyielding unity. The fictional output of a democratic society should be self-dividing, which is to say, it ought to be constituted by ceaseless division. To write or read a presidency provides one such exercise.[13] An extraordinarily contested symbol, the president is never One but forever Two.

---

[13]Claude Lefort, to whom Copjec owes an intellectual debt, confirms this paradox between dread and yearning by ruminating upon how politics and the act of writing inform one another:

Through literary depictions of the president, modern democracy reveals itself to be eternally in-process. The textual president is not a cudgel with which authority figures beat readers into submission; the textual president instead provides a wedge with which each reader can insert her particular interests into the national storyline. Renderings of the chief magistrate remain fundamentally divorced from that which they are said to represent, namely, the metaphysical spirit of the polis. The democratic order strains in futility to locate once and for all its figurative flesh. Through the ceaseless slippage of its ever-unfolding narrative, American democracy sustains the capacity for imaginative change: "The last-minute failure of democracy is the permanent renewal of its enigma" (Plot 2016: 19). The resounding failure of democracy to articulate itself via a universal avatar is, in fact, its singular success. As we shall see in the proceeding chapters, the fictional president arrives always a moment too early—via the illusion of a pre-social essence, an innate Oneness—or a moment too late—as a prescriptive Other against which a society must redefine itself in perpetuity. The envisaged executive is neither proof of the law's encompassing reach, then, nor the sign of an unyielding disciplinary apparatus. Quite the contrary: presidents of American fiction stimulate democratic desire through the perpetual discontentment that accompanies their figuration.

Although some naysayers dismiss the presidents of American fiction as crude vessels through which readers are forced to internalize fantasies promulgated by federal officials, the transmission of this message is never a simplistic one. On one side, authors rearrange POTUS as a symbolic repository with which to make sensible the country's evolving comprehension of itself; on the other side, readers deconstruct these chameleonic characters to make sense of their individual lives as well as their ever-changing relationship with an imagined national community. When they linger on the fictional presidency, readers revisit the foundational dynamism that buttresses America's literature as well as its democratic practices.[14] That is, when audiences approach the executive as a fiction, they begin to undermine the stasis of presidentialism and reinvigorate the vibrancy of a genuinely democratic social order. If we wish to address the domineering function of today's chief magistrates, we must keep alive this complex interplay between readers, presidential iconographies, and the ever-surprising terrain of American fiction.

"Thinking the political goes beyond the bounds of every doctrine or theory. Through writing, it sustains the tension inhabiting it" (Lefort 2000: xlii).
[14]"There is an aesthetic dimension in the political and there is a political dimension in art . . . artistic practices play a role in the constitution and maintenance of a given symbolic order, or in its challenging, and this is why they necessarily have a political dimension. The political, for its part, concerns the symbolic ordering of social relations, and this is where its aesthetic dimension resides" (Mouffe 2013: 91).

1

James Fenimore Cooper's Exceptional Presidents

Any conversation concerning the presidency in American fiction cannot ignore the looming presence of one of America's earliest authors, James Fenimore Cooper, who depicted the first president, George Washington, in his second novel, *The Spy* (1821). *The Spy*, which remains one of Cooper's most successful novels, weaves together various plotlines, including the fictional story of Washington disguised as an enigmatic spy named Mr. Harper and the related tale of Harvey Birch, a fellow spy that works for Washington by cultivating a villainous persona as a British sympathizer to ascertain information for America's foremost Founding Father. Cooper's texts frequently address political concerns within the fledgling country. Indeed, Marius Bewley labels Cooper as "one of the most astute politico-social critics America has ever had" (Bewley 1959: 64).[1] Situated at the germination site of America's interwoven political and literary imaginaries, Cooper developed a complex presidential figure that was representative of emerging national virtues and, at the same time, exceptional due to the figure's capacity to exist outside of the society that he served.[2]

In the aftermath of the War of 1812, Americans started to ask difficult questions concerning their emerging national identity, and a plethora of cultural voices emerged to articulate potential answers. Cooper helped to give rise to a national literature focused on so-called American themes

---

[1]Cooper's contemporaries recognized the author's "desire to be the spokesman for republican values in fiction," although they often found this desire to be problematic "because he (was) obtruding political matters upon the apolitical purity of the historical romance" (Dekker and McWilliams 1973: 14–15).

[2]So complex and difficult was the process of translating Washington into fiction that Cooper later expressed regret at his attempt. See Cowie (1948).

by catering to a specific American audience and constructing a vision for the presidency that could be distinguished from the British monarchy. Importantly, readers must not consider this phenomenon a one-way street in which politics preceded literature; instead, they must recognize how the spirit of the frontier romance also informed the complexities of American politics, especially when it came to the genre's privileged "men of action." As John McWilliams argues, "In successive sentences, one finds details of adventure and weighty statements of political theory . . . (Cooper) turns an exciting tale . . . into a study of the factors underlying the rise of fall of a civilization or a government" (McWilliams 1972: 11–12). Some of this ambivalence was a byproduct of Cooper's cultural context. Obsessed with the legacy of the Revolutionary War, but largely lacking any firsthand experience of that event, various American writers in the early 1820s—an age of nation building widely known as the Era of Good Feelings—sought to rejuvenate the national mythos. The character of Washington effectively filled this need. Barry Schwartz describes how, during this period, "Americans transform(ed) George Washington into a living monument" (Schwartz 1987: 9). According to Schwartz, Americans in the 1820s grasped the significance of Washington as a concrete emblem through which they could retell their most sacred narratives. The chief magistrate, that is, became a screen onto which they could project "their sense of national harmony, their common attachment to a new political unity . . . venerational forms once reserved for the king" (20, 31). On the one hand, then, Cooper presented Washington and his stable of fictional stand-ins for the president as a potent marker of consensus, made possible because the towering man already stood so tall in the American imagination (although perhaps not quite as tall as he stood before the Jay Treaty, a fiasco that undercut some of the goodwill that Washington had accrued). By the time Cooper published *The Spy*, Washington had become a powerful reservoir of positive national feelings.[3] Yet, on the other hand, such hagiographic tendencies do not fully explain the complexity of Cooper's Washington. A small but vocal minority of Americans increasingly dwelt upon the counter-narrative of Washington as a wolf in sheep's clothing—a counter-narrative fueled, in part, by the first president's widely cited concern with his own reputation. Disenchanted of the country's foundational myths, certain writers and readers asked how much of Washington's legendary image was the result of shrewd calculations by a type of Machiavellian prince.

For twenty-first century readers, Cooper's works reflect abiding dangers associated with the office: namely, because of his exceptional position,

---

[3]Schwartz continues, "The American people's regard for Washington had been the clearest expression of what they had in common . . . (he) affirms their attachment to their new nation . . . (and made) incarnate the highest moral principles of a nation, embodying them in a form that can be understood and loved" (Schwartz 1987: 97, 107).

literal as well as symbolical, the president can—indeed, one could argue, must—navigate around governmental and legalistic oversight to act in a unilateral fashion. In response, perhaps the most interesting question that *The Spy* poses is whether the presidency could be reformed or salvaged, or if it remains anti-democratic at its very core. By grappling with this defining tension, Cooper compelled his readers to revisit the radical potentiality that resides within America's emerging legal framework, and to recognize that a president's exceptionality does not inherently impede on the promise of democratic self-expression.

Cooper's president manifests in a variety of guises. While most literary critics today recognize the deep-seated ambivalence of Cooper's prose—its ceaseless wavering between what Cooper called forest freedom and the desire for an ordered, stratified society—fewer critics have scrutinized how Cooper saved his "highest dramatic coloring" for Native American "chiefs" (Zoellner 1960: 410).[4] Through these chiefs, Cooper dwelt upon models of leadership, and his treatment of Washington therefore speaks to a much larger emphasis upon authority figures within his corpus. Said another way, Cooper's concern with Washington and the presidency was hardly relegated to *The Spy*.

Given the generally hagiographic tendencies of the Era of Good Feelings, it is interesting to consider why *The Spy* lingers upon Washington's relatively unpopular decision to hang Benedict Arnold's associate, Major John André, despite the traitor's pleas for mercy. Although Cooper always sensed virtue in Washington, and encouraged his reader to maintain faith in the intrinsic benevolence of America's *pater familias*, *The Spy* nonetheless contemplates how the nation's foremost president must sometimes act in a less than unimpeachable manner to govern his confederacy of rebels. To lead effectively, Cooper's Washington has no choice but to sway citizens, which is to say, to manipulate them, even lie to them, should the nation's overall health require it. Cooper thus added a good deal of nuance to America's understanding of its nascent political profile by contemplating what would later be described, by Carl Schmitt and others, as the state of exception.

Of course, the Cooper of 1821 would not have recognized a phrase like state of exception—a theoretical concept that remained unexplored in detail for over a century. Still, Cooper was well-versed in the closely related concept of presidential prerogative, developed by John Locke. According to Locke, the prerogative of a state leader involves the "power to act according to discretion for the public good, without the prescription of the law *and sometimes even against it*" (Locke 1980: 92, emphasis mine). Many of the so-called Founding Fathers, including Washington, acknowledged the necessity

---

[4]Henry Nash Smith remains one of the most well-known critics to describe Cooper's ambivalence, or his "clash of irreconcilable values" (1950: xvi).

of prerogative and upheld it in their more difficult decisions as president. Strident disciples of Locke, the Founding Fathers harbored "no doubt that national emergency might require presidents to lay the Constitution and the law aside"—a frame of mind that helped Thomas Jefferson to justify, for instance, the controversial Louisiana Purchase (Schlesinger Jr. 2004: 23).[5] To this day, national emergencies have regularly empowered the executive "to act on his own; for a president's final obligation (is) to the preservation of the country" (24). The final section of the chapter returns to the pressing problem of whether or not Cooper laid an ideological groundwork for the unilateral presidencies of figures like Richard Nixon or George W. Bush.

Cooper's fiction interrogates the basis of the American republic by exploring the nation's relatively untested political roadmap, especially in relation to matters of sovereignty (the subject of ongoing discussions surrounding Article II of the Constitution, in which the role of the presidency is rather vaguely outlined).[6] Cue Henry St. John Bolingbroke, a widely read political thinker from England who developed the crucial concept of the Patriot King.[7] Bolingbroke contended that major social reform demands a "great man," a "masterful leader exercising extraordinary powers" (Longmore 1999: 208). In Bolingbroke's words: "There must be an absolute, unlimited, and uncontrollable power lodged somewhere in every government" (Bolingbroke 1970: 55). In Cooper's depiction, Washington stands out as an exemplary Patriot King: a creative symbol with which to ford the river that runs between monarchy and republicanism, colonial subordination and nascent nationhood. As he aimed to (re)establish Washington's greatness in the estimation of a post-1812 American audience, Cooper could not avoid addressing the first president's exceptional status.

---

[5]Presidential prerogative was, however, the source of much disagreement. Following Washington's controversial Neutrality Proclamation in 1793, in which the president appeared to override the legislative branch in foreign affairs, Alexander Hamilton, a vocal supporter of executive authority, and James Madison, at the bidding of Jefferson, entered into a spirited debate concerning the nature of the presidency. Writing under the pseudonyms of Pacificus (Hamilton) and Helvidius (Madison), the two men debated Washington's exceptional status as well as his Constitutional limits. Hamilton said of Washington, "He had a right, and if in his opinion the interests of the Nation required it, it was his duty" (Hamilton and Madison 2007: 16). In response, Madison focused on Locke's concept of prerogative as uniquely un-American; in a footnote, he observed: "(Locke's) chapter on prerogative, shews how much the reason of the philosophy was clouded by the royalism of the Englishman" (58).
[6]Another early American writer of note, Washington Irving highlighted the correlation between the British monarch (George III) and the usurper George Washington in his well-known story, "Rip Van Winkle" (1819), in which a tavern sign marks the differences—and, perhaps more significantly, the similarities—between monarchs and chief magistrates.
[7]Bolingbroke was popularized due in part to the American influencer Benjamin Rush's push to endow Bolingbroke with "prestige of immeasurable significance" (Ketcham 1984: 59). Bolingbroke's unique formulation of the Patriot King became highly relevant during the debates that surrounded Article II: "The idea of a Patriot King . . . was more pertinent and directly useful . . . when the time came to fashion an executive office in the new nation" (68).

He confronted the implications of a Patriot King that must exist concurrently inside and outside of the nation's legal apparatus. The young republic tasks its Patriot King with making final decisions; he must make the law as well as unmake it. Even as the Patriot King gives a physical form to the law, he remains unhindered by it, retaining the privilege to declare a state of emergency and to enact his own will, unencumbered by the demand for consent from the electorate.

T. Hugh Crawford underscores the slipperiness of Cooper's presidential figurehead, which proves "adept at evading the careful gaze of the populace" (Crawford 1991: 409). Cooper cajoled his reader into asking when it might be considered acceptable for a Patriot King to override the will of the people to fulfill his duty and protect the state. Is the president exempt from oversight, given his capacity to break the law in order to maintain it? To answer this question, Cooper tried to strike an equilibrium between presidential "forthrightness"—Washington's unmistakable probity—with "necessary duplicity"—the shadowy demands of federal governance (410). Caught in an eddy of political incertitude, Cooper's Washington maintains a "clearly established moral superiority . . . at odds with the quiet, behind the scenes control he exerts" (Crawford 1994: 65). On the one hand, Cooper crafted a presidential image to convey hegemonic American ideals; on the other hand, Cooper's commander in chief must conduct some of his business behind the scenes in order to exert control while remaining beyond the reach of America's legal branch. National emergencies call for men of action, not the slow, methodical grind of liberal democracy—or so the argument goes. Bernard Crick muses, "Democracies have to defend themselves" (Crick 2002: 71).

Cooper therefore presented fictional executives that were exceptional as well as representative.[8] Giorgio Agamben writes, "The paradox of sovereignty consists in the fact the sovereign is, at the same time, outside and inside the juridical order" (Agamben 1995: 15). That is, Cooper's presidents establish the state's all-encompassing legal authority and, at the same time, remind readers that a leader like Washington must frequently stand outside of the law in order to maintain it. This highly ambiguous position sets the stage for tyrants—presidents that routinely break the law by exerting their personal power—even as it offers a site of possible redemption by illuminating the open-endedness at the heart of any governing regime. According to Cooper, the US presidency straddles a line between inside and outside, norms and chaos. To initiate such a nuanced investigation of Cooper's executives, the reader must first head east—from the seedbed of the presidency into the murky depths of the American frontier.

---

[8]Ross Pudaloff posits that Cooper capitalized upon specific sorts of generic material for the "valorization of a culture politically democratic and socially aristocratic" (Pudaloff 1983: 712).

Natty Bumppo and the State of Exception

In a well-known essay entitled "Uses of Great Men," Ralph Waldo Emerson wrote of his titular characters, "They are the exceptions which we want" (Emerson 1983a: 627). Cooper's fiction similarly reflects a deep desire for exceptional heroes: eponymous great men that do not conform to society's norms; transcendent titans that do not obey existing rules but make new rules for themselves. As a prominent part of this drive to exception, Cooper created the first truly exceptional hero in American fiction, Nathaniel (Natty) Bumppo.[9] A regular in the Cooper canon, Bumppo evades social restrictions on multiple fronts—he remains "too civilized" to coexist with Native Americans but "too wild" to coexist with the so-called civilized.[10] He proves too religious for the woods yet he is too much of a frontiersman for the church. Bumppo, then, exists in a permanent state of exception, in that he acts with neither sanction nor permission from any single community. To be clear, unlike Washington, Bumppo is never a straightforward agent of the law. Cooper's readers would never have expected Bumppo to conform to social standards and the character never tries, at least in any overt way, to compel others to conform to his will. Nevertheless, Bumppo occupies a consonant psychic position with Washington because, in parallel with the fictionalized commander in chief, he can move outside of the law with impunity. Akin to a contemporary superhero, Bumppo uses his exceptional status, which is to say, his idealized symbolic position, not to create laws, but to foster an abstract concept of justice. While one should not too hastily conflate Washington and Bumppo as lawgivers, their function in the public imaginary remains quite similar: they operate at the outer limits of the legal order in order to police that order. To claim that Cooper was ruminating on the presidency when he pontificated upon Bumppo, his magisterial "chief" of the American wilderness, cannot be dismissed as idle conjecture, either, as the author himself spelled out this preoccupation: "I set down Washington and Natty Bumppo as the two only really great men of my time" (Cooper 1838: 229–30). Before turning one's attention to *The Spy*, one must investigate the fictional world of Bumppo, and ruminate upon how Cooper's

---

[9]Henry Nash Smith suggests that "for at least one section of the reading public . . . (Leatherstocking) was a symbol of anarchic freedom, an enemy of law and order" (Smith 2007: 60). Yet Bumppo's supposedly anarchic qualities, if readers divorce them from the ways in which Cooper (and his society) sanctioned them, only tell part of the story. In truth, it is the *legalized lawlessness* that defines Cooper's wayward protagonist.

[10]George Becker details this dual exception. On the one side, Bumppo represents "the America in which Cooper lived, the one which to a certain extent he idealized . . . a wild, rough, expansive country which broke almost all precedent and evaded fixed forms"; on the other side, Bumppo reflects Cooper's "legalistic mind dominated by conceptions of absoluteness and permanence" (Becker 1956: 329).

Leatherstocking novels rigorously examine what will eventually come to be known as the state of exception.

Let us start by defining the state of exception as it has been outlined in political theory. One of the earliest theorists to interrogate the phrase, Carl Schmitt writes: "The state of exception is something entirely different from anarchy and chaos, (because) order still exists in the juristic sense . . . (but) the state suspends law by virtue of its right to self-preservation" (Schmitt 2020: 6). According to Schmitt, the sovereign "does not need the law in order to create the law" (7). Typically, the state of exception manifests during an emergency situation in which the grinding gears of the legal as well as political system are suspended to preserve the state from greater harm. The risk of granting the sovereign these extra-juridical powers—or, allowing the executive to make decisions without consulting other branches of the government—is obvious: once the leader understands him- or herself to be operating from a state of exception, how will citizens be able to check the leader's newfound authority? What will stop the sovereign from declaring an emergency and then ignoring established laws in perpetuity?[11] A constitutional dilemma surfaces as critics come to the troubling realization that a president could at any time suspend the rule of law, as long as he can convincingly articulate imminent dangers facing the republic. Because such a declaration rarely requires objective evidence on the part of the final decider, a suspension of checks and balances remains eternally plausible.

For example, Cooper's *The Pioneers* (1823) focuses on two self-proclaimed great men that exploit the state of exception: Bumppo and Marmaduke Temple. Within the settlement of Templeton, named after Temple himself, these mirror images play oversized roles. Marmaduke rules over the settlement with impunity, while Bumppo, who has long occupied the land on which the settlement now stands, lingers at the outskirts, forcing settlers to confront what he describes as the law of the woods in direct contrast to the legal strictures of Templeton. The plot of *The Pioneers* involves Bumppo "illegally" shooting a deer out of season and duking it out with Temple over his presumed right to do so. A man whose name underscores his aristocratic claims to sovereignty, Marmaduke "ranks among the most wealthy and important of his countrymen" (Cooper 1988: 37). Although Temple proclaims his equality with his fellow citizens before the eyes of the law, his position is quite obviously an exceptional one. He is the namesake for the town. He acts as landlord over the entire settlement as well as the judge that settles legal conflicts in the region. He exercises his privilege to name his cousin, a person with whom he remains "of one blood," as sheriff. The

---

[11]Schmitt records: "The inescapable consequence of emergency law [*Notrect*] came into effect: the person who exercised it had thereby the power to decide whether the conditions required to declare it existed or not" (Schmitt 2014: 157).

man nicknamed "Duke" therefore acts as the settlement's judge, jury, and executioner: "'Duke' is a man who likes to be foremost" (180). In a number of ways, the novel stresses Temple's extraordinary situation, which appears to be rather close to monarchy. Each chapter begins with a Shakespearean quote from one of the Bard's plays concerning doomed monarchs. Moreover, the busts on display in Marmaduke's manor tell their own tale—a George Washington face "with dignified composure"; a non-descript face that could be "Julius Caesar or Dr. Faustus" (64). Caught between the ideals of Washington and the imperial lust of Caesar, Cooper's novel presents Temple as deserving of his exceptional status and, at the same time, it forces readers to confront the sovereign's capacity to impose norms. Like Bumppo and his supposedly ill-gotten deer, Marmaduke engages in legally questionable hunting practices when he joins in a massacre of pigeons and a butchering of fish. And yet, he cannot be taken to task for the deed. Settlers may entertain the notion of suing Temple, but they quickly realize the impossibility of placing meaningful limits on his power.

In his description of Bumppo's woods, Cooper—like Schmitt a century later—recognized the import of *nomos*, a term etymologically derived from fences and forests. *Nomos* underscores the uniquely spatial dimensions of the law. As Cooper's readers witness the struggle between Temple and Bumppo, they confront how land appropriation precedes the legal order, which is to say, how the seizure of land constitutes the legal apparatus that follows in the wake of this seizure. By appropriating the forest and establishing his town, Temple cements his exceptional status as sovereign. Rendering the law spatially visible to the townspeople, he enjoys "the full immediacy of a legal power not mediated by laws; (this act) is a constitutive historical event—an act of *legitimacy*, whereby the legality of a mere law first is made meaningful" (Schmitt 2003: 73, author's emphasis). Every new epoch begins with a spatial reordering. The given leader solidifies his exceptional status by rejecting the fences that precede his reign.

Bumppo too appears to transcend the legal boundaries of the settlement. "There's them living," he opines, "who say, that Nathaniel Bumppo's right to shoot on these hills, is of older date than Marmaduke Temple's right to forbid him" (Cooper 1988: 25). A local woodcutter admits of the Leatherstocking, "The law was never made for such as he" (334). Bumppo proudly fashions himself a "transgressor of the law," a "kind of out-law" (300, 355). When Temple tries to set an example for the citizens of Templeton by putting the aged hunter in jail, Bumppo quickly absconds to his woodland refuge. These representative men enter into conflict because they both consider themselves to be external to the law: whereas the judge "had a great hand in getting the law through," the rustic relic gleefully cries out in defiance: "So much for Marmaduke Temple's law!" (311, 299). One need not read *The Pioneers* exclusively as a story of the cultural clash between old ways and new; instead, by examining the similarities between these two men vis-à-vis their relationship to the law, one gains insight into the state of exception enjoyed by Cooper's proto-presidential figures. Each man makes as well as breaks the law. Depending upon one's perspective, each character can be described as protagonist or antagonist. Temple must be on his guard against possible insurrectionists that would overthrow "civilization"—he incessantly expresses anxiety about the French Revolution, for instance— whereas Bumppo must obey the law of the woods, or, the law of survival, spurred by an ever-present threat of starvation. In this way, Marmaduke and the Leatherstocking enable one another to declare a constant state of exception.

However, as a different set of attitudes about legality took shape in the late eighteenth and early nineteenth centuries, Schmitt contends that Western societies stopped appreciating the necessity of the state of exception and began to repress signs of the extraordinary status enjoyed by the likes of Marmaduke or Bumppo. The rise of liberalism displaced the potency of the Patriot King. Accordingly, Cooper critiqued ineffective and effeminate agents of civilization, including the overzealous surgeon in *The Spy* and the weak practitioner of psalmody in *The Last of the Mohicans*. Although Cooper did laud the role of law and order in the process of nation building, he nevertheless persisted in championing the man of action: an illiberal man who knows when to bypass established laws and make decisions on behalf of everyone else. Importantly, it is Marmaduke's discomfort with his exceptionality—and not the exceptionality itself—that accounts for Bumppo's eventual triumph. Thanks to the increasingly liberal tenets of American society, a good number of Cooper's readers in early America would have been led to believe that, in their country, "the law (is) sovereign" (Schmitt 2020: 15). When it came to matters of the government, liberalism appeared to dictate a belief in complete objectivity. On this front, Cooper's fiction contests a premise laid out by one of the philosophical darlings of the American Revolution, Cesare Beccaria, who argued that the arbitrariness of a tyrant could be overcome by the impartiality of codified laws. But, what if an impartial codified law concurrently demands that elected sovereigns like Washington carve out something like a permanent exception to protect the fragile new order? The indifferent legalism of liberal thought, articulated by figures like Beccaria, merely disguises the enduring sovereignty of Marmaduke—a ruler, as we have already seen, who writes policy as well as revises it. Although he claims to be a servant to the laws of the settlement, Marmaduke operates outside of any rigid, universal legal framework; nonetheless, the judge ultimately retreats from his power when difficult decisions must be made. No longer connected to the brutal seizure of *nomos*, Temple's social standing weakens, because "people who have become settled and live in houses cannot continuously redistribute" (Schmitt 2003: 345). In effect, the very basis of Temple's legal apparatus—his initial seizure of the land—loses its political valence as he becomes more concerned with "dividing and developing," and more intent on eliciting "the functional mode of a state bureaucracy" than asserting power like the prototypical man of action (346, 71). Consequently, Marmaduke's tepid judgment in the Bumppo case "shall be whatever the law demands, notwithstanding any momentary weakness I may have exhibited" (Cooper 1988: 344). Cooper's reader glimpses this type of evasion in the first pages of the text, when the judge repeatedly defers to Natty's "natural right" to prowl the woods (112). The tenets of liberalism have weakened Marmaduke's power as sovereign. Temple's hand-picked sheriff upholds these liberal assumptions when, in the process of adjudicating a dispute between Bumppo and a fellow frontiersman, he awkwardly promises to "appoint a committee" and "draw up, in writing, a set of regulations" (199). In sum, *The Pioneers* reflects the mistaken liberal turn of early American life, including a growing preference for written regulation over sovereign proclamations and a submission to so-called natural rights that disguise the real political power that ushers laws into (and out of) existence. Admittedly, this evasion does come with its own rewards: Marmaduke's late-in-life liberalism allows him to bypass the difficult question of how he first came to own the land, or how he can justify his tyrannical rule over the settlement. As Schmitt observes, the danger of this swelling legalism, divorced from the struggle over terrestrial fundament, may be that societies lose sight of concrete historical processes and thus cloak their "true sovereigns" in darkness (Schmitt 2003: 349). Even as the novel ostensibly looks forward to a day when "justice shall be the law, and not power," Cooper's reader might do well to hesitate on this point (Cooper 1988: 455). Bumppo's triumph over Temple evinces a juridical order that retains within itself openings for a willful individual to claim extra-juridical status. Cooper's prototypical presidents navigate uneven ground between the law and its limits.[12]

An embodiment of American virtues as well as a transgressor of American norms, Cooper's seminal frontiersman Bumppo conveys the tensions inherent to a state of exception. How it is that a community can retain the capacity to suspend or violate the law in order to preserve itself? Agamben phrases the conundrum as follows: "If the state of exception's characteristic property is a (total or partial) suspension of the juridical order, how can such a suspension still be contained within it? How can an anomie be inscribed within the juridical order?" (Agamben 2005: 23). Or, put a bit differently, how can a community grant a chief magistrate the legal ability to act in an illegal manner—that is, to exercise presidential prerogative? The nascent figure of the American president had to conform to the will of the people and then, in moments of emergency, act on his or her own volition. Much

---

[12]Agamben claims, "The state of exception is not a special kind of law (like the law of war); rather, insofar as it is a suspension of the juridical order itself, it defines law's threshold or limit concept" (Agamben 2005: 4).

like Washington, as we shall see in the next section, Bumppo embodies the norms of American society. He distinguishes himself from his seemingly uncultivated surroundings by clinging to what Cooper classified as uniquely American values. Concomitantly, though, Bumppo makes decisions that classify him as an outlaw. He exists in a conceptual gap between the busts of Washington and Caesar displayed in Marmaduke's palatial home—or, more accurately, Bumppo reveals a bridge that connects these great men. Since every fraught moment in the wilderness signals an impending emergency, Bumppo can ignore the laws of the settlement and, in so doing, illustrate how a man of action must maintain his exceptionality if he wishes to aid his society in avoiding ruin. Cooper returned to this tension in his most popular novel, *The Last of the Mohicans*.

With its plot concerning British maidens, protected by Cooper's pair of Patriot Kings, as they are chased through the forest by "savages" during the French–Indian War, *The Last of the Mohicans* probes into the *sui generis* leadership style of the young republic. A gallant British soldier named Duncan Heyward defends the maidens, whereas a sinister Native American named Magua strives to assert his dominance. Meanwhile, Bumppo appears to assist Heyward in adjusting to the "law of the woods" (Cooper 1982: 317). Through the reader's initial glimpse of Heyward, the British are shown to be naïve because they fix themselves within a particular code of conduct (of note, Duncan's name recalls the deposed king from Macbeth, who put far too much faith in his berserker general). European patriarchs apparently rule "by concession rather than by power," and so Cooper's narrative contends that these authority figures invariably fail to thrive in the shadowy margins of the colonies (190). If characters like Heyward are to succeed in their mission, they must strip away pretense and recognize the slipperiness of the Patriot King: "Whoever comes into the Woods to deal with the natives, must use Indian fashions, if he would wish to prosper" (37).

The state of exception empowers strong executives to move outside of the legal apparatus without losing the valence of legitimacy. If he wants to succeed in his mission, Heyward must appreciate "Indian artifices"; he must behave with the natives' "characteristic cunning" (Cooper 1982: 262, 321). Through his antagonistic relationship with Magua, Heyward gradually accepts that command requires an occasional breach of decorum rather than rigid adherence to the rules—that is, a willingness to seize opportunities as they arise rather than to remain anchored to particular principles. The executive must be malleable instead of consistent, as consistency leads to "political ruin" (227). A truly exceptional man can shift his shape whenever necessary. Accordingly, after dealing with the subterfuge of Magua, Heyward practices "subtle speech" and deploys "well-acted sincerity" (105). In contrast, at the close of the novel, an unlikely Native American chieftain condemns one of the maidens to become the property of Magua, based solely on legal precedent. Like the fatally flawed Marmaduke, the elder tribesman subscribes to the illusion of a universal law instead of engaging in exceptional acts to meet exceptional times: in this case, to act morally and save the maiden from her horrific fate. Disenchanted by the legalism of this bad chief, Heyward recognizes that, like Magua, he must no longer be held in check by rules and regulations. "These Delawares have their laws," he remarks, "but I—I have no such obligation" (367). Following Magua's example at last, the British officer, a born-again man of action, seizes the crisis of the stolen maidens as an excuse to exert his own dominant will over others.

On these grounds, one can almost argue that Magua is the actual hero of *The Last of the Mohicans* (although we will qualify this assertion in the next section). A "skillful diplomatist," Magua consistently "shifts his ground" to preserve his own authority, and enacts a series of "ingenius political strokes" (Cooper 1982: 335–36). Magua understands well how to manipulate a crowd. A populist of sorts, he exemplifies the values held by Cooper's Patriot King. Unlike Marmaduke, Magua shifts shapes to control his political future. Grasping the blurred line between criminal and sovereign, he ascends to the top position, hence the novel's incessant refrain: "Magua is a great chief!" Magua proves to be formidable because he can be hero and villain at once.

For Jacques Derrida, the state of exception illustrates how self-proclaimed great men exist outside of the legal parameters of a given society, as both animals and gods. In other words, to be an effective sovereign, one must be seen as capable of suddenly devolving into barbarism, irrationality, or brute force. Unlike the highly civilized Heyward that readers meet at the novel's open, a truly exceptional ruler must be capable of surprise: "The princely beast must itself be double: both lion and fox . . . (one must) make oneself feared as potentially more formidable, more terrifying, more cruel, more outlaw." Indeed, for his part, Magua pretends "to be capable of going crazy, mad, irrational and therefore animal" (Derrida 2011: 88–89). While leaders in the mold of Marmaduke, the early Heyward, or even the punctilious Colonel Munro conform to a predictable set of guidelines, Magua remains external to social norms and so he is well-equipped to respond to unexpected emergencies: "This ability to pretend . . . the prince must be a fox not only in order to be cunning like the fox, but in order to pretend to be what he is not and not be what he is. Thus to pretend not to be a fox, when in truth he is a fox" (91). In other words, Magua embraces the power of politics, which always requires a kind of double-speak: the willingness to stand out as a noble representative while conferring confidence in followers that he is capable of total transformation at a moment's notice. *The Last of the Mohicans* confirms his exceptional position in just these terms: "Does not (Magua) mean to turn like a fox" (Cooper 1982: 103). Heyward compares Magua's art of government to the "barking of a wolf," to which a colonial soldier responds, "When was a wolf known to speak the truth?" (344). But it is thanks to his exceptional status that Magua has, by novel's end, effectively risen to the status of a great chief, and thus put himself, "like a raging wolf, at the head" of his community (377). By presenting himself as always capable of shifting into animality, he sustains an indispensable potential for future transgression. Bumppo too could at any moment switch from hero to villain, should that pivot be deemed necessary to sustain his own authority. Bumppo earns a dangerous reputation among native tribes of the woods because the natives can never be certain whether the Leatherstocking will do "the right thing" or succumb to the animal logic of survivalism (348).

Before turning to Cooper's treatment of Washington, we must conclude our survey of Cooper's output from the 1820s by saying just a bit more about the permeable boundary that blurs the line between beast and sovereign. *The Last of the Mohicans* chronicles masquerades in which human beings pretend to be beasts, including Magua's turn as a carnivorous canine. To penetrate the enemy's camp undetected, Heyward and his companions must disguise themselves as bears and, even less probably, beavers. Donald Ringe writes of Cooper's seminal work, "Very little is what it appears to be" (Ringe 1988: 30). Agamben explores how transgression is built into the social order by gesturing at carnivalesque rituals that encourage citizens to drop the façade of lawful obedience and pretend to be animals. Agamben describes the result through the paradoxical phrase "legal anarchy":

> An essential ambiguity on the one hand, a normative tendency in the strict sense, which aims at crystallizing itself in a rigid system of norms whose connection to life is, however, problematic if not impossible (the perfect state of law, in which everything is rejuvenated by norms), and, on the other hand, an anomic tendency that leads to the state of exception or the idea of the sovereign as living law. (Agamben 2005: 72–73)

In a related manner, Cooper's Leatherstocking tales aim to regulate American behaviors and, at the same time, to treat subversion as a distinct, ever-present, and *healthy* possibility. Following characters like Bumppo, the president must be a perfect embodiment of the spirit of the law (if not always its letter), even as he remains extraordinary enough to understand himself as an outlaw, or a decider empowered to break the law whenever he determines a rupture may be needed.

Both like and unlike Magua, Heyward cultivates his reputation as a fox that can mimic the lion—and a lion that can, when survival depends on it, impersonate the fox. Bumppo underscores this point in his direction to Heyward: "What can't be done by main courage, in war, must be done by circumvention. Put on the skin; I doubt not you can play the bear" (315). Embracing Magua's mutability, Heyward finally asserts: "I, too, can play the madman, the fool, the hero; in short, any or everything to rescue her I love" (262). Given the emergency situation unfolding in the woods, Heyward learns to perform a different part, and so he becomes the sort of hero that

Cooper's reader may not want but which she so desperately needs. In this fashion, Cooper crowned a Patriot King.

To an even greater extent than Magua or Heyward, Bumppo parallels Cooper's other great man, Washington, by remaining fully normal as well as fully transgressive.[13] Cooper's ideal sovereign represents the nation and serves as a composite of the young country's loftiest aspirations. But in times of strife, like the Revolutionary War or the War of 1812, the master must be able to transform into something else: a fox, if cunning throws the nation's enemies off the scent; a bear, if the law of the woods demands brute force or tough, unsentimental decisions; a shadowy secret agent, if the chief magistrate urgently needs answers without oversight from Congress. In a word, Washington and Bumppo, Cooper's uncommon twins, reveal the uncomfortable truth that political action requires an alarming amount of flexibility—a willingness to behave in exceptional ways to address exceptional circumstances. But for obvious reasons, Cooper could not allow his reader to doubt, at great length or with real sincerity, the unblemished character of Washington in particular, or the American presidency in general. Crucially, Cooper did not ask his reader to admire Heyward's bear-like nature; instead, he asked her to see, through Heyward's newfound performativity, the need for a commander to be willing to swing from sovereign to beast, that is, to retain a kernel of anarchy without departing entirely from the bounds of propriety. Cooper's reader must never be duped into thinking that Heyward is actually capable of becoming villainous; rather, she must remain "in on the joke." To achieve these divergent ends, Cooper triangulated his fictional POTUS into a beast (the ever-slippery Magua), a sovereign (early Heyward), and the contradictory middle (Bumppo).

Our President, Secret Friend

Cooper's *The Spy* follows a family caught between British and American forces during the Revolutionary War. Rebels catch the family's beloved son

---

[13]We can extend this line of analysis to Cooper's sea-faring protagonists as well. In *The Pilot*, Cooper fictionalized the maritime American celebrity, John Paul Jones. Once more, Cooper cloaked his real-world hero in a disguise, and the character, known interchangeably as "the stranger," "Mr. Gray," and "The Pilot," remains both "more and less than he seems" (Cooper 1990: 169). Jones announces, "Our security is only to be found in secrecy" (209). Unlike the ostentatious British, this American leader must learn to exploit his liminal status. Through his disguises, the Pilot transgresses as well as transcends: he can be known as a "pirate" to his enemies and a "traitor" to his friends in order to operate from the periphery of the main action; at the same time, he sustains an unimpeachable character, since "he alone can save us" (52). Cooper again directly aligned his exceptional, shape-shifting hero with the nation's Founding Father: when British officers temporarily capture the Pilot, they believe him to be Washington in disguise.

returning home from his fight alongside the British, dressed in an elaborate disguise to visit his aging father. As a result, the rebels must decide a fitting punishment for the native son's transgression. Much of the novel involves the culprit's kin waiting to hear the final judgment issued by Washington. Due to the recent hanging of André, the family feels great uncertainty: to uphold the law unequivocally, will Washington execute their favorite child? Meanwhile, the young soldier's family members have no idea that they have already been visited by Washington in disguise as Mr. Harper, a stranger without obvious allegiance. As family members wring their hands, they also cross paths with Harvey Birch, a neighboring salesman that everyone (incorrectly) assumes to be loyal to the crown. To scrutinize the presidency, Cooper's text again divides it into three interrelated pieces: the beast (the Skinner clan), the sovereign (Washington), and the contradictory middle, or, Birch—a frontiersman who served as a template for Bumppo. Through this symbolic triad, *The Spy* articulates the core tensions that every American president must confront.

By breaking the presidency into these phases, Cooper encouraged his reader to contemplate the internal pressures of the office.

> A certain power to *give*, to *make*, but also to *suspend* the law; it is the exceptional right to place oneself above right, the right to non-right, if I can say this, which both runs the risk of carrying the human sovereign above the human, toward divine omnipotence (which will moreover most often have grounded the principle of sovereignty in its sacred and theological origin) and, because of this arbitrary suspension or rupture of right, runs the risk of making the sovereign look like the most brutal beast who respects nothing, scorns the law, immediately situates himself above the law, at a distance from the law. (Derrida 2011: 16–17, author's emphasis)

The mutually dependent characters of Bumppo, Birch, and Washington challenge any presumed boundary between beast and sovereign. This revelation is hardly comforting for Cooper's readers, though, since it compels them not only to appreciate an endless play of differences, evoked by Cooper's chameleonic style, but to recognize an unsettling chain of similarities between the beautiful and ugly elements of America's nascent government: "There is between sovereign, criminal, and beast . . . a worrying mutual attraction, worrying familiarity, an uncanny reciprocal haunting" (Derrida 2011: 17). Said another way, Cooper's president is haunted by a pull toward transcendence as well as commonality with his fellow "criminals" of the woods. On the one hand, Washington stands above the law, ostensibly looking down from an elevated vantage point; he is a godhead, a divine giver of truth that endows laws with their legitimacy as well as their staying power. To quote Bolingbroke: "A Patriot King is the most powerful of all reformers, for he is himself a sort of standing miracle" (Bolingbroke 1970: 72). On the other hand, however, Washington transgresses—he violates his own code of conduct by lurking in the margins in pursuit of arguably ill-gotten gains, and, most problematic of all, he threatens to murder individuals that follow his example by becoming spies. Is Washington unimpeachable or barbaric? More intriguing still, how is it that Washington can be both unimpeachable and barbaric *at the very same time?*

Straightforward readings of *The Spy* underline Cooper's hagiographic treatment of the nation's first president. Such readings view Cooper's Washington as innately great, an idealized embodiment of the body politic. It becomes difficult, from this well-worn perspective, to separate Washington from the concept of the presidency because, as a sort of godhead, it is Washington himself who endows the office with its assumed aura of greatness, and not the other way around: "Washington's reputation legitimated the presidency" (Schwartz 1987: 47). And it is true, Cooper's text does not outright deny the validity of this worshipful order of things. At the beginning of *The Spy*, when Washington arrives at the family's home in the guise of Mr. Harper, regardless of the fact that the occupants of the home do not know his true identity, they already assume their visitor's strength of character: "His countenance evinced a settled composure and dignity; his nose was straight, and approaching to Grecian; his eye, of a grey colour, was quiet, thoughtful, and rather melancholy; the mouth and lower part of his face being expressive of decision and much character" (Cooper 1997: 13). Although Washington never manifests out in the open in Cooper's story—he only ever enters the narrative in costume, or through the appearance of his distinctive signature in written orders—no one, including Cooper's reader, is meant to doubt his intrinsic worth. Setting aside the future executive's probable lack of sympathy for their brother, one member of the family insists: "I cannot doubt the propriety of Washington's conduct" (48). The unimpeachable Washington endows the novel with its ethical framework. In turn, Cooper's Washington somehow stands outside of politics, in that he does not require the same political education as Heyward; he always already exists on a higher plane. Accordingly, Birch finds his personal fulfillment through Washington's approval of his deeds. "I am alone truly," he remarks. "None know me but my God and Him" (217). *The Spy* never really doubts its hero, clinging instead to uncritical reverence.[14] Beneath his many disguises,

---

[14]Cooper's *Notions of the Americans: Picked Up by a Travelling Bachelor Volume II* expresses this ambivalence in detail. "The constitutional power of the president is not trifling," it admits, "though it is always rigidly subordinate to the law" (Cooper 1963: 220). Even as Cooper recognized the latent power of the presidency, he strove to (re)contain it, in part by assuming its innate goodness. Even though he has "rather more of a voice than any one," the president's "influence should be greater without putting it in his power to defeat the intentions of Congress" (223).

Mr. Harper cannot cloak Washington as the genuine article. Despite a plethora of miscues and counterfeit notes, the mark of Washington's hand cannot be mistaken: "It is a word never to be doubted" (365). The presumed purity of the president's penmanship entitles Cooper's hero to be virtually blameless, certainly, but it also relegates him to the status of fixed icon— hence the complimentary need for Washington to find ways to operate in the shadows. In short, Washington-as-idol proves to be dreadfully boring: "As for Mr. Harper himself, he is stiff and colorless" (Bryan 1970: 200).

On the opposite end of the spectrum, Cooper presented the Skinner family, a ruthless band of marauders out to accrue wealth and power by any means necessary. On first blush, the Skinners are everything that the sacred Washington is not: they effortlessly shift allegiances, lie, cheat, and put on appearances to convey a false sense of authority. They possess none of Washington's laudable traits. They are "men who, under the guise of Patriotism, prowl through the community with a thirst for plunder that is insatiable . . . fellows whose mouths are filled with liberty and equality, and whose hearts are overflowing with cupidity and gall" (Cooper 1997: 289). Although the Skinners practice the sort of spycraft honed by Washington and his devotees, the novel refuses to portray clan members as even potentially good. On the topic of the Skinners, a character remarks: "I could hardly tell my own men from the enemy . . . the rascals change sides so often, that you may as well count their faces for nothing" (381). In contrast, when readers discover the British and American uniforms hanging side by side in Mr. Harper's secret lair, Cooper's reader is not meant to feel disgust or disapproval at Washington's duplicity, which remains unquestionably benevolent. However, upon careful consideration, it remains difficult to distinguish Cooper's sovereign from his beasts.

Cooper's audience must confront the invisible ties that link the legal to the anarchical. Lurking in the margins of the main plot, Washington and the Skinners each retain the privilege to evade the gaze of regulated society. Both extra-legal entities comprehend the importance of the state of exception when they recognize an emergency—the Revolutionary War—and then capitalize on the opportunity to enact lawlessness within the bounds of what is technically lawful. Like the Skinners, Washington maintains an aura of mystery to sustain his dominion: "A premium is placed (by Cooper) on Washington's ability to keep his own counsel, to reveal nothing to others of his true thoughts" (Smith 2009: 38). At the same time, the terror felt by citizens in response to their apparently reckless chief magistrate, who might execute their loved ones without batting an eye, binds Washington to the novel's most animalistic characters. In turn, Cooper's odd bedfellows challenge the boundary that presumably divides the bestial from the divine.

In *The Spy*, an unresolvable tension between the sovereign and the beast resolves itself, or, perhaps more accurately, prolongs itself, through the character of Birch—a spy that remains equal parts protagonist and antagonist. Slippery by design, Birch can be what Washington, that rigid fixture of national coherence, never can be, even in his most cunning disguise: a commander that capitalizes on the state of exception. After all, the performance of Mr. Harper never fully clears the sense of greatness that trails Washington like a pungent odor. As a spy, Birch proves useful to Washington because no one knows with any certainty the moral or political position of the bizarre peddler, and so Birch can move across literal and figurative borders, like the later Bumppo. It nearly goes without saying, though, that Birch is never understood to be an honorary member of the Skinner tribe. While the Skinners openly antagonize him, Washington sanctions Birch's work. This indisputable sign of legitimacy keeps Birch relentlessly tethered to social norms, which is to say, it keeps Birch firmly situated within the bounds of America's juridical code. Birch's tenebrous presence enables Washington to act as a living law—a figure unchecked by the nation's strictures, but still able to exist in a meaningful relation to them. Birch can resemble the Skinners when it means preserving Washington's unblemished record. By dividing his president into three intimately related parts, Cooper contrived an exceptional presidency that could exist above, below, and yet fully within the society that it represents.

Vitally, Birch does not merely allow his merciless reputation to precede him; he actively encourages his neighbors to label him as a British sympathizer and, as a result, he spends his entire life ostracized by his neighbors. His neighbors only realize the truth of Birch's righteous mission upon his death, with the discovery of a note from Washington that explains Birch's dual role in the war. *The Spy* therefore dwells upon the occasional call for POTUS to play the antagonist. Albeit in a different context (an analysis of Christopher Nolan's 2008 film *The Dark Knight*), Todd McGowan asks a series of related questions. According to McGowan, Nolan's film interrogates Batman's darker aspect: the Dark Knight's willingness to be hated by the citizens of Gotham to preserve the social order. To sustain Gotham's hope in a fallen politician, Batman, like the prototypical Birch, allows himself to be perceived as a villain. The finale of Nolan's superhero movie echoes Birch's lament near the close of *The Spy*: "He who serves his country as a spy, no matter how honestly, lives to be reviled, or dies like the vilest criminal" (Cooper 1997: 376). Unpacking the complexity of these sorts of heroics, McGowan writes: "If the heroic exception is not to multiply itself in a way that threatens any possibility for justice, then its appearance must become indistinguishable from criminality" (McGowan 2009: n.p.).[15] As McGowan

---

[15]Emerson espoused: "Every hero becomes a bore at last . . . (the masses) cry up the virtues of George Washington, 'Damn George Washington!' is the poor Jacobin's whole speed and confutation . . . we balance one man with his opposite, and *the health of the state depends on the see-saw*" (Emerson 1983a: 627–628, emphasis mine).

points out, not everyone can be a spy, hence Cooper's delineation through his use of the article "the" in his novel's title: it is not just any spy, but "the" spy. In other words, not everyone can wear two uniforms, or possess two faces, or the entire social order would collapse. At the beginning of Nolan's blockbuster, Batman confronts copycat heroes that ask him why he, and not they, can patrol the outer limits of the law in order to keep Gotham safe. One might pose a similar question to Washington: if he can institute a short-lived state of exception to keep the nation safe, what will prevent other citizens from following the same path? *The Spy* is, after all, a novel about a privileged spy prosecuting a fellow spy for engaging in his own type of espionage. McGowan surmises that the state of exception is always at risk of sliding out of control, into what he deems to be a self-multiplying exceptionality. Cooper's text likewise hints at this threat as Washington's propensity for spycraft seeps ever outward, into characters such as the young soldier on trial. But Washington is decidedly not the equivalent of the Dark Knight at the close of Cooper's text—in part, because Cooper maintained a relatively intelligible distinction between heroism and criminality (although, as we already have seen, such a distinction may prove impossible to sustain in the long run). Not yet far enough removed from the hagiographies of the Era of Good Feelings, Cooper's Washington improbably blends heroism and criminality as central features of the American presidency, and he does so without forfeiting his purity as national godhead. "*The Spy* is a novel in which Cooper can, on the one hand, praise Washington," McWilliams writes, "and then admit that Washington's fellow officers could only win independence by underhandedly employing the Skinners" (McWilliams 1972: 55).[16] Thanks to its triune president, *The Spy* can have its cake and eat it too.

In the final tally, Cooper's proposed solution to the problem of how to depict the state of exception proves problematic. In an attempt to rescue her brother from Washington's harsh judgment, one of the family members of the prosecuted spy argues that her brother is a "good spy" because he practices subterfuge "openly, manfully, and bravely" (295). But what exactly is a spy that does his work openly? Is not the concept of a transparent spy an oxymoron? A character quite reasonably inquires, "Ain't one spy as bad as another?" (295). That is, how can Washington be a "good" spy, while other spies operating in a similar vein are considered to be "bad"? In the end, the incongruities of Cooper's presidency—sovereign or beast; hero or criminal; representative or exception—are unsatisfactorily resolved for

---

[16]Although the principle of presidential prerogative may have been indispensable in Cooper's estimation, he nevertheless expressed wariness. In *A Letter to His Countrymen*, Cooper recorded: "I see far less apprehension of executive than of legislative usurpation in this country. Still, I am willing to admit that the president has too much authority for our form of government" (Cooper 1834: 90).

readers through Cooper's return to literary as well as political archetype. However, when the novel insists that "the time must arrive when American will learn to distinguish between a Patriot and a robber," Cooper's readers might respond with skepticism (247). *The Spy* has, in fact, been asking them to do the very opposite by revealing that the distinction between patriot and robber is always already an illusion.

With that being said, Cooper maintains an obvious difference in kind between Washington and the novel's beasts. In problematically racialized terms, Magua's "Indianness" marks him as inherently, irredeemably evil, whereas Washington's privilege as a white male manifests through Washington's unflinching ability to separate the morally upright from the sinners. To Birch, the chief magistrate declares: "I saw in you a regard to truth and principle, that, I am pleased to say, has never deceived me" (397). Just as Washington cannot be deceived by appearances, Cooper's reader is never meant to suspend her certainty in the proceedings; *The Spy* never truly asks its reader to lose faith in the potency of POTUS as a force for social betterment. In this sense, *The Spy* anticipates an important hitch at the close of Nolan's *The Dark Knight*: the police chief's son watches Batman ride away, having witnessed firsthand the hero's sacrificial decision to adopt the persona of the villain. But if the audience is "in on the joke," which is to say, if Nolan's audience shares the boy's perception and never falters in its knowledge that Batman remains intrinsically good, even when performing the supposedly useful role of criminal, doesn't that knowledge weaken the entire premise of the state of exception? Said another way, if Cooper's reader never wavers in her belief that Washington represents the best of humanity, does she ever truly recognize the complex overlap between sovereign and beast? How would she not always already succumb to a blind faith in the unwavering goodness of the president?

In addition to this pressing matter of perception, I think what matters most here is the question of whether or not the president *must* operate from a state of exception. Could Cooper have envisioned a presidency that did not require ceaseless crises in order to justify his actions? Or, could contemporary readers envision such a presidential figure today? From one perspective, Bumppo and Washington are both condemned to exceptionality, since their positions vis-à-vis the social order remain entirely circumscribed by a drive to extra-legality—positions detached from the foundations of democratic governance. It can be argued that audiences only care about these heroes because these heroes sustain a radical contingency. In this regard, the sociopolitical dangers of the power possessed by Bumppo and Washington cannot be overstated: with his willingness to celebrate, or at least make more palatable for his audience, the chief magistrate's exceptionality, Cooper came quite close—*avant la lettre*, of course—to legitimizing the imperial presidencies of the twentieth and twenty-first centuries, with their blatant disregard for democratic oversight. Even worse, Cooper's state of exception could confirm Agamben's worrisome statement that "there is nothing outside of the law," which is to say, that even the law's potential openings for revolutionary upheaval can be subsumed under the purview of an oppressive regime (Agamben 1995: 29).

But could a nation like the United States function without the exceptionalism of Cooper's Patriot Kings? One could surmise that America's system of government necessitates a president that is not a rigid monument to national wholeness, but the marker of a hole within the social order, the indeterminable nature of the nation's (extra)legal foundations. Had Cooper exorcised his exceptional chiefs from the collective consciousness, his work might have been cited as an endorsement of authoritarian designs. Without the attendant tensions of Cooper's fictional presidents, his readers might have isolated a romanticized national essence and, in turn, downgraded the extra-legal position of their Dark Knights. This tradeoff may seem desirable, but it would have left readers with a reduced capacity to imagine the radical contingencies that underlie the structures of authority that oppress them.

It may be the greatest strength of Cooper's The Spy, then, that it never resolves its internal conflicts. In their final correspondence, Washington tells Birch: "In me you will always have a secret friend" (Cooper 1997: 400). The closing moment of The Spy thus confirms the importance of truth as well as secrecy in the figure of the presidency: a symbol that must hold in balance assumptions of true character with a recognition that, in unusual circumstances, certain things must be kept secret. Although Cooper's romantic impulses occasionally drove him close to naïve idolatry, his works nevertheless reflect a (merciful) paradox that accompanies depictions of the chief magistrate—legalism and illegality; icon and iconoclasm; sovereign and beast; democrat and authoritarian. To view presidential figures as pure exceptions would be to follow the Skinners, or to lack even a basic aspiration of articulating the common good; at the same time, to view authority figures as totally uncorrupted by the state of exception would be to fall prey to a kind of essentialism and elevate Washington into the rank of authoritarian leader. Consciously or not, Cooper charted a trifold negotiation of normative, lofty ideals, the abject precariousness of the law, and the unsettled position that a Patriot King must hold. It is only by scrutinizing the shifting faces of the president—without, and this point remains paramount, jumping into an illusory reconciliation—that one can understand the vital function that POTUS retains in America's political imaginary. The power of contradiction holds sway. Given the nature of the rest of this book, I ought to pause and assert the requisite function of American fiction in formulations of the presidency. That is, Cooper revealed, to an increasingly democratic populace in the 1820s, why an executive was so vital. The resultant literariness of the office has allowed generations of readers to grapple with its ambiguities and to avoid transforming the president into either an unsavory unilateral force (like, say, George W. Bush) or a romanticized embodiment of national exceptionalism (like, say, Barack Obama). Returning to Cooper's ambiguous corpus, readers might consider how the foundations of American literature correlated intimately with nascent renderings of the Patriot King. Indeed, such a return allows readers to comprehend how fictional presidents have played—and must continue to play—a paramount role in orienting the American project.

2

George Lippard and the Gothic President

In terms of mass appeal, no American writer has shaped popular visions of the presidency more than George Lippard.[1] Lippard's fiction places the nation's first president in fantastic situations in order to craft a compelling caricature. While his stories tend to dwell on Washington's experiences during the revolutionary years, they remain messianic, which is to say, they always gesture at Washington's eventual ascent to the presidency. More specifically, Lippard's depictions of Washington defined the would-be president through Gothic conventions and, in the process, generated an image of the nation's leader imbued with a sense of the sublime and sensationalized through associations with abject as well as unimpeachable female bodies. Lippard played with the presidential body as both corporeal form and disembodied spirit. His amalgamation of myth and materialism forged a deeply unsettling image of the commander in chief.

Washington remained enormously important to Lippard throughout his life. Indeed, Lippard "devoted more pages to the treatment of Washington than any other writer of fiction up to the present day" (Bryan 1970: 214). The secret society that Lippard launched employed the name Washington as an honorific for its members: "Moving up through its hierarchy there were Chief Washingtons and Exalted Washingtons and one Supreme Washington, who was, of course, Lippard" (Poe and Butterfield 1955: 286). Washington also appears countless times throughout Lippard's corpus, including in the three major publications to which this chapter will attend: *Blanche*

---

[1]Few American authors have been as prolific or as popular as Lippard. His best-known work, *The Quaker City: Or, the Monk of Monk Hall* (1845), was the best-selling American novel prior to the publication of Harriet Beecher Stowe's *Uncle Tom's Cabin* in 1852.

of Brandywine; Or, September the Eleventh, 1777: A Romance (1846), *Washington and His Generals "1776"; The Legends of the American Revolution* (1847), and *Adonai, The Pilgrim of Eternity* (1851). The plots of these texts are simplistic: Washington enters into battle, overcomes horrific obstacles, and emerges triumphant. In these three works, Lippard crafted an uncanny president-in-waiting, a fictional executive whose Gothic characterization proved requisite to Lippard's vision of a radical democracy to come.

Before analyzing Lippard's treatment of Washington, though, I must devote a word to Lippard's politics and the backdrop against which he forged his unique political profile. During the 1830s and 1840s, America, and especially the city of Philadelphia, experienced a tremendous amount of turmoil as banks failed and seeds were sown for widespread mistrust of elites.[2] Aligning himself with the marginalized, Lippard engaged in religious as well as racial riots that took place in Philadelphia, going so far, in 1848, as to stake his career in a weekly magazine, *The Quaker City*, dedicated to the advancement of social revolution. Concurrently, following the Jacksonian turn, Americans of many stripes experienced a sort of democratic rebirth. In the 1840 presidential contest between Martin van Buren and William Henry Harrison, nearly eight of ten eligible voters cast a ballot—a statistic that suggests "national politics was becoming popular, and popular politics national" (Altschuler and Blumin 2001: 36). While the preceding Era of Good Feelings was characterized by a gulf between the masses and ruling elites, the election of 1840 revealed a resurgence of "broadly felt" democratic feeling: a "newly awakened electorate . . . (experiencing) ephemeral bursts of enthusiasm" (46). Working for a Democratic law firm dedicated to populist causes, Lippard played a major part in perpetuating these "ephemeral bursts," especially through the bodily sensations of his urban Gothic tales. Lippard's dedication to somatic responses was not a mere secondary issue, but the primary matter at hand, as his dream for American society very much involved the "merging of vibrant materiality and radical politics" (Reynolds 2015: 61). By definition, radical democracy induces dramatic leveling, and so even the most homely of façades—or the most stately of busts—cannot repress for long the potential for an unhomely demolition of the status quo. These ruptures remain of the utmost importance for any good faith attempt at constructing a democracy.

Because I begin by designating Lippard's Washington with the term uncanny, let us look at several ways in which the Freudian concept can be applied to Lippard's presidential portraits. First, according to Freud, the uncanny is marked by a subject that surmounts primitive beliefs but can

---

[2] "The masses were suffering because of the bad decisions of an unaffected, wealthy minority" (Williams 2013: 170).

never fully shake them; for his part, Lippard contrasted brutal historical realities of the American Revolution with mystical associations tied to a heavily romanticized leader. Second, feelings of uncanniness occur when something that has been repressed recurs, or, something that has been concealed becomes uncomfortably exposed. Lippard recognized the power of this second definition when he contrasted natural bodies, typically dead or dying, with the metaphorical body of an elected sovereign (a traditionally bloodless symbol). Finally, the fiction writer—Freud claimed—can best maximize the impact of uncanny sensation: "He deceives us into thinking that he is giving us the sober truth, and then after all *oversteps the bounds of possibility*" (Freud 1925: 405, emphasis mine). Lippard frequently overstepped the bounds of possibility by startling readers accustomed to established norms. This drive to shock the system, to truly unnerve the elites, advances Lippard's claim that democracy demands uncanny moments, and that these uncanny moments need to be facilitated primarily by writers of fiction. In a word, oscillating between misty monument and vibrant materiality, Lippard's Gothic depictions of Washington underscore the radicality of democratic politics.

But why was vibrant materiality in particular so crucial to Lippard and his fellow democrats, and how did this concept inform his stories of the first president? Lippard was committed to the embodiment of certain ideals that could be tangibly felt, which is to say, by the physical bodies fighting and dying in factories as well as the streets of Philadelphia. Thanks in part to his own religious upbringing, Lippard remained "attentive to the corporeal and material aspects of earthly existence" (Streeby 1996: 451). Unlike many of the period's hagiographies, which treated Washington as a noble yet anemic symbol, Lippard channeled perceptions of Washington through the reader's sensorium to endow his audience with a renewed appreciation for how flawed economic and political ideals had taken a significant toll on the young republic's corporeal concerns. In effect, Lippard prioritized a fleshy version of Washington the revolutionary: a visceral figure created in response to the sheer weightiness of America's forgotten working class. He forced his reader to interrogate the manner in which the nascent democracy articulated its unwieldly beliefs.

On a related front, much analysis remains to be done in terms of understanding the president as an integral part of a larger textual system— that is, as a literary trope situated within a historically circumscribed system of meaning making. Lippard's future president did not manifest in isolation; instead, Lippard grafted Washington onto relatively recognizable plotlines, alongside a set of familiar characters and within familiar literary settings. Although previous studies have mostly understood the president to be a stand-alone icon, Lippard's texts allow critics to interrogate the president as a complex generic construct. His fictional president was informed by Lippard's idiosyncrasies as a writer—what Christopher Looby describes as his "unsettling literary style"—as well as the prescribed expectations of generic movements within the nineteenth-century literary marketplace (Looby 2015: 3).[3]

Lippard's presidential tales contrast the young republic's idealistic messages—such as the messianic plotline of American progress, tied to the prophetic voices of its Founding Fathers—with an acutely sensationalized mode of delivery. The "ideological freight" of "martyred bodies" consequently clashes against a commercial impetus to keep "the reader fascinated" (Shapira 2018: 24). Accordingly, the first section of this chapter analyzes Lippard's Washington in terms of syntax (the mythological coherence attached to the presidency) as well as semantics (the specific tropes that serve as building blocks to forge presidential narratives). While the syntax of Lippard's Washington stories echoes other hagiographies of the period, the semantics of these works depart dramatically from the output of Lippard's contemporaries. David S. Reynolds describes this collision of elements as a byproduct of Lippard's status as an author "whose hyperbolic reverence for America's republican ideals impelled (him) to go to unprecedented sensational extremes to expose what (he) saw as the betrayal of these ideals" (Reynolds 2011: 170). To read fictional presidents in this manner encourages scrutinizing the uneven relationship between metanarratives associated with the presidency and the peculiar building blocks designated to comprehend individual administrations: the terrifying tyrant, the pastoral shepherd, and so forth.[4] In sum, one can revisit how the tensions attendant to genre dovetail with the tensions of early American politics, including the divided nature of the president as a democratic king with two bodies (a concept developed in the final section).

In Lippard's telling, the disincarnate premise behind the American government, comprised of vague claims concerning freedom, equality, and boundless prosperity, becomes unnerved by the bodies that litter Lippard's literary landscapes. The grotesque and perfected bodies that manifest in the pages of his thrillers challenge as well as affirm metanarratives connected to the presidency. From mutilated corpses to abstract ideals, Lippard's fiction remains replete with unsightly as well as inspiring bodies, as he exploited fleshy frameworks to educate and enthrall—two agendas that

---

[3]David S. Reynolds articulates the dynamic as follows: "Lippard was at once the most intensely patriotic and the most militantly radical novelist of the pre–Civil War period. His veneration for America's Founding Fathers verged upon the religious, as witnessed by his long, very popular collections of historical 'legends' in which he mythologized the heroes of the past. At the same time, his perception of the distance between democratic deals and the horrors of industrialized America impelled him to write lurid exposés" (Reynolds 2011: 205).

[4]David S. Reynolds argues that Lippard's works are "filled with hyperbolic reverence for the Founding Fathers and, at the same time, with vitriolic bitterness against the perceived inequities in nineteenth-century American society, which they regarded as a nightmarish realm" (Reynolds 2011: 184).

were rarely synchronized.[5] Lippard articulated the mythological cohesion of the presidency via the perfect symmetry of Washington's body, Greek like in its harmonious proportions; at the same time, and due in no small part to its Gothic surroundings, Lippard's executive form functioned as a shrewd strategy for selling stories. In unorthodox moments, Washington's body offered a rejoinder to accounts of the young nation's grandiose purpose. Lippard thus unleashed "uncanny, spectral forms that troubled exceptionalist fantasies" (Streeby 2002: 2). For Lippard, Washington's body, and the surrounding bodies that define it through points of contrast, encouraged readers to confront disembodied ideals that the United States had proclaimed in theory but never exemplified in practice. Familiar and unfamiliar at once, conjured from vaporous spirits and anchored to bodily existence, Lippard's Washington unveils a nation in search of itself: its burgeoning Christian nationalism; the ideals trumpeted by nationalists to suppress acknowledgment of the physical condition of real-world laborers; and sensationalist oddities greedily consumed. In his own eclectic manner, Lippard used his portrayals of Washington to undercut any simplistic telling of how American readers were to understand their chief magistrate. His Gothicized presidency compels contemporary readers, in turn, to reconceptualize their country's haunted iconography.

Gothic Body, Gothic Soul

The idea of the presidency evolves alongside literary genres. In Rick Altman's terms, Lippard tarried around tensions between syntactic expectation—the dominant storyline that initially advanced Washington to his state of supremacy—and semantic signal—the sensationalized treatment of Washington as a maiden in distress, or a beheaded corpse. In effect, readers cannot isolate the president in American fiction, or, truly, in American culture at large, from issues of narrative coherence, or from the marketable tropes employed to fabricate presidential narratives. Lippard's tales of Washington sustain an ongoing deification of the Founding Fathers; concomitantly, they transmit this message by tapping into sensations that are unorthodox in presidential accounts of the era: specifically, the physical sensations aroused in highly sought-after Gothic stories. As George E. Haggerty argues, "Gothic form is (. . .) affective form" (Haggerty 1989: 8). Consequently, this line of inquiry proves to be an inquiry into bodies, into lived forms—religious, political, and aesthetic. Lippard's treatment of

---

[5]Chad Luck contends that, in Lippard's fiction, "The production and persuasion of readerly affect (. . .) is, as a result, brimming with revolutionary potential" (Luck 2014: 188). On multiple levels, Lippard engaged with the interplay between bodies and literary affect.

the commander in chief invites readers to ruminate upon how they might disentangle real-world bodies from the abstract ideals to which those bodies have been incongruously wed. Once more, the results are uncanny, in the Freudian sense of the term, as a crucial slippage occurs between the familiar and the unfamiliar, or, the mighty edifice and its immanent undoing.

Lippard's Washington is a curious creation, an amalgam of religious imagery and sensationalist plots. A practitioner of syncretism in both his art and his liturgical habits, Lippard juxtaposed the "soul" of his stories—their metaphysical assumptions—with distinctive physical forms in ways that could be quite jarring. In an overtly political sense, Lippard aligned pieces of a hegemonic national narrative that was beginning to come into focus during his lifetime, only to revel in its immanent decomposition: "(Lippard) rips signifiers from the signifieds that have gathered around them in the general culture. He *deforms* these signifiers by transplanting them to utterly new settings or characters" (Reynolds 2015: 48, author's emphasis). Rearranging political and aesthetic elements in bizarre ways, Lippard relied extensively upon the language of the Gothic.[6] The results were unquestionably captivating. In short, Lippard successfully capitalized upon "the extraordinary energy generated by the play of contradictory forces" within and between genres (Altman 2009: 556).

But how did Lippard intend for his readers to respond to the presidency in particular, with its attendant religiosity and far-fetched idealizations, and how did these intended responses correspond with, or diverge from, the common expectations of Gothic reading? On the one hand, Lippard infused the idea of the president with Gothic sensations as the thrills and chills of the revolution directly informed the executive's prominent place in American life. He manifested the future president's Gothicism through the enduring folklore of the bloody battlefields as well as the eerie graveyards that surround them. At the same time, Lippard sustained a sycophantic account of Washington's greatness, despite—or, perhaps, precisely because of—the grotesque stylization that he infused into his narratives of presidential excellence. With a style that some critics have described as puerile, Lippard depicted Washington through literary conventions such as the haunted house and the sublime wilderness.[7] Lippard's Gothicized presidency invokes

---

[6]Michael Denning summarizes the author's overall strategy: "Lippard achieved his figurative energy by appropriating the conventions of the Gothic" (Denning 1998: 92). Although Denning recognizes Lippard's reliance upon Gothic tropes, he does not reflect upon their prominence in Lippard's depictions of Washington. Denning presents the works on Washington as naively patriotic. I would disagree: Lippard's Washington stories remain some of the most haunting narratives within his corpus.

[7]J. V. Ridgley records, "(Lippard's) art, crammed with the clichés of popular culture and the slogans of proletarian social protest, was remorselessly lowbrow" (Ridgley 1974: 78). William Alfred Bryan laments the "ill-advised Gothic scenes" in Lippard's fiction (Bryan 1970: 216). I

an ever-elusive border between form and formlessness: an unorthodox style that manages to convey the requisite messiness of radical democracy.

Since gloomy settings are a staple of Gothic narratives, it comes as little surprise that a Gothicist like Lippard projected Washington's wartime exploits against a terrifying backdrop. There were syntactic as well as semantic reasons for Lippard to erect decrepit mansions within his retelling of Washington's rise to the presidency. Syntactically, the metaphor of a decrepit domicile conveyed the rotting timbers within twin national frameworks, British as well as American. Semantically, the portable features of these unhomely homes—the creaking floorboards; the shadowy windows; the moldy cellars—aided Lippard's effort to conceptualize, through points of distinction, Washington as a timeless structure in his own right (an important point to which this chapter will return). The problem of course was that young America did not actually possess ancient buildings. Lippard had to transpose well-worn tropes that signify an eroding establishment, that is, the haunted house, from its British origins to vacant American lots. On this front, Lippard followed the lead of another Pennsylvania writer, one of his main inspirations and the man to whom he dedicated his novel *The Quaker City*, Charles Brockden Brown. Brown too faced the difficult task of turning the virginal American landscape into a Gothic canvas in the seminal haunted house story of American literature, *Wieland; Or, The Transformation: An American Tale*. Like Brown, Lippard filled the pages of his stories concerning Washington with spooky edifices to augment his transgressive message. He recycled the haunted house convention to erect a textual embodiment of everything that he believed to be sick and dying in American life. Among these ruins, his Washington broodily stalks.

More than mere window dressing, these macabre settings carry with them a specific political message: "Gothic novelists employed their gloomy settings as a shorthand for the hierarchies of aristocracy . . . which they detested and which their revolutionary age fatally undermined" (Bailey 1999: 5). From Horace Walpole's prototypical Castle of Otranto to the bifurcated abode of Edgar Allan Poe's Usher family, Gothic structures have long conveyed a palpable political purpose.[8] Lippard's crumbling mansions stand out against the carnage of the revolutionary battlefield. These structures, as well as their sensational surroundings, establish the mood of the text, while at the same time underscoring Lippard's political agenda: to expose readers to a fundamentally unjust society in need of urgent reform. "The old mansion rises in sullen gloom, its dark walls tottering as though about

---

would counter that it was only by reworking the relationship between underlying message and stylistic trappings that Lippard could capture the unsettled state of nineteenth-century America.
[8] Dale Bailey continues, "The haunted house becomes a strikingly versatile metaphor; transcending the glossy clichés of formula, it drags into light the nightmarish tensions of gender, class, and culture hidden at the heart of American life" (Bailey 1999: 24).

to fall" (Lippard 2007: 497). Although it is likely jarring for readers today to imagine a preeminent president riding through Gothic circumstances, Lippard's corpus routinely includes such unusual tableaus.[9] By priming his reader for supernatural shock and awe, negative as well as positive, and by stroking revolutionary sentiment, Lippard juxtaposed one of America's most formulaic literary settings with one of America's most formulaic figures (the archetypical president).

Lippard took his readers on a veritable tour of Gothic abodes. In *Blanche*, readers spend a good deal of time wandering the creepy corridors of Rock Farm, "that dark and gloomy mansion . . . a fit scene for legends of horror" (Lippard 1846: 32). One of the story's maidens finds herself imprisoned in the inner recesses of the imposing manse. As shrieks echo through the hallways, the maiden races from room to room, pursued by invisible as well as visible monstrosities. At last, she approaches a door, around which flashes "red gleams of light"; when she opens it, there stands "a woman's form (. . .) in the centre of that large and gloomy chamber with the beams of a lamp falling over her face . . . like a spirit from the other world. That wan face, that look—oh God, I shall never forget it" (175). Lippard's *Washington* sends its reader into yet another pair of ancient mansions set in the eye of the storm of a bloody revolutionary battle: Chew's House serves as "the embrace of death" for disoriented soldiers, an "impregnable" structure with "lurid lights" flashing in every blackened window (Lippard 2007: 51). Lippard's reader becomes increasingly upset by "the horrid howl of slaughters, the bubbling groan of death." She must "tread carefully, or (her) foot will trample on the face of that dead soldier"; the ceiling, at one point, appears to be dripping blood—it turns out to be wine and, in a Poe-like scene of "ludicrous horror," soldiers forfeit the struggle to drink the blood wine (53–58). Turning to yet another dilapidated residence, *Blanche* describes Block-House as a "strange old mansion . . . as sad and desolate as the tomb . . . like some strange sepulcher, in which the dead of long-past ages lie entombed" (87–90). Block-House confirms the thesis of Lippard's twice-told revolutionary legends: burned by the brutal British, it offers a grim reminder of the merciless nature of colonization. While Lippard's Washington never sets foot in these impure houses—although he does enter into adjacent catacombs—one cannot overlook how Lippard's texts supplement a presidential life story with midnight constitutionals in dank dwellings. Both the syntax and the semantics linked to the American haunted house emotionally heighten Lippard's pseudo-biographical sketches of the

---

[9]Not coincidentally, Lippard was a regular correspondent with Poe and one of Poe's staunchest defenders. One cannot fail to see the influence of Poe, for example, in the freakish outsiders that stalk the character in *Blanche*. One is a man named "Blood" and the other is a woman named "Death," recalling the oddities that populate Poe's story "King Pest."

nation's first president, and prepare the reader to be thoroughly unnerved by what they discover within.

If the reader's eye wanders away from these otherwordly mansions, she quickly confronts another Gothic aspect of Lippard's Washington fables— the sublime wilderness. Lippard routinely shifted his readers gaze from gross façade to ethereal mist. Charles Brockden Brown likewise appealed to the American wilderness to inspire a sense of wonderment before the ever-present unknown.[10] For Lippard, the valley of Brandywine in Pennsylvania remained "rife with incidents of supernatural lore" (Lippard 1846: 48). Specters linger at every wood line, hovering at the margins of the so-called civilized realm, beckoning American soldiers to their doom. Lippard's *Washington* asks its readers: "Does not the awful silence of these primeval woods . . . strike your hearts with a deep awe? (. . .) There is something fearful in this ominous silence . . . the abyss" (Lippard 2007: 341, 344). When soldiers eventually enter the ominous forest, the effect is immediate. The sublime, which is to say, the mind's inability to grasp the enormity of the unknown, infuses every moment of Lippard's text with trepidation as well as reverence: "Your mind is awed by tremendous hills . . . every scene around you seems but the fitting location for a wild and dreamy tradition" (59).

The sublime horizon of these stories amplifies the expansiveness of Washington's imagined transcendental soul—a bombastic gesture at the nation's prophetic grandeur. In *Blanche*, the figure of Washington calls to mind "the sublimity of Godhead" (Lippard 1846: 237). On first blush, the metaphysical idealism surrounding Washington dwarfs the carnal human being from Mount Vernon. Lippard's novel augments the reader's sense of smallness by turning to an impenetrable obscurity that engulfs the revolutionary battlefield. These landscapes are eternally formless, blurry, and blanketed in murk: "As the dim moonbeams gleaming through the gathering mist and gloom, shone over glittering arms, and dusky banners, all gliding past, like phantoms of the Spectre Land" (Lippard 2007: 35). While this ominous unrealizability may chill the reader, these texts concurrently dare the reader to dream, which is to say, they incentivize the reader to long for a better future. Lippard's vision of democracy demands an openness to unexpected change. In this sense, Lippard's Gothicism retains a vital sense of dissatisfaction: a remembrance, thanks to the story's innate formlessness, of the hard work that remains to be done, and a preservation of the strife that must continue to propel the nation toward that more perfect union. A democratic body politic must of necessity remain hazy around the edges.

---

[10]In *Edgar Huntly*, Brown points to "this chaos of rocks and precipices . . . a desolate and solitary grandeur . . . sanctity and awe . . . I was probably the first who had deviated this remotely from the customary paths of men" (Brown 2006: 71).

Yet the politics of the sublime remains a complicated matter. On one front, Lippard's sublime evokes the timelessness of Washington; the reader's mind reels when the narrator asks it to perceive the president-in-waiting as one example in a long litany of eternal heroes dating back to Jesus Christ.[11] From another vantage point, however, this murkiness—this undefinable essence; this relentless uncertainty—actually *undermines* Washington's status as a stable reservoir of national virtues. Shrouded and ephemeral, the presidency perhaps lost a bit of its coherence as Lippard rushed to exploit readerly sensations. In other words, for Lippard to Gothicize the president-to-come involved forfeiting specificity and relinquishing the clarity of the Washington myth, one that was only just starting to coalesce into a legible script. His readers may have been titillated by the author's evocations of the sublime, but Lippard's aesthetic choices may have helped to deny American readers firm footing before their nation's foremost symbolic representatives. Even as ardent nationalists were evoking Washington to embody the metaphysical soul of a nation, Lippard held that the uncanniness of Washington as a national figuration—his standing as both moldy monument and monstrous mist—was precisely what he needed to convey his own radical agenda.

Feminized Forms

Lippard's texts concerning Washington leave readers in a complicated position through his deployment of yet another Gothic convention: the maiden in flight from the madman. His fiction presents maidens running from the talons of men who have lost any tether to reality. In *Blanche*, one such maiden, echoing the women of Matthew Lewis's *The Monk* and other British sensationalist texts, is forced to marry a monstrous man. Lippard's British men commit atrocities against innocent American women with regularity. They steal full-bodied American daughters with "necks of alabaster," "bosoms of snow," and so forth (Lippard 1846: 137). Understanding well the literary marketplace of the mid-nineteenth century, Lippard dove into grotesque subjects like rape without an overriding concern for propriety.[12] A question naturally arises: how could the disturbing abuse of a maiden's body possibly be harnessed for the benefit of presidential hagiography? Interestingly, Lippard did not portray Washington rescuing young women in

---

[11]Poe and Butterfield write that, for Lippard, "The heroes of our revolution were not just great men to him; they were demigods" (Poe and Butterfield 1955: 288).

[12]Daniel Stein describes Lippard's work as a mixture of ideological conviction and a shrewd awareness of marketplace trends, texts that suggest a willingness on the part of their author to "negotiate the tension between a moral absolutism geared toward the politicization of readers and the narrative demands of serial storytelling" (Stein 2017: 64).

peril; instead, he periodically aligned the president with the maiden. In one such scene, a band of British soldiers capture Washington and threaten to undermine the revolutionary cause. With a melodramatic flourish, the novel synthesizes the name of its idealized maiden with the name of its idealized president-to-be: "WASHINGTON-BLANCHE" (243). The text invites its reader to feminize Washington's body and, thus, shudders at the thought of British madmen violating sacred American figures. The familiar generic distress of female forms under siege carries over into the less familiar distress of a presidential body taken against its will. Of course, the synthesis of Washington and Blanche remains a strange one, given the fact that Lippard's story supposedly recounts Washington's climb to national dominance. The generic expectations of a Gothic maiden can be read as undercutting the logic of Washington's unimpeachable greatness. Never one to shy away from the risk of incongruities, Lippard transposed the figurative body of a haunted house, set against an unspeakable frontier, into a divided female form.

Lippard's feminization of the future president's body, in tandem with the future president's juxtaposition with the unknown, more specifically, with death—moves necessitated by generic norms—produced an unusual amalgamation of national mythos and the American Gothic. Lippard encapsulated these tensions within what Poe famously (and problematically) called the "most poetic" of tropes: a dying woman. Lippard's narrators describe beautiful feminine remains in startling detail: "A corse, on whose fair proportion rude eyes would gaze, a lifeless body, whose voluptuous outlines, would be trampled under horses' hoofs, or whose young bosom, would be torn by the carrion vultures of the battlefield." At the same time, his texts mark the discarded female body as "a beautiful incarnation of maidenly innocence" (Lippard 1846: 213, 215). For Poe and his literary disciple Lippard, this distinction remained crucial since, like the haunted house, it exposed a thinly veiled rot beneath the allure of the nation's most idealized forms. Elisabeth Bronfen argues that in many Gothic works the female corpse is "polluted . . . a carrier of death . . . the beauty of Woman is conceived as a mask for decay . . . the source of life clothed in beauty but infested by the ferments of death" (Bronfen 1992: 67). And yet Lippard's female bodies, idealized and stripped of their materiality, also serve as vessels for a timeless essence that floats high above the mortal coil: "From the very rankness of the mould, that encloses the Mother's Form, from the very eyes and skull of Death, fair flowers bloom beautifully into the light, and with their fragrance sanctify the graveyard air" (Lippard 2007: 360). In a similar fashion, Lippard's Washington is a delicate treasure under siege as well as a personification of universal beauty.

In other words, Lippard's Gothic stories of Washington muddy the proverbial waters through their reliance upon female corpses. One could argue that when women die in Lippard's legends, they are thought to "go home," to be liberated from the curse of human existence; in contrast,

Lippard's texts commonly celebrate Washington's body for its materiality—its vitalism; its domineering presence. Unlike the feminine corpses scattered throughout the future president's life story, the foremost American executive appears to be endowed with a solid, earthly form. Despite this perceived tendency toward corporeality, though, Lippard's Washington actually serves as both an ethereal subject, one that magically transcends his corporeality, and an abject body, one that recalls the radical situatedness of American citizenship. This ambivalence marks Washington as very much aligned with the female corpse in the Gothic tradition. Lippard's gendered legends struggle to reconcile Washington as syntactic subject—his generalizable purpose as an emblem of the lineage behind American freedom—with Washington as a semantic unit—a human vessel, endowed with fleshy, if mathematically flawless, features. Lippard's Gothicism presents readers with problems concerning the link between the figurative soul and the textual soma of presidential myths. That is, his tales blur Washington-as-ideal, the uninterrupted plotline of a purportedly eternal story, with Washington-as-form—a fully actualized embodiment; a flesh-and-blood human being. Aligned with the female corpses of American fiction, Washington's body allowed nineteenth-century readers to visualize the bifurcated nature of America's emergent political imaginary: a metaphysical boundlessness alongside the unbearable suffering of vulnerable citizens, often driven into the trenches by madmen.

Lippard's Washington stories incessantly guide the reader's gaze to the sensible earth to glimpse abject corpses (the grim toll of a sanguinary revolution). Lippard was far from alone in his willingness to expose his reader to gory human remains.[13] Yael Shapira scrutinizes the Gothic corpse as "an image of the dead body rendered with deliberate graphic bluntness in order to excite and entertain" (Shapira 2018: 1). From the highbrow Graveyard poets to the cheap thrills of anatomical instruction, the nineteenth century witnessed the growth of a veritable cottage industry that churned out assorted depictions of the corpse. Transposed into an overtly political key, Lippard's countless bodies "call into question official, abstract, and decorporealizing national narratives" (Streeby 1996: 451). Against propagandistic abstraction, Lippard demonstrated the importance of an embodied nationalism—one that had to acknowledge the ongoing destruction of human capital, especially on the factory floor. By "repeatedly sketching pictures of endangered, mutilated, or destroyed U.S. bodies," Lippard intended to unify his readers via the stable formulation of Washington's

---

[13]Xavier Aldana Reyes comments, "The Gothic (is) inherently somatic and corporeal. It relies on the reader's and/or viewers' awareness of their own bodies, particularly of their vulnerability and shared experience of projected pain through vicarious feelings" (Reyes 2014: 2).

physical presence.[14] However, Lippard's reader only arrives at this endpoint through repulsion at the sight of countless lifeless carcasses: "Lippard's dead bodies distress the reader by forcefully concretizing the experience of alienation" (Luck 2014: 212). On the one hand, then, Lippard's readers encounter the disembodied story of America's metaphysical greatness, "the predominance of abstracted national politics divested from material bodies"; on the other hand, Lippard's readers stumble upon "legions of dead bodies that register the invisible victims of nominal yet immaterialized democracy" (Emerson 2015: 124, 128). Lippard meant for his grotesque corporeality to inspire a different sort of social arrangement: a democracy that could cater to the real corporeal needs of actual human beings. Even as British overlords and America's would-be tyrants were intent on diminishing the human form, extracting its soul and leaving the shell to decompose in the gutters of war, Lippard emphasized the bodily demands of a better future. Lippard shifted from recycling pieces of a national narrative that overlooked the material needs of its citizenry to imagining a society that could pump life into its citizens and, in so doing, aid them in more fully embodying American ideals.

Lippard believed that only the bluntness of a mangled corpse could adequately convey his political message. Lippard deployed mutilated bodies, around which Washington navigates, to expose his audience to the gross decay obscured by the lofty ideological formulations being sold by the most strident of nationalists. According to Lippard, every unjust declaration of power over another life involves a body used up, a corpse stripped of its vital life essence, and an enslaved form reduced to mere mass. The unvarnished quality of Lippard's extraneous bodies, not to mention their sheer quantity throughout his corpus, recalls Washington's supposed *raison d'etre*: an urgent need for a second revolution. Lippard's Washington stories confirm the corpse as a catalyst for a kind of political transformation that was previously thought impossible. Time and time again, Lippard's characters come face-to-face with a hideous corpse, and respond by utterly changing the course of their lives. In *Washington*, a young man looks upon the hanged corpse of his father, a spy executed by American rebels. The details of the encounter are unsparing: "The burden of the fearful fruit which (the branch) bore . . . the blackened face and staring eyes, and protruding tongue glowed horribly in the sunlight" (Lippard 2007: 346). Exposed to the unsavory side of warfare, the youth proceeds to enact vengeance on one of his father's killers. Extending this storyline, *Blanche* describes what follows: the father's body, "a blackened mass," sprawled on the pile of ashes—"a ghastly wreck of humanity . . . (a) shapeless carcass, dumb and motionless" (Lippard 1846: 65). The cycle of violence continues

---

[14]Julia Kristeva notes, "Abjection, when all is said and done, is the other facet of religious, moral, and ideological codes on which rest the sleep of individuals and the breathing spells of societies" (Kristeva 1982: 209).

as the sight of this tortured body rallies other rebels into action. A rebellious leader recalls that "mangled mass of scarred flesh, with the peeled skin and whitened bones," in order to radicalize his listeners, "each eye fixed upon the corpse" (114). These hanged and burned bodies presumably goad onlookers into deliberate political action. And, for the purposes of this book at least, the most startling example of a corpse fomenting insurrection appears in a dream in which Lippard's reader must confront what would have happened to Washington if he had betrayed his nascent country. In a profoundly disquieting scene, the text impels its reader to watch a public beheading of the first president: "The head falls upon the saw dust . . . the life-blood falls in a torrent upon the quivering body" (171). Rendering the president as a victim in the feminized Gothic mold, Washington's corpse affirms a need for continual revolution. Lippard's readers must somehow reconcile, then, the sublime and abject faces of Washington with the transcendent yet tortured female forms of the Gothic tradition.

The President Incarnate

Lippard's Washington is a confused icon. Cloaked by the dusk of war, he stands out as a well-defined, singular entity at a degree of removal from the cadavers that clutter the ground. He almost always stands erect among the rankness of unanimated bodies. And yet, as we have seen, Washington's body is also feminized, assaulted, even brutally decapitated. Caught between Gothic sublimity and Gothic corporeality, Washington manifests at the intersection of foggy formlessness and morbid materiality. The future president's body provides a temporary placeholder for a mythic lineage leading to the birth of the United States; concomitantly, the future president's body occupies actual space, with genuine weightiness. In Lippard's treatments, Washington ultimately emerges as "the Incarnation of some great principle" (Lippard 1846: 163).

Much more than a routine corpse, Lippard's Washington serves as an imaginative, dialectical site—a meeting point for the metaphysics of freedom and the necessity of freedom finding finite form. Washington stands, very much alive, against the vaporous battlefield, and his bodily presence remains full of muscular vitality: "How grandly his form towers in the mist . . . the form of Washington is in the centre of the fight, the battle-glare lighting up his face of majesty" (Lippard 2007: 37, 40). Lippard's texts emphasize Washington's extraordinary visibility: his profile, sharply defined against the dusky air; his upright posture, prominently displayed above the prone position of his dead contemporaries. "All around was bloodshed, gloom, and death; mist and smoke above; (. . .) mangled corpses below," and there, unmistakable, available to the eyes of all, "(Washington's) tall form" (41). Placed in contrast with "the form of Death," Washington—a "towering form" with a "muscular chest"—is definitively "seen by every eye in the interval of the battle-smoke" (63–65).

Washington's tangible body emblematizes the strength of America's body politic, replete with carnal principles abandoned by the Philadelphia foremen intent on regurgitating platitudes in their disregard of the suffering of the working class. All around Washington's grand physique, disenfranchised individuals fester.

> While they tell the mass of the people that Washington was a saint . . . they draw a curtain over his heart, they hide from us, under piles of big words and empty phrases, WASHINGTON THE MAN. You may take the demi-god if you like, and vapor away whole volumes of verbose admiration a shadow, but for my part, give me Washington the Man. He *was* a Man. The blood (. . .) flowed in his veins. (Lippard 1846: 334–35, author's emphasis)

As this passage suggests, *Blanche* revolves around the juxtaposition of moribund bodies with the robust form of a president-in-waiting. The text consistently reflects on the perfect proportions of Washington's body by calling to mind classical Greek sculpture. At the same time, the novel recycles the term sinew *ad nauseam*—a term which stresses tough materiality, the corporeal presence of a presidential figure not carved in stone but made of genuine musculature: "His form so tall, so muscular . . . a beating heart" (237). Situated between ethereal mist and mangled corpse, Lippard's Gothic president blends Christian reincarnation with the burgeoning mythology of America's Forefather.

Lippard aligned Washington with Christ by incorporating the future president's body into a dynamic unfolding. Initially, the fictionalized Washington conjoins with a vast, disembodied spirit: "The ghosts of the mighty-head, come crowding to the portals of the Unknown . . . the martyrs of New World Freedom" (Lippard 2007: 78). Russ Castronovo argues that, among Lippard's contemporaries, democratic freedom was ostensibly "most complete when most disembodied. Envisioned as word and not flesh, construed as syntax and not an accretion of semantic meaning" (Castronovo 2001: 33). Concurrently, however, Lippard's Washington cannot ignore the "senseless carcasses, with the arms rent from the shattered body . . . sunken jaws . . . gory chest" (Lippard 1846: 72). From spirit, to senseless matter, to idealized form, Lippard's Gothic trinity upholds the general thrust of Christian thought: "This man of kingly presence . . . not this figure of mist and frost-work, which some historians have called WASHINGTON— but Washington, the living, throbbing, flesh and blood, Washington!—yes, WASHINGTON THE MAN" (107). The promise of New World freedom achieves its cumulative articulation in the tactile yet quixotic body of the first chief magistrate. Simply put, Lippard's Washington endows sacred word with flesh: "Washington looked like the Ideal image which all future time will delight to worship" (Lippard 1846: 236).[15] Washington here reincarnates the ideals of the New World and endows them with a "proud form . . . dilated to its full stature" (345). Utterly autonomous as well as intimately intertwined with the ghostly heroes of yore, Lippard's representations of the future president's body possess profound political, theological, and aesthetic resonance.

Lippard most thoroughly visualized a presidential reincarnation in *Adonai, The Pilgrim of Eternity*. Adonai, a traveler through time and space, decides to visit the New World, a land "made holy by the deeds of Washington" (Lippard 1851: 42). Upon his arrival at Mount Vernon, Adonia hears Washington's disembodied voice and longs for a return of the hero, whose name is "the holiest synonym of Liberty" (43). *But the spirit is not enough*. Adonai recognizes that freedom means nothing if it is not embodied; Washington must appear to Adonai "in bodily form" (45). Contrary to archetypical portraits by the likes of Parson Weems, Lippard articulated national aspirations that had to be endowed with a concrete shape (Casper 1999: 90). Lippard's text merges Washington's spirit, and the spirit of his age, with the recently deceased carcass of a forgotten laborer. "The Arisen Washington" materializes in a majestic form that appears to "dilate and grow even within its faded garments" (Lippard 1851: 51). The body of the American president-to-come brings freedom back from the dead, cyclically, through the form of a working-class citizen.

As Lippard's narrator looks to the death bed of later president John Adams, *Washington* expounds upon the vital theme of presidential reincarnation: "Every moment the waves come higher; the ice of the grave comes slowly through the concealing veins, up the withered limbs; the mist of death gathers around the old man's eyes" (Lippard 2007: 451). Lippard's reader stares down at the dying president and surveys a graphic process of decay. Adams' son, John Quincy, who later goes on to serve as president himself, also watches the scene unfold: "Let us from the crowd of mute spectators, select a single form. Beside the death pillow . . . gazing in his father's face . . . the son, the Statesman and the president" (451). The abject flesh, the deathless spirit of freedom, and the singular form of a president-in-waiting: Lippard's Gothicism blends with Christian nationalism to exemplify an intimate link between Gothic semantics and presidential syntax, or, putrefied body and patriotic soul.

Through a series of dialectical shifts, Lippard's once-and-future president reveals something significant about Lippard's aesthetic preferences.[16]

---

[15]Lippard stressed the connection between Washington and Jesus Christ in numerous ways: "Washington was assailed because he refused obedience to the King. Think not my friends, to escape the trial of your Saviour, if you follow in his footsteps" (Lippard 2007: 415).

[16]Steven Bruhm writes, "The pained body in Gothic fiction becomes the conduit through which one's identity vacillates—now felt, now numbed; now empowered, now silenced; now self, now other" (Bruhm 1994: 148).

The dedication page for *Blanche* establishes that the novel to come will encapsulate flesh as well as word: "The story will live when I am dead" (Lippard 1846: v). Lippard deliberately designated *Blanche* as his "child": a tactile entity conceived to propel "divine thought" into the physical realm. "This page alone," he argues, "Shall rescue their names, their deeds, from the silence of the grave" (337–38). For Lippard, only the work of art adequately expresses the dialectic of the American spirit—a merging of ageless syntactical elements, like universal freedom, with concrete semantics, like mildew-stained structures. Nineteenth-century sensationalist novels habitually interchanged text and body, as corporeality and literary manifestation influenced one another.[17] Lippard's words give shape to deathless concepts that demand a vessel. The textual form of this message is made explicit in the preface to *Washington*: "Some of the brightest gleams of poetry and romance, that illumine our history, or the history of any other land and age, I have endeavored *to embody*" (Lippard 2007: 12, emphasis mine).

This recurrent focus upon reincarnation speaks to the conflicted nature of the presidency as an uncanny concept. Specifically, Lippard's texts gesture at a political theology that has driven the story of the American presidency. Ernst Kantorowicz describes how, in a medieval context, the superhuman perfection of the king was an immutable emblem, meant to encompass the body politic. Medieval theorists and practitioners had to come to terms with the king's anatomical reality. Later, when determining the fate of Charles I, the British Parliament had to isolate the body natural—a living man to be executed— from the body politic—the godhead king that must endure beyond the death of any lone monarch. Ever since, historians and political scientists have employed the phrase Royal Christology as a shorthand for the complex ways in which the king's two bodies enter into something akin to a holy trinity (Kantorowicz 2016: 16). Yet before the birth of modern democracy, doubt could not "arise concerning the superiority of the body politic over the body natural," since the body politic had proven "more ample and large" (9). Lippard's unsettled *persona ficta* underscores thorny issues surrounding the king with two bodies in a distinctively American context. In particular, Lippard remained much less liable to forsake the body natural in his deification of a national essence.

On the one hand, Lippard sustained the undercurrent of Royal Christology by positioning Washington within an uninterrupted whole; on the other hand, Lippard compelled his readers to revisit the trope of king with two bodies and ask how the concept functions within a uniquely *democratic*

---

[17]For more on the intimate relationship between text and corporeality in sensation novels, see Talaraich-Vielmas (2013).

social order. At times, Lippard challenged the ancient prioritization of body politic over body natural by returning to a central theme bantered about by Christian socialists of his day—namely, the value of a vibrant materiality. "Lippard's eternal social verities are drawn from the teachings of Jesus, whom he saw and represented as a laborer who came to lead his fellow laborers, and these verities are made flesh by . . . George Washington" (Ziff 1981: 97). Said another way, Washington's fleshy actualization mattered more to Lippard than the whispered words, like liberty, equality, prosperity, that accompanied the future president's name. After all, one must remember that the radical implications of democracy are that every single body matters as much as every other body, and that every citizen can—indeed, must—strive to feel, at the level of her sensorium, princely pleasures.

Hopeful but horrified by the prospects of his own vision for a radical democracy, Lippard may have turned to Royal Christology to preserve the nation's metaphysical foundation in the face of its imminent deconstruction.[18] In the aftermath of the American Revolution, and the fall of the *ancien régime* in France, modern democracy emerged alongside the horrifying threat of a truly open-ended society. Without a king, modern democracies would have to come to terms with an "absent body," the monarchical body that had previously provided "an index of social unity and identity" (Lefort 2006: 167–68). To some extent, Lippard responded to this unsettling rupture by preserving within his fiction "the phantom of the theologico-political," and transposing the Royal Spirit into a new carnal principle, one more consonant with the increasingly powerful concept of "the people" (182). Even as Lippard disassembled an emergent consensus surrounding the country's preeminent Founding Father, he restored an illusion of certainty through his secular trinity: an unbroken national essence, the laborer's broken body, and the mediating presence of once-and-future president Washington. Lippard's imagined president thus played an invaluable role in staving off a perceived breakup of social unity in the wake of painful democratic revolutions.

But before writing off Lippard's radicality as covert conformism meant to restore an ancient religiosity within a newly politicized social order, we must return once more to the acutely Gothic dimensions of his portrayals—dimensions which are not merely supplemental, but of the highest possible significance. *It very much matters that Lippard opted to Gothicize Washington's body.* In Lippard's portrayal, Washington's body is not simply another body to be utilized on the road to redemption. The hidden narrative behind Lippard's Washington is driven not by an unbroken *telos*,

---

[18]See, for instance, Jules Michelet's treatise, *History of the French Revolution*, in which he posited the spiritual underpinnings of post-revolutionary France in ways that clearly echo Lippard's strategies in the American context: "The wished-for spring which promises a new light to the world. What light? It is no longer (. . .) the vague love of liberty; but a determined object, of a fixed and settled form" (Michelet 1967: 440).

but by genuinely startling tensions. Lippard's Gothicized executive provides readers with a window into the somatic suffering, palpable anxieties, and sensational hopes of the American working class. And without these sorts of unruly ruptures, contended Lippard, American democracy could not endure.

Lippard's American Gothic turns readers inward by pivoting from hyper-rational detachment to a lived experience, with racing pulse and creeping skin. If modern democracy was to avoid the trap of false certainty through monarchical forms—that is, if modern democracy was to exorcise what Claude Lefort labels as the "royal phantasmagoria"—it would require a fleshiness, a textual tissue, one that would be neither pristine nor predetermined but porous, even, on occasion, decaying (Lefort 2006: 179). The results are definitively uncanny: Lippard's vision of democracy remains familiar as well as unfamiliar, a syntax at constant odds with its semantics. It was Lippard's Gothic proclivities that allowed his readers to glimpse the genuine radicalism of his political imaginary, and to salvage the president's body, at least in theory, from the fate of its kingly counterparts (the titillating as well as terrifying specter of Robespierre lurks everywhere in the margins of this discussion). Due to the Gothic valence of Lippard's Washington, readers cannot bypass the future president's body in favor of hazy virtues, nor can she reduce the American subject to a cadaver left to die in ditches. Instead, Lippard encouraged his readers to conceptualize the president's body as a suture with which to conjoin myth with materialism. Without Lippard's privileging of the uncanny, his renderings of the presidency would have devolved into empty platitudes, divorced from the everyday lives of Americans, or meager forms to be rejected whenever the mood strikes. It may not be too rash, then, to speculate that Lippard's radical democracy could only be upheld through the circulation of Gothicized presidents.

3

William Wells Brown and the Disembodied President

William Wells Brown's *Clotel; Or, the President's Daughter* tells the tale of the child of Thomas Jefferson, who is left to pursue her freedom after being abandoned by her famous father. Adapted from Lydia Maria Child's short story "The Quadroons," as well as a rumor—later proved to be true—that Jefferson impregnated one of his slaves, Sally Hemings, Brown's novel is at once highly conventional and surprisingly distinctive. *Clotel* ruminates upon how the president, an icon of federal consensus, occludes much of the messiness of antebellum America. Indeed, in its very title, the executive defines the daughter, nearly overriding her name as the book's primary descriptor. Concurrently, however, empty words associated with the chief magistrate function as a reminder of political unrest, unveiling how America's foremost sins must be addressed with something more substantive than platitudes. Brown thus presented the figure of the president as a fictional device for building consensus, especially on the issue of citizenship, as well as a reminder of the vital gaps that orient a democratic society.[1]

A former slave from St. Louis, Brown published his monograph while engaged on his lecture tour in England following the passage of the Fugitive Slave Act of 1850. He would go on to revise and republish the novel on four separate occasions. This chapter focuses exclusively on the earliest iteration

---

[1]Brown was not alone in using the figure of the president to achieve these ends. During this era, contributors to *Freedom's Journal*—one of the earliest abolitionist publications—frequently turned to images of the president to articulate their political message. David Walker, for instance, often referenced Thomas Jefferson "as a major source of ammunition for his takedown of the country" (Jackson 2019: 53). And editor Samuel Cornish insisted that freed people of color were "as truly Americans, as the president of the United States and as much entitled to the protection, rights, and privileges of the country as he" (qtd. in Jackson 2019: 50).

of *Clotel* since many of that book's most salient critiques were forged in tandem with Brown's interrogation of the symbolic role of the commander in chief.[2] By ruminating upon the friction between noncorporeal ideals associated with the executive as the young republic's premier avatar and the nation's inability to realize these lofty ambitions—or, to express its values corporeally, in the lived experience of actual human beings—*Clotel* offers an incisive commentary on the failures of early American governance. Yet even as Brown's work undermines the premise that the country's proclamations of freedom and equality could manifest in physical form without its leaders addressing systemic oppression, it nonetheless upholds a number of Jeffersonian appeals. *Clotel* is thus a complex artifact that reflects the core political tensions of its moment.

By the 1840s, it seems safe to assert that the American president had become the most visible emblem of the nation's grand metaphysical narrative. In the aftermath of the War of 1812, George Washington became nearly deified as a supreme manifestation of America's assumed greatness. Shortly thereafter, the Jackson administration of the 1820s and 30s advanced that the presidency was the paramount fetish for the will of the people. The much-hyped election of William Henry Harrison in 1840, in which nearly 80 percent of eligible voters cast a ballot, further demonstrated a swelling significance of the executive in the public eye. At the time of *Clotel*'s publication, then, the president was the signifier par excellence of the prowess of the federal government; he rendered the body politic as a corporate entity, incarnated as what Ralph Waldo Emerson called an exceptional man. Indeed, the president in Brown's day would have been the closest thing to a royal *persona ficta* promulgated by the fledgling democracy. But America's status as a fledgling democracy also complicated this urge to craft a cogent Cult of Personality around the executive. How could a godhead be tolerated within a democracy—a mode of governance meant to level the proverbial playing field? More significant still, what were writers like Brown to do with the chasm that separated this godhead, who presumably embodied the nation's egalitarian values, from the agonies of freed black men being denied the fruits of citizenship? After all, the lionization of POTUS meant precious

---

[2]Notably, with each passing iteration, Brown relied less and less upon the US presidents to tell his story, ultimately replacing figures like Jefferson with less controversial politicians of a lower stature. After its inaugural release in England, never again did the subtitle "President's Daughter" grace the cover of Brown's perennial narrative. In the 1867 version of his story, re-titled *Clotelle; Or, The Colored Heroine: A Tale of the Southern States*, Brown left virtually no trace of a presidential presence. Although the heroine retains some oblique connections to American politics—her great-grandfather is a Senator, and her father is a Congressman—their government roles have no discernible impact on the narrative. Gone are all presidential referents, including the crucial moment that takes place beneath the Washington monument (discussed in the following section). Without the Presidency as a touchstone, I would argue that Brown's text loses some of its political potency.

little to marginalized subjects denied opportunities to transpose Jefferson's nonrepresentational ideals into their daily lives.

The previous chapter analyzed the president's radical embodiment at the hands of sensationalist writer George Lippard, and explored how Lippard turned to the figure of Washington to negotiate between a timeless spirit ("the spirit of '76," to borrow a colloquiual phrase of the day) and the need for that spirit to be made flesh. Lippard's fictional president offered readers an awkward avatar with which to consider the republic's paragons in conjunction with its shortcomings. Brown's work parallels Lippard's by conveying incongruities between the nation's fantasy of itself, which supposedly culminates in the icon of the president—namely, liberal universalism, or the belief that every individual remains constitutionally liberated—and flesh-and-blood bodies, the carnal expression of this fantasy (or, more accurately, the *failure* to generate such an expression). Yet there are crucial differences between the presidential sagas of Lippard and Brown. While Lippard exploited the image of Washington to articulate the nation's potential, as evidence of his populist sympathies with laborers exerting blood, sweat, and tears, Brown's American presidency more often marked a *disembodiment*, especially in the context of the fight for federal citizenship. In Brown's estimation, the lofty ideals behind the office had not yet congealed in a satisfactory manner. The presidential promise was the stuff of legend, not lived reality. Said another way, the avatar signified the unrealized potential of America's founding documents. A stand-in for the young republic's values, Brown's tribune continually clashes against the palpable restrictions of being black in America.

The paradox of the presidency remains vital to Brown's story. While analyses of *Clotel* attend almost exclusively to the novel's eponymous yet ever-elusive Jefferson, Brown's novel deals with a wide array of presidents as well as would-be presidents. From Washington to Andrew Jackson to Henry Clay, Brown's book returns time and time again to chief magistrates as well as presidential candidates. Brown's sheer insistence upon this theme suggests a probing interest in the office and its function within the political imaginary. But Brown's presidents only show up in the margins of the text. Jefferson floats through the novel as an idea, never a human being. The bodiless logic of the presidential myth—the premise that American ideals of freedom and equality could surface in a singular being; the delusion that any individual could one day become president—contrasts sharply with Brown's plethora of discarded bodies. *Clotel* dwells upon somatic, abject corpses, disease as well as decay, and the disjuncture between personal character and phenotype to expose that America's purported principles and the lived experiences of its citizenry remain incommensurable. That is to say, in Brown's estimation, a democracy cannot fully self-actualize until every subject, every citizen, can conceive of him or herself as a proper signifier for the country, or, to imagine him or herself as intimately related to the chief magistrate.

Through its ruminations upon the so-called Founding Fathers, Brown's story literally and figuratively orbits around America's assumed political inheritance, the fantasy work of *jus sanguinis*. Russ Castronovo writes of nineteenth-century fiction: "Revolutionary 'blood' does not always follow predictable pathways and instead gets lost in questions of race and dismemberings of the fathers' law . . . the metaphoric continuity of the nation in which the sons remember the blood of the fathers confronts the tangles of miscegenation" (Castronovo 1996: 3). Brown illuminated the blockage of this model of inheritance through his extended commentary upon young Clotel's physical frame. Although her imagined essence remains infused with Jeffersonian talking points, and other high-minded concepts associated with the presidency, the social value of these presumably inherited qualities quickly becomes moot due to Clotel's ostracized black body. Brown revealed the pathways for transmitting the law of the metaphoric father to be deeply congested. Brown depicted the presidency as a similarly conflicted site: a vague yet alluring body politic in tension with a limited yet vital body natural.

To understand why the figure of the president was so crucial to Brown's vision, one must consider the ways in which this prominent figure, especially in the wake of Washington's reign, came to serve as a shorthand for federalism proper, and how Brown participated in specific debates surrounding the proposed citizenship of freed black men in the years leading up to the ratification of the Fourteenth Amendment in 1868. While on the speaker circuit in England, Brown advocated for a path to American citizenship for former slaves such as himself. Living as an expatriate abroad, he collaborated with revolutionaries and argued, alongside self-defined radicals like Martin Delany and John Dick, that "America's ideals were hollow" (Bonner 2020: 83). Christopher James Bonner tracks how in the 1840s and 1850s the relatively fuzzy topic of citizenship in the United States, dictated at the state level, opened an opportunity for freed people of color like Brown to petition for a stronger sense of legal as well as cultural belonging. To attain national citizenship for the disenfranchised could theoretically forge "a legal order in which citizen status connected individuals to the federal government through a web of rights and obligations" (5). In effect, the elusive promise of citizenship—with its inherent impetus toward centralization as well as its reflection of a growing need for a symbolic confederation to bridge the schism between freed black subjects and their native land—mirrored a promise presumably embodied in the personage of the president. Simply put, *Clotel* longs to give a real body to what the executive metaphorically represents (a protective parent; a well-defined citizenry). Brown's dependence upon presidential iconography underscores his belief that a renewed federalism could resolve many of the uncertainties plaguing freed people of color: "Black activists (like Brown) sought a relationship with the federal government that would make real the egalitarian language of the nation's founding documents" (66). In *Clotel*, petitions for citizenship and a strong federalism merge with fantasies of inheritance, nativity, and the absence and/or presence of father figures. By placing Brown's text into conversation with his activism concerning federal interventions in the matter of citizenship, readers can begin to comprehend why the presidency plays such an oversized part in this text. As Hannah Arendt argues, "(Positive laws) guarantee the pre-existence of *a common world*" (Arendt 1994: 465, emphasis mine). Along these same lines, conservative philosopher Edmund Burke once observed that the liberal promise of unimpeded freedom for the subject lacked a recognizable framework for transmitting cultural norms. Burke's critique uncovered a pressing need for metaphorical guardians. Brown, too, looked to fashion a clearly defined community, with a shared sense of obligations, as part and parcel of America's evolving political imagination. In search of a common world that could establish citizenship for freed slaves, Brown's inclusion of a paternal commander in chief speaks volumes about the hopefulness that a host of black activists felt regarding centralized governance in America.

Yet the figure of Jefferson remains uncommonly ambivalent given his peculiar position as someone who fought on behalf of state's rights and, paradoxically, as one of the chief magistrates most routinely fetishized as an exemplar of the young republic's collective essence. Although *Clotel* invokes an absent POTUS to highlight the lack of a dependable conduit between the country's founding documents and its egregious violations of human rights, it also upholds the dream of a robust federal government, for which the executive serves as utopian ideal. Maurice Gauchet observes, "Democratic society, at its most profound, is one of conflict, but one in which there is no one who does not dream of social unity" (Gauchet 2016: 184). From Brown's perspective, disembodied presidents could rupture the (white, male) fantasy of a coherent national narrative; at the same time, however, the nearly theological presidency could manifest a latent unity, a metaphysical wholeness that could incorporate freed people of color. Brown thus used the precarious president to diagnose what was ailing American democracy and to chart a possible path toward citizenship for all. Brown's POTUS remains the problem as well as the resolution. In turn, *Clotel* strives to make sense of incongruities that continue to haunt the American presidency, nearly two hundred years later.

The Meta-Executive

Romantic ideals associated with Jefferson serve as the political unconscious of *Clotel*. Figuratively, Jefferson's blood courses through the protagonist's veins and infuses her with a rare, almost superhuman excellence. Moreover, Jefferson's ideological vision defines his daughter's position in the world, since Clotel is said to inherit Jefferson's insurrectionary impulses and, concomitantly, she cannot escape from the gravitational pull of his fallacies of self-governance. Although he remains almost wholly missing from the diegesis of the novel, Jefferson exists between the words, in the margins of every page. Brown pushed his reader to conceptualize the Founding Father as a blank page, a *tabula rasa*, onto which everything else must be written. And this void of whiteness at times lulls the reader into assuming that Jefferson's metaphysical musings are a natural—rather than heavily constructed—backdrop.

Clotel repeatedly gestures at liberal assumptions like natural rights. In the early days of the republic, Jeffersonians advanced "the right to enjoy perfect liberty as one of those inherent and inalienable rights which pertain to the whole human race" (Brown 2003: 100). Indeed, *Clotel* periodically shares this belief in the imperatives of liberal universalism. While one "may . . . debase and crush (the slave) as a rational being," *Clotel* maintains that "the idea that he was born to be free will survive it all . . . it is the ethereal part of his nature" (127). Jeffersonians held that existential freedom was a hereditary condition and that certain malevolent rulers would obscure that reality by condemning citizens to perpetual unfreedom. The resultant fallacy of a totally disembedded individual endured long past Jefferson's presidency, of course, but the name Jefferson has nonetheless abided as one of its primary signifiers. Inheritors of Jeffersonian ideals purportedly possess free will before their inculcation at the hands of society—a popular characterization that whitewashes the legal structures that foster genuine liberty. Clotel invests herself in this ill-defined, *a priori* order of things. The specter of Jefferson's ideals, his status as political unconscious, infiltrates the heroine's consciousness to such a degree that she unwittingly falls into the trap of assuming that these vague ideals will hold true for her as well (a human being classified by her society as mere property). Yet Clotel cannot ignore indefinitely the incongruity between her Jeffersonian sense of unfettered self and the fact that she occupies a physical body classified by the government as black: a fact that bolsters not her assumed natural rights, but the property rights of her self-declared Forefathers. Not completely convinced by the Jeffersonian ideals that he occasionally parroted, Brown complicated the Jeffersonian narrative by lingering upon the "twists, internal contradictions, and dark digressions" that interrupted the Founding Father's declarations of an effortless inheritance for the nation's citizens (Castronovo 1996: 13).

It nearly goes without saying that the liberal universalism that Jefferson ostensibly "passed on" to his literal and figurative children depended upon a presupposition of whiteness. As many critics have noted, liberal universalism continues to make sense only in the context of white male privilege: the privilege of owning private property; the privilege to vote; and the privilege to hold the highest office in the land. The disembodied presence of a chief magistrate like Jefferson can never actually emerge from the shadows of

Brown's text because it has little relevance for a slave like Clotel. As long as she has one drop of what the dominant system deems non-white blood, her Jeffersonian birthright must remain unrealized. John Ernest writes of nascent American culture, "African Americans found themselves variously misrepresented, omitted, or problematically inserted into white nationalist histories" (Ernest 2009: 153). Brown's characters must confront the story of what America supposedly stands for in tension with alienated bodies that cannot revel in the nation's so-called poetic spirit. Brown repeatedly returned to this uneven interchange: "Characters dwell in the spaces between apparent skin color and the legal/social privilege metaphorized through racial color" (Senchyne 2012: 149). That is, *Clotel* distinguishes the Jeffersonian delusion of a disembedded subject from the embeddedness required by the nation's material practices (including, significantly, the creation of its literary texts).

In Brown's novel, the president not only materializes *through* words but he also *is* words, first and foremost, which is to say, Brown's novel represents the presidency as a signifier decoupled from what most white male readers might expect the presidency to signify. The meaning of the president's words proves stubbornly elusive as Brown's text reveals the substance behind presidential words to be sorely lacking: "Sad to say, Jefferson is not the only American statesman who has spoken high-sounding words in favour of freedom, and then left his own children to die slaves" (Brown 2003: 131). *Clotel* recycles language from one of Jefferson's most famous works, the Declaration of Independence, in a bid to expose the chasm between the grandeur of what the words supposedly mean and the feebleness of ink lines, scratched on a pitiful piece of parchment. Said another way, the imagined spirit of the law runs up against its symbolic inscription. For example, Andrew Jackson—a general in the War of 1812 and future commander in chief—champions black soldiers by declaring that "the President of the United States shall hear how praiseworthy was your conduct in the hour of danger, and the representatives of the American people will give you the praise your exploits entitle you to" (135). Consider the circularity of this particular moment: a future president addresses a sitting president; a doubled presidency—one who makes the declarations, and one who receives them. Within this completely self-enclosed presidential circle of privilege, Brown's reader finds nothing but circulating texts that have been decoupled from any solid referent. It nearly goes without saying that Jackson's black soldiers never received the aforementioned entitlements. What is this president, or chain of presidents, then, but a series of unfulfilled signifiers, missives without a conceivable destination?

Again, Jefferson's lyrical poetry and Jackson's high spirit, rendered so ubiquitous in American discourse as to be left largely unexamined, appear seamless only if the reader does not pause to acknowledge real-world strictures surrounding skin color. Whiteness remains an overlooked canvas as the words of presidents Jefferson and Jackson blend in with a liberal

universalism that has frequently posed as colorless. With his insertion
of Clotel's black body, Brown revealed how Jeffersonian principles have
never manifested via legible characters. Word and flesh are fundamentally
severed from one another. In this way, *Clotel* exacerbates existing divisions
between the president as an aspirational marker of national coherence
and the president as a supplement, a fetish, a reminder that such romantic
notions are impossible. On one side, the Jeffersonian meta-narrative, upheld
by white authors seeking to reproduce their own advantage, reads like a
"high commission sealed by a Spirit divine . . . the embryo elements of all
that is useful, great, and grand in Northern institutions" (Brown 2003:
155). However, Brown's novel recognizes that these embryos do not truly
germinate into healthy offspring. It therefore confronts the genetic as
well as generic dead-ends that separate the president from his daughter.
Consequently, the textual dimensions of Brown's presidency—its status as
a vainglorious inscription, a pale substitution, a vow and never the thing
itself—maintain a ceaseless dissatisfaction. The president's words never
quite hit their mark because the intended message of liberal universalism
only ever produces more words, or, presidential maps to be deciphered
exclusively by presidential eyes. A more precise union never materializes
between these vague words and the felt expectations of disenfranchised
people of color inhabiting the United States.

From a certain vantage point, *Clotel*'s presidential stories appear to
be devoid of substance. One of Brown's fictional slave owners reads the
speeches of Clay, a Senator well known for his multiple attempts to ascend
into the presidency, when deciding whether or not to send her emancipated
slaves back to Africa. Unable to articulate a better plan, Clay's words do not
catalyze a more righteous position; instead, the would-be president's words
evince an *inability* to communicate, a signal that the nation's commission
requires a more equitable transposition of its principles into embodied
experience. What makes such a failure to communicate interesting,
especially for the purposes of this book, is its correlation with the concept
of the presidency. *Clotel* underscores a basic premise tied to the metaphor of
POTUS: an urgent need to make real, to make tangible, the nation's latent
metaphysical mythos. The absent body of federalism must be routinely (re)
incarnated.[3] In this way, *Clotel* impresses upon its readers the complicated

---

[3]In profound ways, Brown's novel demonstrates how the presidency functions within the larger
grammar of American literature. Through his interrogation of this schism between the form and
formlessness of the body politic, Brown's *Clotel* reflects a significant characteristic of American
literature: namely, its dialectical underpinnings. In Herman Melville's "Benito Cereno," the
mutinous Babo remains a potent as well as highly visible character within the story—at least,
until the novella reveals that the entire narrative has been uttered by an unreliable, and invisible,
white narrator. In Ralph Ellison's *Invisible Man*, which dedicates its epigraph to "Benito
Cereno," the disenfranchised narrator pines after potency as well as visibility, and yet, once he

manner in which the president shapes as well as stages modern democracy. The Sisyphean dimensions of the presidential promise—the impossible notion that a singular avatar for federalism could ever make visible the pluralist underpinnings of democracy; the fantasy that any subject could feasibly become president—would have resonated with former slaves like Brown, who was desperately trying to preserve a kernel of hope amidst widespread disillusionment.[4]

Bodiless Presidents and Somatic Slaves

Brown's text unveils the schism between Jeffersonian ideals and black bodies most vividly in the novel's dramatic scene atop Long Bridge in Washington, D.C., in which Clotel, pursued by slave catchers, leaps to her death in the Potomac River rather than succumb to the evil institution from which she has fled (we will return to the symbolic resonance of the bridge in the final section). Castronovo cites Clotel's suicidal plunge as further evidence of how disempowered individuals in nineteenth-century America, especially women and slaves, considered freedom to be achievable only through release from their earthly bonds, since the legal system disassociated their physical form from the principles that it trumpeted elsewhere. When Clotel destroys her body, she affirms a tacit connection between liberty and the sort of disembodiment necessitated by America's liberal platitudes. Nonetheless, *Clotel* is filled not only with floating spirits, but also with damaged bodies and corpses. The novel derives a good deal of its stylistic identity from a parallel boom in sensationalist fiction among writers including Lippard, Susan Warner, and Harriet Beecher Stowe, particularly in her novel *The Minister's Wooing*. With his distinctive approach to the material realm, Brown also established a new way to trace the contours of an imagined presidency.

First and foremost, in unexpected moments, a number of the characters in *Clotel* perish from communicable disease.[5] Even as Brown's white characters

---

sees that canonization means serving as a puppet for the perpetuation of a racist status quo, he realizes that power comes not from visibility (often tied to blackness), but invisibility (often tied to whiteness). Like Brown, Melville and Ellison place paramount metaphysical assumptions of whiteness in dialogue with the legibility of black bodies.

[4]According to Brown, a presidential icon does not "embody power, because whoever moves to the central stage in the pole of the political cannot overcome the blind spot that makes it unable to successfully claim a permanent monopolization of the visibility of the social" (Plot 2016: 19).

[5]Peter Dorsey insists that these "hurried" and "rather abrupt" deaths are a sign of Brown's weaknesses as a writer; I would counter that these hurried deaths play a pivotal role in establishing the importance of bodies in *Clotel* (Dorsey 1995: 263).

pontificate on America's principles, they too are ravaged by disease, and so their bodies are symbolically leveled, given a weightiness—a somatic dimension—that the novel otherwise reserves for black corpses. Mr. Peck, a devious plantation owner, succumbs to cholera: "In less than five hours John Peck was a corpse" (Brown 2003: 123). In short order, Clotel's mother, the mistress of Jefferson, yields to yellow fever. One of the novel's most outspoken critics of the institution of slavery and so, readers might assume, the least likely to be killed off, expires: "In the midst of the buoyancy of youth, this cherished one had dropped and died . . . oh what a chill creeps through the breaking heart when we look upon the insensible form, and feel that it no longer contains the spirit" (159). These unforeseen deaths accelerate as the novel progresses, spreading in viral fashion and in ways that become increasingly difficult for the reader to stomach. Listing the causes as yellow fever, small pox, or cholera, Brown's novel slowly teases to the surface the gruesome face of death itself: "Fiery veins streaked the eye . . . mucous secretions . . . gums were blackened . . . sank under a delirium . . . yellowish spots . . . a fetid odour . . . mouth spread foan, tinged with black and burnt blood." When the viral carnage is complete, "nearly 2000 dead bodies lay uncovered" (173). But why does Clotel dwell upon these deceased figures? In one sense, this sensationalism affirms Brown's conventionality as a writer, as the poetic deployment of the dead remains a staple of fiction from the era. At a deeper level, though, Brown's text employs grotesque scenes to draw sharper distinctions between the body and the soul. The polluted bodies of Clotel defy the calm, collected meta-narrative of Jefferson's ghost. In other words, Jeffersonian assumptions of personal autonomy and innate rationality cannot account for the indiscriminate course of a biological disease. All human beings remain equally vulnerable to pathogens; death retains the title of ultimate leveler. Accordingly, Brown's free person of color proves to be little more than a future carcass, especially when the subject in question has already been devalued by the ideology of the day: "No graves were dug for the Negroes; their dead bodies became food for dogs and vultures" (181). To convey this point, Brown frequently gestured at Ovid's Metamorphoses, including gestures at Actaeon and his hungry dogs. While presidential ideals are regularly treated as immutable constants in American discourse, Brown's individual bodies change—and sometimes radically, without any warning.

In the case of slaves like Clotel, Brown demonstrates how readers cannot easily reconcile metaphysics associated with a national essence with the uncertainty of corporeal existence. Recent scholarship on Clotel interrogates Brown's approach to this issue of disembodiment. Judith Madera, for one, analyzes the novel's omnipresent materiality. "It was this veneer of stability that Brown's entire literary corpus aimed to disrupt," she argues. Clotel depicts "a living, fleshed-out struggle" (Madera 2015: 31). Because bodily energies must eventually be "inscribed and realized," reformers must pay more careful attention to the body itself in their efforts to conjure the evolving spirit of the law (Chakkalakal 2012: 30). That is to say, Brown's readers must not ignore the disjuncture that *Clotel* highlights between the lived experience of black subjects and abstract ideals espoused by Jefferson's disciples. This process is not just theoretical; it involves the lived labor of actual human beings. Slaves are "like other people," Brown's text recalls. "Flesh and blood" (Brown 2003: 137).

Crucially, *Clotel* also expounds on the issue of disembodiment by shifting the reader's gaze to a number of presidential bodies. The bodies of presidents are certainly strange things. The nation has not infrequently been engrossed by the dead or dying body of a chief magistrate. There has been a relatively widespread fascination with the aging of presidents during their time in office—their graying hair, their diminishing mental faculties, and so forth. Yet these widely circulated corporeal scenes are offset by the impression of an untouchable president, carved into stone or memorialized by nearly sacred texts that resist deconstruction. To paraphrase Jean-Paul Sartre, the Founding Father's imagined essence precedes his existence. Preserving Jefferson as a kind of poet-legislator, his promoters have etched the third president into the annals of history. Yet despite his eloquent prose, Brown argued that the character of Jefferson never brought forth breathing citizens with a pulse—or, citizens that were not always already doomed to confuse death for an expression of personal freedom. As such, *Clotel* reverses Jefferson's well-known slight of America's first African American poet, Phillis Wheatley: "Among the blacks is misery enough, God knows, but no poetry" (Jefferson 1999: 147). Against Jefferson's pronouncement that Wheatley lacked the ability to translate spirit into word, Brown's novel implies that it was actually Jefferson who lacked this capacity.

Readers witness Clotel's literal and figurative failure to thrive as the novel's consanguine protagonist is sold as chattel: "This was a Southern action, at which the bones, muscles, sinews, blood, and nerves of a young lady of sixteen were sold for five hundred dollars" (Brown 2003: 50). Brown's readers are disturbed by the sheer physicality of the young lady, that is, her reduction to sinew and nerves. A harsh divide resonates: "Thus closed a Negro sale, at which two daughters of Thomas Jefferson, the writer of the Declaration of American Independence, and one of the presidents of the great republic, were disposed of to the highest bidder" (51). Brown's readers must watch the abject mistreatment of black bodies as these bodies are excised from the comforts of a broader Jeffersonian narrative. Southern colleges, the reader learns, utilize black bodies for unsavory experiments, while slave owners deploy "religious instruction" not as the meaningful cultivation of an enriched subjectivity but as a calculated move "to make slaves more trustworthy and valuable as property" (102, 111). Over and over again, *Clotel* frames the commodification of the human body as being at odds with the larger mythos of American life. The character of Clotel exemplifies this tension after her husband, another stand-in for Jefferson, abandons her to pursue a higher social status. Her husband grapples with the excellence of Clotel's immaterial character against his legal impetus to consider her as a material good. "True, she was his slave," he thinks to himself. "Her bones and sinews had been purchased by his gold, yet she had the heart of a true woman . . . that graceful figure, weeping in the moonlight, haunted him for years" (89–90). In other words, Clotel's imaginary essence—a true woman; a graceful figure; a spectral, haunting vapor tied to the moonlight—remains closed off from the physical world. At the same time, although infused with the supposed spark of genius that she supposedly inherited from her God-like father, the worth of the daughter of Jefferson can only ever amount to a certain value in gold. Even worse, "the fact that they were the granddaughters of Thomas Jefferson, no doubt, increased their value in the market" (174). The legalistic view of Clotel's body inhibits her from embodying the principles that figuratively course through her bloodstream. The assumed fecundity of the American president—a symbolic reservoir of cultural optimism—proves, at last, infertile.

In another instance of a would-be president failing to register in physical form, *Clotel* records an incident at a hotel in which a preeminent politician, Daniel Webster, former Secretary of State and a well-known candidate for president in 1836, is mistaken for a black man and denied service. Webster appears to be darker skinned due to poor lighting and so a hotel official refuses to allow him into the upscale hotel: "It was not till (the official) had been repeatedly assured and made to understand that the said Daniel Webster was a real live Senator of the United States, that he perceived his awkward mistake" (Brown 2003: 149). Once more, the prominence of the presidency has been eclipsed by the body natural. Webster's lofty reputation cannot overcome the initial, somatic response of a hotel worker. Legalistic strictures placed on the body trump the greatest political pedigree.

Let us return, then, to the fate of Clotel's body after she flings herself from Long Bridge. Under assault by slave catchers, she elects to kill herself. On the one hand, upon diving from the bridge, she vanishes, erased by the nation's grand meta-narrative: "Thus died Clotel, the daughter of Thomas Jefferson, a president of the United States; a man distinguished as the author of the Declaration of American Independence, and one of the first statesman of that country" (Brown 2003: 185). Suppressed even in her final moment of transcendence, Jefferson's name renders his daughter mute. She becomes a footnote to her own eulogy. Her body subsequently washes up on the banks of the Potomac; random onlookers then "deposit" her carcass into a "hole dug in the sand" (186). Suffering a gross indignity, Clotel's corpse does not receive a proper burial but finds itself covered in sand, subsumed by erosion and the ever-shifting force of time. A calloused poem is composed in honor of her demise: "That bond-woman's corpse— let Potomac's proud wave / Go bear it along *by our Washington's grave*, /

and heave it high up on that hallowed strand, / to tell of the freedom he won for our land" (187, author's emphasis). This memorial poem maintains that Clotel's corpse is fortunate to be associated with one of the nation's most revered symbols. At the same time, her abject precarity contrasts sharply with the perceived constancy of Washington's grave-marker. The poem reveals her body to be an "it," an object to be "heaved" onto the hallowed ground—hallowed not by her presence, but by the presence of the erstwhile president's deathless remains. The poet eagerly seizes Clotel's corpse as a political prop with which to herald the first president's supremacy within the American imagination. The tale tells of the president's supposed greatness, not Clotel's, as it washes over her needless demise with proclamations of freedoms hard won. The president's spirit, the spirit of "our Washington," remains aloof and disembodied; in contrast, her society has reduced Clotel to detritus, mere debris cast on holy ground. The narrative recited by worshippers of Washington has virtually nothing to do with the story of a black corpse that has been discarded haphazardly upon his monument. Brown's novel dwells on this encomium to emphasize once more a chasm between the presidency and material oppression of American residents, one of whom has now been reduced to scant sediment and summarily deposited onto the base of an imposing façade.

A President without Politics

In sum, Jefferson is both everywhere and nowhere in Brown's narrative. He is not a father, in any tangible sense, but an idea. At the height of its complicity with Jeffersonian logic, *Clotel* practices an "unreflexive traffic with humanism," thereby diminishing the value of politics proper—with its power struggles and antagonisms—in favor of immovable moral truths (W. Brown 2002: 375). "Always mistrustful of power . . . the moralist inevitably feels antipathy toward politics as a domain of open contestation" (377). Catering to the indeterminate nature of American liberalism, William Wells Brown occasionally depoliticized his message by resorting to a blanket moralism (the other face of sentimental fiction from the period). At times, Brown's text grants Jefferson's ideals near theological significance and renders them as unquestionable as gravity. For example, *Clotel* laments the lot of the slave for being "stripped of every right which God and nature gave him, and which the high spirit of our revolution declared inalienable" (Brown 2003: 152). Of course, the notion of inalienable rights from a high spirit means virtually nothing to Clotel herself, a fatherless "alien" who has been stripped of communal belonging. Nevertheless, the novel persists in presenting young Clotel's natural rights as a repressed truth. Brown's flattened moralism, which aborts democratic wrangling, dovetails all too easily with Jeffersonian assumptions that seem preordained as well as untainted by the vagaries of political contest.

Put differently, Brown's imagined presidential essence proves oppressive because it restricts the reader's imagination by positing an apolitical, immoveable set of intrinsic values (e.g., the tacit endorsement of liberal universalism). Before breaking apart this correlation between Brown's flattened moralism and presidential essence, Brown's readers ought to recognize how this uninterrupted correlation has been historically aligned with constructions of whiteness. George Lipsitz, for one, demonstrates how a "relationship (endures) between whiteness and asset accumulation . . . (and so) the language of liberal individualism serves as a cover for coordinated collective group interests" (Lipsitz 1998: viii, 22). Proponents of Jefferson's vision assume that white privilege is an organic offshoot of liberalism when, in fact, it remains part and parcel of a specific group's political agenda. That is, powerful white men have relied on the apparent naturalness of unequal arrangements to cover up their own asset accumulation and justify their own oppression of others. By allowing the consensus behind bodiless presidents to hover over his text, instead of interrupting its presumed coherence, Brown can be viewed as at least partially complicit in affirming the undemocratic underpinnings of the young republic. The ceaseless flow of Jefferson's figurative blood from father to daughter provides *Clotel*'s most consistent analogy for an essentialist—read: undemocratic—worldview. Even slaves like Clotel can apparently relish in an innate "insurrectionary feeling," which is to say, thanks to her mighty bloodline, Clotel can sustain "the unconquerable love of liberty the heart may inherit" (Brown 2003: 179, 184–85).[6] The text's undefinable insurrectionary feeling reveals itself to be different from Jeffersonian logic in degree rather than kind. The driving force of *Clotel* may be read as biological or spiritual, but it is never political.

One example of the novel's preference for a defanged liberalism over political engagement occurs during the breakdown of Clotel's marriage. Brown's affinity for the redemptive power of interracial marriage resonates throughout his work: "Marriage is, indeed, the first and most important institution of human existence . . . (it) awakens every germ of goodness" (Brown 2003: 45). According to the text, if Clotel's husband would only have appreciated his private existence with Clotel, he would have been spared a great deal of personal anguish. Nevertheless, he abandons his seemingly happy union to pursue his political ambitions. Like Jefferson before him, who famously casts aside his daughters to enhance his reputation in Washington, Clotel's spouse expresses his "ambition to become a statesman," and so

---

[6]Elizabeth West notes, "Brown reflects on the legacy of slave insurrectionists, suggesting that their desire for freedom originates or has been ignited by their mixed racial identity" (West 2012: 180–81).

he destroys his domestic refuge (66). Here Brown's book prefers a Biblical basis for the social order over a political one, relying upon an imagined love that stems from "the bulwark of Christianity and liberty" (74). Over and over again, crude political opportunities lure Brown's characters away from moral cornerstones. And so the novel rejects the very premise of political contestation.[7] Elsewhere, a character wastes many hours "over the writings of Rousseau, Voltaire, and Thomas Paine," when—or so the text claims—he should have been forsaking political philosophy in favor of a more holistic framework (74). *Clotel* thus decouples institutional reform from political strife.

Consider the events of Chapter XXII, in which Clotel shares a carriage ride with an assortment of politicos. The presidency once more structures Brown's prose at a foundational level: "It was on the eve of a presidential election, when every man is thought to be a politician. Clay, Van Buren, and Harrison were the men two expected the indorsement of the Baltimore Convention" (Brown 2003: 162). The carriage scene denigrates American politics when a farmer, in an overt nod to Jefferson's agrarian sensibilities, refuses to play any part in the politico's game. When an aspiring politician asks him who he supports in the upcoming election, the farmer responds, "I work for Betsy and the children." The pundits of the carriage ask the Jeffersonian farmer to which party he belongs, and the farmer responds, "I belong to the order of married men" (162). Once more, Brown's text clearly prioritizes the private institution of marriage above electoral conflict when it inserts one of Jefferson's heroic farmers into the middle of a politically divided carriage. Implying that there are higher rewards in life than electoral success, a critic of the banter among the passengers notes with disdain: "Your palms of victory and crowns of rejoicing are triumphs over a rival party in politics" (167). Clotel herself does not take part in the campaign discussions of her fellow carriage passengers, and, if the logic of the text holds, Brown's reader should rejoice in her detachment. Like the Jeffersonian farmer, Clotel's aloofness marks her as morally superior. But her relatively uncomplicated moralism, her *silence*, simultaneously marks her as a woman, a slave, and a piece of property. When *Clotel* presents barriers to political participation as a much-needed balm for what Brown perceived to be an overly politicized society, one might respond by asking how the insidious institution of Brown's story could be reformed without sustained political intervention.

Clotel never articulates how the reform of an institution like slavery could take place without political intervention. In truth, it could be argued

---

[7]Deak Nabers argues that, according to *Clotel*, "the law is itself a form of slavery, that legal prerogative challenges divine authority, that political action involves a kind of blasphemy" (Nabers 2005: 103).

that the narrative's applause for apolitical righteousness remains as abstract, and unhelpful, as Jeffersonian ideals. Beneath the power plays of overly ambitious young men like Jefferson or Clotel's husband, there endures a *tabula rasa* presumed to be reasonable and *a priori* correct: "Liberalism believes that by confining divisive issues to the sphere of the private (. . .) should be enough to regulate the plurality of interests in society. *But this literal attempt to annihilate the political is bound to fail*" (Mouffe 2006: 111, emphasis mine). For skeptics of the liberal tradition, the variegated desires of a heterogeneous population can never be managed in this fashion, since "antagonistic forces will never disappear and politics is characterized by conflict and division" (69). If political struggles constitute the human being, as Aristotle claimed, the attempt by Brown to reconcile all of his novel's internal divisions will prove to be an impossible one.

Yet the reader must complicate *Clotel*'s tacit endorsement of Jeffersonian ideals when she shifts her gaze to how the American presidency informs the fantasy structure of the novel. In a word, the presidents of *Clotel* compel critics to discover the text's hidden political potential. The *absence* of presidential fulfillment resonates like a kind of Jeremiad: a promise that the nation's founding ideals might one day be embodied upon that distant City on a Hill. The character of Clotel closely mirrors the presidential figure on this front because, despite their rigid moral veneers, both figures ultimately withhold satisfaction from Brown's readers. Indeed, it is their unrealized potential that confirms their enduring value as signifiers of American democracy.[8]

President, Interrupted

With its desire for metaphysical wholeness alongside its drive for deconstruction, *Clotel* reflects an abiding conflict within the American experiment, particularly on questions surrounding the proper scope of the federal government. Nowhere is this conundrum more palpable than in Brown's unsettled figurations of POTUS. Like Clotel, the president occupies a liminal position. On the one side, the executive opens a productive schism within the young republic's divided carriage; on the other side, the president remains above the fray, evidence of an intrinsic love of liberty that sustains itself *sans* political wrangling. Brown's president acts as a fictional suture designed to conjoin, however uneasily, an affirmation of the nation's desire

---

[8]Peter Dorsey comments, "At the end of *Uncle Tom's Cabin*, Stowe asks her reader to 'feel right'; Georgiana, who has 'felt right' throughout *Clotel*, puts those beliefs into practice and in so doing becomes a 'liberator' more powerful than any found in Stowe's work" (Dorsey 1995: 262).

for metaphysical ideals with its unconscious drive to incompleteness—or, the nation's need for federal guardianship alongside its hunger for individual freedom. Instead of celebrating the text's heterogeneity or outright denouncing its homogeneity, Brown's readers might focus on the novel's vital contradictions. With her higher poetry as well as earthly form, Clotel affirms the ambivalence of the presidency (and vice versa). In Brown's title—*Clotel; Or, the President's Daughter*—a semi-colon separates as well as links independent clauses. The semi-colon grammatically marks an ongoing friction between federalism and personal autonomy. Furthermore, the conjunction "or" grammatically marks that the disparate terms, the president and the daughter, are of equal weight. Clotel remains the possession of the president and, conceptually at least, his peer.

Brown's text presents Clotel and the president as related liminal beings that straddle a line between emancipatory open-endedness and rigid ideological convention. Symbolically speaking, the site from which Clotel leaps to her watery death, Long Bridge, fosters a tenuous connection between the political struggles of Washington and the peaceful sanctuary of Arlington Place, a house "occupied by the distinguished relative and descendant of the immortal Washington" (Brown 2003: 184). Long Bridge metaphorically conducts the mercurial demands of the populace to the "distinguished" and "immortal" nerve center of the body politic: the first president's ancestral home. Brown's book dwells upon Clotel's position between these two loci; her prison stands "midway between the capitol at Washington and the president's house" (183). The protagonist's precarious placement between the Capitol and the president alerts readers to a fundamental blockage in the arteries of the nation: an inability for the so-called immortal essence of the nation to pass from the president's lips to the ears of the people. An inability of the word to be made flesh.

Echoing its confused figuration of Jefferson's daughter, *Clotel*'s ambiguous framing of the president as apolitical—omnipresent; foreclosed—as well as political—disruptive; contested—reflects an ever-shifting relationship between the noncorporeal and incorporated dimensions of American government. Federalism in the form of a president provided Brown with a reassuring centralized entity with which to combat state legislatures on the matter of citizenship and, at the same time, a convenient illustration of America's aborted promise of egalitarianism. Brown's fictional presidency is therefore the key with which to unlock his text's greater political significance.

Brown's novel argues that the installation of human rights for freed black men requires a coherent community with comprehensible parameters. Again, conservative philosopher Edmund Burke reacted against the imprecise nature of Jeffersonian liberalism by calling for an "entailed inheritance"—or, a clear-sighted transmission of rights from corporate entity to embedded subject (Burke 2009: 33). Aesthetically speaking, the figure of the president serves as a federal pillar onto which the young republic can scaffold a vision of human rights. While Brown's chief magistrate unquestionably remains an artificial construct that necessitates deconstruction to avoid fetishism or cultish devotion (a trap into which, as we have seen, Brown occasionally fell), Brown nevertheless clung to the importance of a commonwealth, a "common world" that can be articulated, for instituting protections for would-be citizens (Arendt 1994: 302). To shield a person without a home from being torn apart by the torrents of history may require the solid grounding of a coherent body politic, visibly encased in something like a presidential body. Brown needed tangible bodies: the body of a forgotten, stateless being (a homeless daughter) as well as the body of a father figure who could confirm the existence of a homeland in which actual rights would be conferred on fully recognized citizens. For Brown, the metaphor of a parental president assisted in staging an argument on behalf of citizenship for free people of color.

Appropriately enough, the critical reception of *Clotel* remains deeply divided.[9] Detractors critique the novel for its affirmation of America's hegemonic values. Richard O. Lewis, for one, stresses Brown's "intense regard for the family unit as an institution" (Lewis 1985: 130). Other critics of Brown's narrative salute its self-reflexive qualities.[10] Elizabeth West comments, "With its central paternal figure, Thomas Jefferson—leading patriarch of American Enlightenment and the Republic—Brown's *Clotel* is arguably a critique of the man and the ideals" (West 2012: 171). According to its celebrants, Brown's text remains incongruous, cacophonous, and heterogeneous, in content as well as form. Yet given Brown's ambivalent relationship to federalism, readers should hesitate in firmly taking a side. Through his assembly of presidential figures, Brown signaled his text's collusion with Jeffersonian thought and, concomitantly, underscored the text's democratic undercurrents. Like the character of Clotel, Brown's executives push readers to navigate between their desire for consensus alongside their drive to difference.

In closing, Brown's presidency exists as a site for wrestling with the manifest as well as latent content of American democracy.[11] Whenever the text outwardly professes a desire for an avatar with which to depict

---

[9]It is worth observing that critical reception remains divided *when it happens at all*. Ann du Cille states, "*Clotel* remains a book in need of both reading and readings, an originary, enabling text in want of analysis and deep theorizing" (Du Cille 2000: 451).

[10]Katie Frye writes, "Beneath its affectation of the tragic mulatta and its ostensible reliance on the structure of the sentimental novel lurks a topsy-turvy world and gender politics . . . showing the destructivity, fragility, and instability of white ideology" (Frye 2009: 528). She adds: "(Brown) demonstrates the inherent insecurity of representations of race" (539).

[11]Reiterating Brown's claims many years later, Maurice Gauchet articulates the democratic impasse: "The problem of reconciling the imperative to represent the will of all of the citizens with the existence of a conflict between their interests that is recognized, at least tacitly, as irreconcilable" (Gauchet 2016: 194).

the general will—a Jeffersonian romantic core—the text unconsciously drives toward dissolution, the realization that this romance can never be fully actualized. Simultaneously, whenever the text professes a desire to tease apart the signifier and the signified—the president and the people—it unconsciously drives toward reconciliation: a nearly theological realization that there must be at least a kernel of consensus if American citizenship is to mean anything at all. The president sparks political discord even as it affirms an intrinsic unity.

Brown's complex cast of presidents unclog the political pathways of his novel. On one hand, the acutely political dimensions of the president, which is to say, the cracks and fissures that divide the proverbial carriage, classify POTUS as a democratic symptom. The metaphysical promise of Brown's fictional president stands in constant tension with the paltry forms that it eventually adopts. On the other hand, the chief magistrate offers a beacon of federalism that cannot be dismissed out of hand because the lack of any embodied national identity presages—as Burke so keenly foresaw—a denial of rights that could only ever be assigned through citizenship.

It would be a mistake to conclude, however, that Brown's imagined presidency confers on Clotel's life a greater significance. To do so would be to repeat Jefferson's erasure of Clotel from her own eulogy. Let us, then, reverse this equation: through Clotel's story, Brown's book confronts the self-dividing nature of the American presidency. Wedged between the letter and the spirit of the law, Clotel encourages Brown's audience to contemplate the bisected character of the executive. By spotting the slave standing at the midpoint of a conduit that channels the partisan energies of the Capitol to and from the commander in chief's "eternal home," readers can interrogate the failures of the storied presidency as well as its indispensable value for stateless beings (i.e., for disenfranchised individuals who have been stranded for far too long, questing after the disembodied dreams of their federal Forefathers).

4

The President in Books for Boys

Andrew Shaffer's best-selling novel *Hope Never Dies* (2018) presents a hyper-masculinized fantasy of duo Barack Obama and Joe Biden, nicknamed "Joe Tingler," uniting to solve a local murder. Albeit with tongue planted firmly in cheek, the text recycles an array of recognizable tropes from the hardboiled detective genre, depicting Joe as a hobbled but persistent hero with existential angst and a chivalrous streak. This exercise in machismo was clearly not just for laughs; Shaffer deployed generic signposts to guide his readers into imagining Biden as a president who could get the job done (he was eventually elected in 2020). The stunning success of Shaffer's narrative raises several questions: have American audiences elsewhere framed the presidency in such explicitly generic terms? Are there other examples of American audiences consuming the president via cheaply made yet exceedingly popular genres, especially genres aimed directly at young men? If so, how exactly have these works fashioned the political imagination of countless readers?[1] Following the dictates of genre fiction, the imagined presidency instigates enduring problems (e.g., lawlessness or excessive prudence) as well as possible solutions (e.g., pedantry or adventurousness). In turn, fictional POTUS reflects the ideological tensions attendant to American masculinity through its uniquely unsettled generic profile.

Although the American president appears extensively in so-called books for boys, which is to say, books targeted specifically to adolescent male

---

[1] The distinction between children's and adult literature was not definitively pronounced in the nineteenth century. Books for boys were often marketed for children as well as adults, the most famous example being the works of Mark Twain. Edmund Pearson comments, "The reading of dime novels was not exclusively confined to boys, or to rude and uncultivated men. Stories of this type have always been enjoyed by everybody" (Pearson 1929: 45–46).

readers, few scholars have studied the phenomenon in detail.[2] Critics could reasonably insist that due to growing market pressures to churn out stories quickly and without deviating from popular plot structures, the inclusion of the president has rarely added anything more than a sense of gravitas to a given text. After all, storylines remained largely unchanged from concurrent adventure tales, and so critics tend to add these texts to a pile of purportedly hackneyed writing from the period. Yet fictional executives open wide a conceptual dilemma for young male readers by invoking emotional surpluses via thrilling adventures—even as the texts dictate a model for appropriate behavior. In these tales, the president's alignment with the law complicates the palpable pleasures that his oversized presence cultivates; the president as symbolic lawgiver, that is, helps to repress the emotional surpluses of impressionable lads. But one must remember that repression is always already return. POTUS functions as normative injunction and exception, all at once.

On one hand, the president in books for boys served as a blueprint for behavior throughout the first half of the nineteenth century. Literary analysts refer to his period of juvenile literature as the Didactic Era, since the vast majority of publications focused on old-fashioned conceptions of duty. Writers like Samuel G. Goodrich, known under the pseudonym Peter Parley, as well as Jacob Abbott stubbornly refused to cater to the needs of immature readers. They wrote tracts that were heavily pedantic. Goodrich's *The Life of Washington*, for one, includes reading comprehension questions at the bottom of each page and depicts Washington as a stone-faced Stoic: "Silent, diligent, and methodical; dignified in his appearance, and strictly honorable in all his conduct" (Goodrich 1842: 8). Writing a bit later, Abbott catered to a Puritanical sensibility, particularly in his Rollo series—a set of books that have since been classified as "docile, earnest, literal" (Jordan 1948: 14). Abbott wrote for well-established families within an evangelical Protestant tradition and, as such, his prose could be rigid and sanctimonious. Within his American History series, he published a treatment of George Washington, a book that, although it claims to deliver "both entertainment and instruction," spends most of its time reeling off historical facts in a rote fashion. The concluding section of Abbott's text would no doubt strike many contemporary readers as quite dull due to its lengthy exposition concerning plans regarding national infrastructure. No one could accuse Abbott of making Washington's life very exciting or pandering to an overzealous crowd. In the hands of authors from the Didactic Era, the fictional president exists as yet another measuring stick for moral instruction.

---

[2]Russ Castronovo offers one of the few studies of juvenile presidential biographies. See Castronovo (1996).

Nevertheless, one recovers from Abbott's book on Washington early signs of a shift in progress: even as Abbott continued to breed docility, he acknowledged the changing appetites of America's young audiences (indeed, the preceding chapters show how the seeds for a pivot into generic sensationalism were already sown by the likes of James Fenimore Cooper, George Lippard, and William Wells Brown). Abbott recognized that he had to "awaken" in childish minds "interest in the history" as well as a "desire for future instruction" (Abbott 2017: v). In other words, because of a mercurial literary marketplace, Abbott was compelled to paint Washington as "an extremely picturesque and dramatic character" (15). The author needed to "convince parents that fiction for children might be made *pleasant as well as moral*" (Nye 1975: 61, emphasis mine). A split emerged between Abbott's didactic prose and his adventurous preface: a fissure that opened into a chasm in the decades that followed. Provisional lines were drawn between pleasure and the law, or desire and discipline. Abbott and his ilk conceptualized the presidency as an internally conflicted trope, one with pedagogical as well as passionate purposes.

Meanwhile, authors in the mid- to late nineteenth century pivoted to the dime novel, frequently under the employment of publishing giants like Street & Smith as well as Beadle & Adams. The resultant books for boys featuring fictionalized presidents displayed little fidelity to the assumed historical truths on display in publications from Goodrich or Abbott. May Hill Arbuthnot comments upon the liberties taken by writers from this later tradition, as they cast "known facts into dramatic episodes complete with conversation" (Arbuthnot 1953: 317).[3] Championing this cultural shift, Arbuthnot declares that "children love action," complains about a tendency among American teachers to focus on the implausible story that Washington never told a lie—the stuff of Protestant prudes, in her estimation—and notes the failure of educators "to introduce George Washington (as) the best wrestler, the highest jumper, the hardest riding youngster" (519). No longer bound to strict guideposts, writers in the dime novel tradition presented the chief magistrate as precocious, mischievous, and a source of adventurous thrills.

By depicting POTUS interchangeably as marble statue and provoker of bodily sensations, nineteenth-century books for boys tended to strip the president of political intrigue in favor of formulaic satisfaction. Publishing firms routinely rendered the president's story as one of individual prowess in which, even in the face of massive societal issues, "the remedy is never found in a social attack on the problem but rather in single-handed effort" (Curti 1937: 764). For many ideological reasons that we shall unpack shortly,

---

[3]Later juvenile stories about presidents, such as Ann Weil's *John Quincy Adams: Boy Patriot*, included wild conjecture, invented scenarios, made-up dialogue, and ample free indirect discourse.

depictions of the president during the age of the dime novel were "far more interested in plot, action, romance, and mystery than in the social, political, and philosophical implications of American historical events" (772). During the Didactic Era, and then in residual traces throughout the remainder of the century, the image of the president provided young male readers as well as their parents with a pedagogical touchstone to supplement the residual values of the Era of Good Feelings, fast fading from favor. At the height of the dime novel's influence, the image of the commander in chief offered readers a fantasy of openness via boundless external and internal frontiers (accompanied, ironically enough, by ever more circumscribed emotional parameters). And while it might be comforting for readers today to imagine that the tricks of the didacts and dealers in dime novels no longer inform modern perceptions of the presidency, the recent success of *Hope Never Dies* suggests otherwise.

A survey of the president in books for boys must address an ongoing friction between moralizing and sensationalism. According to Daniel T. Rodgers, a great splintering materialized between the morality tale and the adventure story. As we have seen in preceding chapters, the break was never a clean one. Still, it is safe to say that authors of dime novels sought "a heady infusion of romantic ideals" to escalate "the imaginative stakes" (Rodgers 2014: 133–35). As a result, characterization gradually became secondary to "stirring and surprising incidents" (139). Many dime novel writers stripped away historical or political overtones by privileging the executive's private prowess. Nevertheless, dime novel writers also preserved clichés from the Didactic Era as they clung to the basis of the morality play, pitching concepts like work ethic to "a new level of abstraction" (152). The president in books for boys thus sutured bland moralism and unending adventure into a fantasy structure aimed primarily at male readers: the executive as an exemplar of the law *and* a perpetually dissatisfied exception to the rules. By exploring the ambivalence of these stories, one can reconsider how the presidency continues to foster widespread political as well as aesthetic desires. Said another way, one might scrutinize the interplay between residual values from the Didactic Era and emergent values conveyed by dime novels to gain insights into how generations of readers have grown up dreaming about American masculinity alongside literary depictions of the president.

Francis C. Woodworth and the Napoleonic President

As a writer of juvenile literature, Francis C. Woodworth, who regularly published under the pseudonym Theodore Tinker, anticipated many of the themes featured in works by writers such as Oliver Optic and Horatio Alger. Woodworth capitalized upon the image of a would-be president to convey righteous lessons to his target audience, or—as Russell Nye writes—"to introduce young people to their culture and to provide them with minimal equipment to fit into it" (Nye 1975: 60). At the same time, Woodworth's *The Young American's Life of Fremont*, written on behalf of presidential candidate John Charles Fremont, holds that its specific mode of storytelling matters more than its content, which is to say, it presents an adventurous life, told through an acutely adventurous style of writing. Torn between Transcendentalist influences and the incipient demands of the dime novel, *Life of Fremont* exemplifies awkward attempts to transmit a cogent image of the chief magistrate into the imaginations of juvenile readers.[4]

One of the early transcontinental surveyors, and later a candidate for president, Woodworth's Fremont foreshadows Alger's industrious heroes. Fremont's father "made the best of his misfortune. He went to work" (Woodworth 1856: 24). This work ethic rubs off on the younger Fremont, who comprehends that wealth means little when compared to "ambition . . . industry, and energy, and perseverance." The blossoming progeny recognizes that opulent wealth would only "be in his way. It would clog his greatness" (18–19). Woodworth's Fremont therefore obeys a set of recognizable middle-class values, including a Protestant dedication to labor as an end-in-itself. Woodworth's work maintained an underlying pragmatism—an insistence upon "being reasonable" and resigning oneself to a middling life of honorable toil. "It is one thing to hear stories about thrilling adventures, by land and by sea, and quite another thing to ground one's-self" (86). In a word, *Life of Fremont* enforces a pattern of social respectability by exploiting the gravitas of the presidency as a vehicle for communicating a lesson on appropriate manners. One could argue, though, that Woodworth does not need the presidency to tell his tale; for his story, the office is almost completely auxiliary. Fremont only interests Woodworth's readers in the lead-up to his political career. Subsequently, *Life of Fremont* loses its coherence at the precise point in which the story moves from Fremont's salad days to his career in Congress. Although Woodworth had little use for the presidency or its political function in American life, he readily grafted his usual tale of moral instruction onto the narrative of a presidential campaign in which a young man rises through the ranks.

Writing in the mid-1850s, Woodworth idled at an intersection between his Transcendentalist forbearers and the forthcoming world of the dime novel. The famous publisher of dime novels Beadle and Adams formed in 1856, the

---

[4]Woodworth was hardly alone in his uneasy admiration for Napoleon. Ralph Waldo Emerson, patriarch of the Transcendentalists, wrote at some length about Napoleon as a "great," if complicated, man in his lecture, "Napoleon; Or, the Man of the World."

same year in which Woodworth published *Life of Fremont*. At times, *Life of Fremont* reiterates the preoccupations of pedagogues like Ralph Waldo Emerson, Henry Wadsworth Longfellow, and Bronson Alcott. It is a story that constantly compares its childish reader to a germ "to be cultivated." The narrator makes this case plain: "Cultivate this little flower of fortitude in your heart" (Woodworth 1856: 39–40). In these instances, Woodworth-as-Transcendentalist wished his reader would visualize adolescents as a veritable garden that, with proper caretaking, would grow more bountiful, perhaps even becoming president. Likewise, Woodworth's text depicts Fremont as a sort of Thoreau analog (of note, Thoreau's magnum opus *Walden* was published just two years prior to *Life of Fremont*). On the common man, Woodworth's narrator notes: "With his riches, he has made a multitude of wants . . . I think it isn't wise to make too many wants" (97). And like Emerson, Woodworth railed against too much education, viewing traditional pedagogical designs not as a pathway to discovery but as a narrowing of one's ability to imagine alternatives, or an impediment to one's individual will. Finally, Woodworth derived his pedagogical strategies from Alcott's model: rather than sermonize, Woodworth's narrator, like Alcott himself, prefers a Socratic method. "You would like to take a part in the conversation," he muses. "You would like the liberty of asking a question now and then . . . it was a great deal better to have the boys understand me, than it was to have my stories go on smoothly" (17, 20). Woodworth's depiction of POTUS borrowed an array of devices from Transcendentalism, an American school of thought that was highly influential in the years preceding the Civil War.

At the same time, however, Woodworth recognized the changing marketplace of American fiction, and his *Life of Fremont* borrows from the dime novel, a tradition still in its infancy. He noted that while his book was meant to educate young men, it was "chiefly, *not solely*" designed for that purpose (Woodworth 1856: v, emphasis mine). Anticipating a divide to come, Woodworth embraced greater sensationalism by employing what detractors of the dime novel would come to view as vulgar, cheap thrills. Woodworth's narrator Uncle Frank acknowledges to his immature audience: "I thought you would like to hear a few wild-oat stories" (Fremont 1856: 28). He fills his narrative with action sequences, quite a few of which prove to be only tangentially connected to Fremont himself: "The scenes in the life of my hero, although they are mostly peaceful and harmless, are stirring enough, and thrilling enough, to suit anybody's taste" (14).

Life of Freemont correlates Fremont's "spice" with Woodworth's privileged mode of delivery through a prolonged commentary on the art of storytelling. Uncle Frank likens Fremont's adventures through the American wilderness to the young listener's traversal of his compelling narrative. "Don't let any hard words lie in the way of your understanding," he advises. "It is as necessary to us in our expedition, to clear away all these obstacles to our getting along as it was for Fremont and his men to use those mauls in order to make a path" (Woodworth 1856: 142). By comparing the obstacle of advanced word choice with the obstacles faced by a transcontinental expedition, Woodworth manipulated the sensorium of his male minors, pushing them to approximate the titillations of the protagonist through a distinctive listening and/or reading experience. Uncle Frank understands the weight of his status as a storyteller, and he does not disappoint his assembly of boys: "You'll find (these tales) racy, take my word for it. I have no fears that there will be any sleeping while I read" (254).

A conundrum quickly comes into view: can Woodworth's reader be thrilled as well as educated by Uncle Frank's words? It may prove rather difficult to balance the demands of the Transcendental sermon with dime novel sensations. How is Woodworth's audience to make sense of the conflicted figure of the would-be president, being forged from similar fires? *Life* recounts how Fremont was expelled from school for a torrid love affair, the aforementioned wild oats, before marrying a young woman without her father's blessing. Woodworth spun tales of Fremont's impulsive behavior as a sign of Fremont's perseverance, or his pluck. But mere pages later, the text describes the hypothetical executive as eminently reasonable: "He was a practical youth, as he has since been a practical man" (Fremont 1856: 46). So which will it be—practicality or passion? Woodworth's text lauds Fremont's writing style as "very plain, very simple, very earnest, very truthful"; but Uncle Frank's—and, by extension, Woodworth's—style regularly runs counter to these values, which is to say, the style proves meandering, hyperbolic, and full of rhetorical tricks (101). Readers are left, like Fremont in his passage over the Rocky Mountains, to sort out whether they wish to take the "sensible course" or the "heroic one" (102–03). These disparate courses become so entangled with one another that Woodworth's juvenile readers would have likely struggled to grasp the precise contours of the presidency as an imaginary site at which the two roads could converge.

One of the most unsettling aspects of *Life of Fremont* is the book's insistence on comparing Fremont to the French leader, Napoleon. According to Woodworth's depiction, Fremont, like Napoleon, harbors "gigantic schemes for exploring the wildest portions of our continent" (Fremont 1856: 26). Woodworth's Fremont maintains just the right amount of Napoleonic audacity, and his journeys into the unknown rival Napoleon's conquests, "splendid as they were" (103–04). Of course, given the well-known realities of the situation in Europe, Woodworth had to temper his favorable comparison: "I would rather have chiseled on my tomb-stone the story of such an act as (Fremont's), than the record of the greatest achievement of Napoleon." According to Woodworth, Fremont's conquests, unlike Napoleon's, "were, many of them, almost bloodless" (203). Indeed, many of the glaring inconsistencies in *Life of Fremont* tarry around the subtext of American imperialism: by blending heroism with pragmatism, romantic boldness with the cold water of realism, Woodworth lionized Fremont's Napoleonic nature while at the same time rubbing away some of the tyrant's rougher edges. But Fremont's conquests are *almost* bloodless—that is, for Woodworth at least, these conquests preserved the right ratio of risk and reward, moral uprightness and rousing adventure. The story of Napoleon was "one of the great means by which the imagination of Europe (and the United States) was charged with the deep and heart-pumping excitements of empire . . . (yet) sentiment had been powerfully organized against Napoleon—depicting him as an emperor and despot" (Green 1979: 36). In other words, Napoleonic tales stimulated young men with the prospect of imperial expansion and, concomitantly, they created a point of contrast at odds with a presumably natural, righteous, and emotionless American advance across western territories. At times, American growth became not an adventure story, but a morality play—a system rendered boring due to its assumed inevitability.[5] The story of Fremont as future president remains charged enough to fire the immature imagination and tedious enough to impose a sense of constancy, even normalcy, onto American conquest.

Balanced on the fault line running between pedantry and exhilaration, presidential candidate Fremont embodies the ambivalence at the heart of the nation's westward expansion. Historically speaking, this enterprise was not "almost bloodless," but bloody in the extreme. Consider the horrors that Woodworth mapped onto his "unknown country," including the "wild beasts and wild Indians" (Woodworth 1856: 171). In a rush to produce "tingling" in his readers, Woodworth's story reduces the Native American population to a corral of faceless, shape-shifting demons, prowling at the periphery. These stock characters are comical as well as grotesque. From one perspective, they remain "thoroughly wild" and their threatening presence enlivens the narrative; from another perspective, they prove thoroughly "uninteresting," "dull and sleepy" (91–93). In Woodworth's story, American imperialism comes across as a bold as well as daunting adventure, the likes of which stir the fantasy life of boys, and a reasonable, well-thought-out, thoroughly adult endeavor. Woodworth crafted his image of the president against the backdrop of a delirious frontier lifestyle without, in the process, losing the changeless underpinnings that middle-class parents preferred for the eyes of their sons. Still, Woodworth's racialized excesses—the driving force behind many dime novels in the years ahead—often overpowered the genteel comforts meant to accompany them. POTUS as a symbol of national righteousness became for Woodworth an after-thought, abandoned

---

[5]Martin Green extends this argument further: "Humanism, perhaps especially Anglo-American humanism, is powerfully oriented . . . away from expansion and adventure" (Green 1991: 42). However, he notes, in spite of this resistance to adventure, it is the sensations of the adventure story that marshal young and old readers alike into compliance with the agenda of empire building.

at opportune moments in favor of intoxicating encounters with the Other. Sensations tied to a specific genre like the frontier romance overwhelm all real-world concerns associated with the office. But what are the costs of saturating the political imaginary of American men with such cheap thrills?

The Ambivalent President

Written on behalf of Ulysses S. Grant's presidential campaign by Oliver Optic, the pseudonym for William T. Adams, *Our Standard-Bearer: Or, The Life of General Ulysses S. Grant* pleased Grant so much that he invited its author to his inauguration. The contours of the text dovetail with the contours of popular literature for young men (Optic's genre of choice in non-election years). One can locate traces of the dime novel throughout Optic's book for Grant: its exuberant rallying cries; its unrestrained prose; its strong emphasis on action and suspense via prolonged scenes of military engagement. Like Woodworth, Optic crafted a pseudo-biography of Grant that would appeal to green readers through stirring machismo, jingoism, and cult worship. One can track, here, the relationship between Optic's presidential adventure story and the dime novel, as both formulas paradoxically drew from the "innocuous boyhood pleasures" of Beadle & Adams's "genteel, moralistic" tales (Denning 1998: 10, 60). Stirred by idealized as well as restless presidencies, authors like Optic fashioned America's political fantasies in tandem with the dime novel tradition.[6]

It is vital for readers to remember that the dime novel, although perhaps a bit sensational to contemporary tastes, was in its day marketed as "realistic . . . a more accurate and vivid picture" (Denning 1998: 13). Borders that contemporary readers might want to install between reality and fantasy remained highly permeable for writers like Optic. For example, Optic's narrator announces that phrenologists—the pseudo-scientists that were said to be able to "read" a person's skull—are entirely too restrained to do justice to Grant's grand destiny. "I can almost worship him," Optic's narrator admits. "Towering in lofty preeminence above every other man . . . I am an enthusiast!" (Optic 1868: 16). The text uses prophetic moments to declare the inevitability of Grant's election, tying Manifest Destiny to the predetermined greatness of the president. Optic's untouchable Grant exudes a sprawling, cosmic resonance. Grant's followers hail Grant as "their own

---

[6]This vacillating relationship between Grant and his assumed authority resonates with a larger trend in children's literature: "Adolescent characters themselves often create repressive parental figures to dominate them. The adolescents, in turn, rebel against this perceived domination in order to engage their own power," which is to say, these characters learn to see "repression as a precursor to empowerment" (Trites 2000: 54–55).

deliverer," "the nation's saviour," and an "immortal man" (139, 18, 20). Optic deployed the word sublime to gesture at the unspeakable excellence of his subject matter—a surplus that drew the ire of Optic's critics. Louisa May Alcott, for one, lambasted Optic's output as "optical delusions" (Alcott 1875: 198). Unperturbed, Optic stressed a state of perpetual awe at the feet of Grant, ushering his readers into a state of mesmerism before a nearly divine president.

Yet Optic's employment of the word sublime betrayed an underlying threat: Grant, as well as the nation that he embodies, was *fundamentally inaccessible*. The president is only a symbol, after all, and never the thing itself (or, the embodiment of an imagined national essence). Although Optic's text does at times worship Grant, it periodically undermines such an inflated notion: "The American people are no man-worshippers" (Optic 1868: 58). How can both of Optic's sentiments ring true at once? First and foremost, *Our Standard-Bearer* is meant to be a heart-pumping adventure. Despite its incessant idolatry, the text can neither escape its open-ended character nor evade the premise of ceaseless change that courses through its generic veins. Consider the following moment: "Glory and honor, also, to the people who sternly pull down and cast out their heroes . . . neither the soldiers nor the people blindly worship Grant. It always has been, and still is, possible for him to fall" (59). Grant stands above reproach and yet his exceptional status stems precisely from the fact that he is fallible, which is to say, his eventual triumph only impresses readers because it follows a passage of thrilling uncertainty. With its focus on underdogs rather than unimpeachable giants, the dime novel is structured upon a degree of dissatisfaction. Even as he elevated his presidential subject above public scrutiny, Optic had to preserve an unfinished quality in order to make the story exciting for boys. After all, it is this unfinished quality that fuels the reader's desire and makes the story rousing in the first place.

No effortless reconciliation can be found in these oddly tame yet contested cultural artifacts. Fredric Jameson argues, on the subject of genre, "To resolve the opposition . . . would destroy it" (Jameson 2015: 26). Stitched into its very fabric, books for boys produced pedantry in tension with high-flying passions. Reach as they must for the solid ground of an unmoving final word, a final president, Optic's book returns obsessively to the thrill of unfinished business. The dissatisfaction that structures his book for boys is not a simple byproduct of formulaic fodder, then, but an indispensable aspect of successful presidencies. One must wait with bated breath as the plot moves through its distinctive moments of uncertainty: the election, the passage of bills, the re-election, and so forth. In the end, however, Optic's text reasserts the chief magistrate as a fantastic compensation for the loss of control triggered by its generic arousals—a tendency, we shall see momentarily, that Alger would augment. In Optic's books for boys, the conflicted figure of the president delivers comfort as well as intoxication in equal measure. A subgenre in its own right, representations of the American presidency helped to create problems and then facilitated their resolution.

In the years that followed, Optic's pupils profited from this paradox of pedantry and passion. Perhaps the most famous of all the adolescent fiction writers from the nineteenth century, Alger followed his mentor Optic in his use of the executive's image to impart moral lessons, most visibly in his pseudo-biographies of Abraham Lincoln and James Garfield.[7] Alger learned his trade under the watchful eye of Optic and published his most famous work, *Ragged Dick* (1868), in Optic's *Student and Schoolmate* magazine in the same year that Optic released his pseudo-biography for Grant. Like Optic before him, Alger, a minister by training, composed manuals for proper behavior in the guise of adventure stories. His works thoroughly blur the line between titillation and education. While most of Alger's naysayers focus on his didacticism, fewer of them have attended to Alger's books on the presidency, opting to present the author as strictly apolitical. To borrow Voltaire's phrase, critics have tended to view Alger as lecturing readers on how to cultivate their own garden, and they assume that Alger "avoided the social issues of the day" (Nye 1975: 74). Even detractors that do ruminate upon the political underpinnings of Alger's output have undervalued the significance of his fictionalized presidents. Carol Nackenoff, for instance, argues: "Alger's fiction is otherwise almost devoid of explicit reference to political figures . . . his conception of American candidates and issues was rather pedestrian, and his views unsophisticated" (Nackenoff 1994: 110). Elsewhere, Jordan D. Fiore wonders why Alger did not do more with the idea of the presidency: "Since the story of Lincoln's rise to fame parallels in many ways the pattern of (. . .) books that Alger wrote, one might wonder why he did not recognize and use the Lincoln theme earlier" (Fiore 1953: 248). In fact, Alger's presidential books for boys should not be categorized as aberrations because they reveal a great deal about the disjointedness within his entire corpus. Presenting POTUS as a totem of American progress as well as a pedagogical tool, Alger vacillated between mystification and disenchantment, romance and realism, fuzzy nostalgia and revisionary politics.

Alger's *The Backwoods Boy: Or, the Boyhood and Manhood of Abraham Lincoln* demonstrates the author's ambivalent position. For good reasons, Alger has been categorized predominantly as a pedantic writer. Attempting to compress his outsized subject into an existing framework, Alger was unwilling, or perhaps unable, to deify the former president. He opted instead to highlight certain quotidian aspects of Lincoln's life that Lincoln's other biographers had passed over. For one, Alger's narrator presents Lincoln as

---

[7]Frank Mott observes, "Alger's name has become a by-word for the boy's success story . . . he wrote at least 135 of them" (Mott 1947: 158).

a jokester, before admitting, "I am not prepared to recommend my young readers to imitate Lincoln in this respect" (Alger 1883: 11). Alger's story later celebrates Lincoln for his basic social graces in passages that feel rather diminutive given the enormity of the persona in question. Alger had very little interest in the mythologized rail-splitter himself; instead, Alger exploited the cultural cache of the Lincoln brand *to retell the same story that he always told*. In one aside, Alger's pseudo-biography critiques Lincoln's step-brother for his lack of industriousness and frugality by connecting the idle, shiftless step-brother to a self-made man that Alger's narrator once met on a boat. The text ties the lionized laborer to Lincoln with only the barest of threads. What Alger really wanted to convey in these passages had almost nothing to do with the presidency—and yet the executive remained front and center.

Seldom depicted as a larger-than-life presence, Alger's Lincoln nonetheless adds a degree of gravitas to Alger's typical lessons on punctilios. On highlighting Lincoln's love for wrestling, Alger's narrator notes: "I have told this story partly because I know my young readers would be interested in it, partly to give an idea of the strength and athletic power of the hero of my story. But wrestling contests would not earn a living for young Lincoln" (Alger 1883: 15). Given his proclivity for instructing juvenile male readers on improving their work ethic, Alger turned away from Lincoln's physical prowess to focus on the president's "honest and efficient" job as a store clerk (15). As a result of this focus on youthful manners, Alger's narrator has less and less to say as the narrative moves from Lincoln's adolescence to his notable public life. By the time the text arrives at Lincoln's political career— what one might assume to be the real meat of the matter—Alger's prose has become almost completely derivative of well-known Lincoln biographies. Having retrofit the adolescent Lincoln into his residual rags-to-riches formula, Alger's book has precious little to say concerning the mature man or his politics. The demands of genre thoroughly subsume the presidency.

In order to consider Alger's presentation of the presidency in terms that are not merely derivative, or, as a presentation in which the commander in chief does not simply affirm the writer's pre-existing template but reveals the template's internal tensions, one must go further back in Alger's career, to his fictionalized biography of Garfield, entitled *From Canal Boy to President*. This presidential tale strictly obeys the rules of Alger's Ur-plot: the figure of Garfield re-enforces the "traditional middle-class virtues of industry, integrity, piety, social respectability, neatness, punctuality, temperance, kindness, and generosity" (Cawelti 1961: 79). At the same time, as a result of Alger's patented didacticism, *Canal Boy* willingly exposes its fetishized figure to be a trope—a stylized, and decidedly unnatural, literary device. Blurring boundaries between the Didactic Era and the Gilded Age, Alger negotiated traditional demands for national fealty with the demands of a less restricted literary marketplace. In Alger's hands, the presidency becomes a political signpost as well as a commodified trope.

Before addressing the complexities at play, however, let us examine *Canal Boy* as a recognizable Alger story on at least two fronts: its emphasis on the benevolence of American progress and its praise for the innate goodness of the American middle class. Alger's depiction of Garfield reaches back to recover an uncomplicated, and completely imaginary, time before the economic tumult of the Gilded Age. John Cawelti discovers in Alger's prose "a reassertion of the values of a bygone era in an age of dramatic change and expansion" (Cawelti 1965: 120). Put a bit differently, Alger's fictions as well as pseudo-fictions "desire to maintain continuity of identity and experience while the world was being radically and unalterably transformed ... an unchanging moral universe" (Nackenoff 1994: 131). Alger's image of the executive gives tangible form to a set of prescribed behaviors that Alger promoted as an evergreen aspect of American life.

Accordingly, Alger's work aimed to instill in untested men an ethical framework. It comes as no surprise, then, to read that Garfield endures, from the moment that he walks out of his "rudely-built log-cabin" to look "earnestly" across the clearing in front of his abode, as "a sturdy and indefatigable worker" (Alger 2018: 11, 15). Alger's president remains wired from birth to labor his life away. Alger's Garfield maintains a firm grasp on "the immutable principles of right or wrong" and heeds the advice that is given to him by a wise elder: "All you need to do is work" (40, 55). Garfield mirrors Alger's stock characters with almost no deviation. Here again, readers must listen to a familiar litany of laudable traits: Garfield pays his way in the world; his years of poverty enable him to attain the "highest dignities"; he knows implicitly that he can never "afford to be idle" (60–62, 71). Perhaps what would surprise contemporary readers the most, though, is the degree to which Alger focused upon the dreams that Garfield *forfeits*—a strange shuffling of priorities, given how this character eventually ascended to the highest office in the land. Although many of his disparagers dismiss Alger as a proto-libertarian, interested exclusively in personal freedom and monetary success, in truth Alger's books fostered a Protestant work ethic that encouraged only modest ambition. Relatively disinterested in the presidency, Alger's Garfield "worked hard, but he always enjoyed work . . . by no means (was he) impatient for higher honors" (Alger 2018: 205). Readers watch as the future president becomes disenchanted of a life at sea, a romance that gradually "wears off" in favor of more practical occupations (21). Life at sea, his mother insists, is "a fairy story," and because Garfield conducts himself as a "reasonable boy," he eventually succumbs to her argument against childish fantasies (23–24). *Canal Boy* does little to exploit its subject as a means to inspire lofty goals; instead, it doubles down on work as an end-in-itself. On finishing Alger's tale, one has the sense that Garfield could have emerged as a grocer instead of POTUS and Alger's Ur-plot would have gone almost entirely unaltered.

Like many nineteenth-century writers of juvenile literature focused on the president, Alger strangely depoliticized his subject. His goal was to inculcate proper behavior in young men, it seems, and not to rally voters into a dependable bloc for an upcoming election. Going one step further, Alger's villain of choice, Garfield's assassin, allowed the author to cast politics proper as a pernicious social ill. The assassin is "a wretched political adventurer, who, inflated by an overweening estimate of his own abilities and importance . . . (kills Garfield) in the foolish hope that his chances of gaining would be better under another administration" (Alger 2018: 229). In a word, *Canal Boy* focuses at length on Garfield's assassin to condemn political activism of all stripes. A political adventurer in pursuit of power and privilege: there is likely no character more wretched in all of Alger's universe. In contrast, Garfield declares himself to be a politician without a political profile, which is to say, he stands out as a man unwilling to act as a "slave to party," a man who obeys "his own sense of right" (208). In a refrain that appears throughout books for boys concerned with the presidency, Alger established Garfield as a perpetual outsider who dislikes the political arena. Political strife, or, the Aristotelian strife that constitutes human beings as political animals, does not exist in Alger's stories. Any semblance of politics is always "embedded in profound agreement" regarding a "proper" work ethic (Lhamon 1976: 26). In Alger's telling, Garfield's cumulative position as commander in chief—a highly politicized charge, one cannot deny—has almost no bearing on the course of an otherwise exemplary life.

At the same time, *Canal Boy* does not focus on probity to the exclusion of all other values. The text also emphasizes a need for values that it pins to adolescent males—namely, pluck and precociousness. Like Optic, Alger did not have the luxury of advancing a reductive moralism without the window dressing of the dime novel. Alger's narrator takes pains to assert that Garfield is not "sanctimonious," and the future president remains open to many "social pleasures" (Alger 2018: 103). Garfield gets into several scrapes, including a white-knuckle adventure on a flat-boat. Readers are meant to view Garfield not only as a studious and hard-working but also as an adventurous youth. Alger's presidency remains imbued with romantic overtones. His president is both an action-packed dreamer and a pristine exemplar of moral goodness. Two faces: one part doctrinaire, one part devil. Michael Denning describes the dialogic aspect of Alger's work: "His 'reforming' fiction used the sensational format like a ventriloquist dummy, trying to capture and reshape its audience" (Denning 1998: 171). That is, Alger's texts borrow thrilling traits from the dime novel to market what are actually "genteel, moralistic narratives" (60).[8] Alger's presidential

---

[8]John Cawelti views the Alger tale as "a nostalgic reincarnation of the ideal *eighteenth-century* merchant . . . with enough of the fantastic and unusual to be exciting" (Cawelti 1965: 122, author's emphasis).

stories represent an ongoing tension between sensationalism and sermon at the *fin de siècle*, a tension that helped to define popular perceptions of the presidency for generations to come.

And yet, because Alger continually intruded on his narrative to guide the reader through the path of moral correction, his texts unconsciously handle the president not as a naturalistic man to be emulated, but as a trope, a tool with which to indoctrinate. Said another way, by transforming Garfield into an archetype in a relatively unchanging formula, Alger unwittingly revealed the executive to be just another fictional device (albeit a device with extraordinary staying power). This realization threatened to undermine the self-made mythos to which Alger wanted his audience to subscribe. Not unlike Woodworth, Alger's narrator engages in metacommentary by pulling back the curtain to expose Alger's function in steering the reader's imagination. "My chief object in writing this volume," the narrator declares, is "to commend its subject as an example for boys" (Alger 2018: 144). A list of Alger's pedantic interruptions would be an extensive one. By making himself a highly visible character, indeed, perhaps the most visible character within his stories, Alger unknowingly exposed the formulaic underpinnings of the presidency, thereby demystifying POTUS as the stuff of romance and opening an avenue through which readers might approach this over-heated subject with a greater degree of critical distance.

In sum, works by Optic and Alger expose a core ambivalence within depictions of the president in books for boys. They glorify a predictable moral essence beneath the garb of a seductive dime novel; they are genteel and stimulating, sanctimonious and gratifying. "Each Alger novel defuses its own lively conflict: it arouses then souses itself" (Lhamon 1976: 25). But these pseudo-biographies concurrently wear their moral instruction on their sleeve and, in so doing, they underscore the formulaic nature of the presidency itself. This tendency has never fully gone away: the office continues to function as a didactic device for juvenile males despite, or perhaps because of, its outward appearance as feel-good escapism. The icon of the president endures as both a symbolic lawgiver and an undisciplined adventurer.

A Prison-House of Genre

Adolescent literature from the nineteenth century habitually marginalized the president, either by burying the political aspects of the man, and thus losing sight of his social significance, or by tabling his story to give audiences what they "really want"—namely, the affective experiences that were the stock-in-trade of the dime novel. Roger L. Nichols comments, "Working under intense time pressures, (dime novel) authors could not afford the luxury of careful characterization" (Nichols 1982: 50). Books of this ilk are "mostly action and little characterization" (53). So what does this heightened sensationalism reveal about the image of the president, especially as it was cultivated in the imaginations of American boys? Why should we care that these writers depicted the president primarily as a man of action, relatively devoid of character? For one, the nascent demands advanced by young readers as well as their parents during this period complicated the dignity associated with the office. As early as the mid-nineteenth century, constructions of the presidency bowed to the whims of the popular entertainment industry—an issue with which readers in the early twenty-first century remain all-too-familiar. This obsequious position became increasingly problematic as the entertainment industry peddled racist visions connected to American imperialism.

Consider William Makepeace Thayer's *From Pioneer Home to the White House*, an entry in a long series of books written by Thayer entitled "Log Cabin to White House." Thayer's best-known contribution to the series tracks Lincoln from his eventful boyhood to the apparently yawn-inducing time that he spent serving in the federal government. What particularly interests me in this text is Thayer's over-indulgence in supposedly arousing scenes of confrontation between frontiersmen as well as women and so-called Indians—confrontations pilfered from the pages of the most crude of the dime novels. "Dime novel Indians were seen a savage and inferior beings. Story after story contains reference to their blood-thirsty and savage nature . . . (the dime novel also maintained) the assumption that (Indians) lacked either the physical or mental capacities of the whites" (Nichols 1982: 50–51). Of course, by 1883, countless flesh-and-blood Native Americans had been either killed or forced *en masse* onto reservations, and so Thayer's work reveals the extent to which these flesh-and-blood peoples had been transformed into a trope for general amusement among predominantly white male audiences. The executive and visions of American masculinity were similarly transformed in dialogue with these stock characters. Instead of a robust characterization of Lincoln as an avatar for American virtues, the first two-thirds of *Pioneer Home* offers action sequences propelled by imagery designed for uncritical bigots.

Caricatured Indians populate Thayer's fictional world and furnish much of the text's exigency. *Pioneer Home* opens with a tense tale of Lincoln's grandfather in conflict with a tribe on the prairie. Caught up in the need for endless action, the book sprints from brief exposition on Lincoln's lineage to a tangential tall tale that has virtually no narrative purpose other than to stimulate the reader's baser emotions. In this tangent, a man drags his dead son across the river as he is pursued by so-called savages, and a group of adventurous boys must intervene to stop the captivity narrative in progress. Thayer's narrator points out that Lincoln's elders were "great storytellers," known for their "yarns," but Thayer never addressed the fact that he himself recycled these yarns as part of what purports to be an objective biography (Thayer 1882: 27). Thayer's mouthpiece muses that these "harrowing tales" supply Lincoln with "anecdotes and some useful information" (28). The confusion here between yarn and historical account, between anecdote and useful information, speaks to the unsettled nature of the text, as both an account of the presidency and a competitor in the marketplace of books for boys. Thayer's narrative never pauses to resist its own propulsion and consider how these two agendas may be at cross purposes.

Digressions into racialized sensationalism punctuate *Pioneer Home*. Wandering away from its casual focus upon Lincoln, the book reminisces about frontier life through white-knuckle recollections. In one story, a woman left alone on the homestead with her children tricks an "Indian" into giving up his gun and then threatens "to blow his brains out"; in another subplot, a solitary woman bravely wields an axe to dispatch a handful of what Thayer calls savages (Thayer 1882: 55). Removed from plot advancement, these digressions foreground Lincoln against the backdrop of a rip-roaring frontier. This distinctive backdrop, in turn, would have certainly influenced the fashioning of its subject (the president) within the political fantasies of American men.

Perhaps the most vexing example of this phenomenon occurs when Thayer's narrator describes Lincoln's journey with a friend by raft down the Ohio River. This "exciting and perilous business" reads like a reverse Huck Finn narrative: the book details a fight between Lincoln and a one-dimensional group of vile slaves. As they fight "for their lives," Lincoln and his friend—like Thayer's immature male readers, at least according to the publisher's calculus—become "thoroughly aroused and excited" (Thayer 1882: 165–66). Although Thayer's narrator includes a throwaway line about how Lincoln realizes that the institution of slavery "made them that way," the impetus of the scene cannot be missed: Thayer included this tangent to stimulate male minors, whose appetite for chauvinistic violence was simultaneously being cultivated by the dime novel tradition as a whole.

What was lost in Thayer's compliance with the demands of the dime novel industry? One can argue that Lincoln's humanist ethos, the very bedrock of his public persona, grew a good deal cloudier due to Thayer's inclusion of this story. It is not as though Thayer's critics would wish to erase these moments from Lincoln's personal biography; if accurate, the scenes reveal important inconsistencies in the sixteenth president's public persona. However, one could reasonably expect Thayer to have provided green readers with a bit more context, or at least a more penetrating commentary upon the irony of Lincoln's gleeful violence against slaves. What these readers receive, instead, is an action sequence devoid of moralism and replete with harmful stereotypes. Henry Nash Smith writes, "The outworn formulas had to be given zest by a constant search after novel sensations . . . killing a few more Indians meant, in practice, exaggerating violence and bloodshed for their own sakes, to the point of an overt sadism" (H.N. Smith 2007: 92). The idea of the presidency came to hold a similar inflection. That is, *Pioneer Home* subsumes the presidency within the conventions of the dime novel and thereby demonstrates how the economic pressures of the marketplace for adolescent fiction overwhelmed all other concerns—moral, political, and so forth.

A similar phenomenon can be seen in Edward S. Ellis's pseudo-biography of William McKinley, *From Tent to White House: Or, How a Poor Boy Became President*. As a result of the Spanish–American War, and America's growing imperialist presence on the world stage, it should come as no surprise that Ellis's book is replete with distorted portrayals of Spanish-speaking people.[9] Following the Mexican War of the 1840s, dime novels capitalized upon "the xenophobia enflamed by the expansionists who wanted all of Mexico as a war indemnity. American novels fought the war in the pages of the dime novel as well as on the battlefield" (N. Smith 1980: 526). In other words, the dime novel and the fiery rhetoric of American imperialism mutually informed one another, and Ellis added to this volatile mixture his figuration of POTUS: a character concocted in the crucible of sensationalized, and racially charged, language. The famous writer of *Seth Jones; Or, The Captives of the Frontier*—incidentally, one of Lincoln's favorite novels—Ellis marginalized McKinley within his own narrative by wandering widely into the stirring (and lucrative) field of bloody conflict. Ellis preferred to "quicken the pulse and thrill the heart" rather than engage in substantive reflection upon America's political circumstances (Ellis 1901: 39). Why not exploit the fictional executive to model empathetic or intellectually curious attitudes for American boys?

Instead, Ellis's narrator endeavors to thrill his readers by treating Spanish-speaking individuals as stock characters, adapted from the very worst aspects of the dime novel tradition. Spain's record in the New World purportedly involves "perfidy, ferocity, treachery, murder and every hideous crime"; like Thayer's so-called Indians, Ellis's Spanish villains lack any "common sense" and celebrate "treachery and cruelty"—traits that are supposedly "inherent" to this "mob of murderers" (115). In Ellis's treatment, Spanish soldiers prove to be a living embodiment of profligacy, exoticism, and pure excess, "unspeakable miscreants" fueled by a "ferocious nature" (118, 120). On the one hand, Ellis intended to legitimize the role of the United States in the Spanish–American War through his demonization of the enemy, and his spectacular jingoistic displays were meant to set the young man's heart aflutter. As Ellis's text guides the reader's eyes across scenes of grotesque suffering among Cuban victims—described in lurid detail—it simultaneously commands the reader to feel revulsion toward the perverse Spanish actors, as well as pity (and paternalism) toward the unfortunate Cubans. In spite

---

[9]Edward S. Ellis employed racial stereotypes of Native Americans throughout his fiction. For instance, in *The Steam Man of the Prairies*, he portrayed so-called Indians as being "like demons," "varmints," "treacherous dogs," and "phantoms" (Ellis 2016: 23–25, 29, 89).

of the text's categorization as a biography of McKinley, then, the fleeting presence of the chief magistrate serves only to supplement Ellis's cultural reinforcement of a young male's blossoming imperialist sensibilities.

Costs and Comforts of a Clichéd Commander in Chief

To attend to the president in books for boys does not merely entail understanding better how generic confines have been exploited by various administrations; it also requires understanding better how popular genres have prescribed the actions of presidents, that is, how well-read formulas have restricted a real-world chief magistrate's capacity to greet unprecedented events with something beyond purely derivative responses. Notably, real-life presidents like Herbert Hoover or George W. Bush have eagerly exploited a symbolic reservoir of materials associated with the American frontier. But when unexpected events occur—a Great Depression, or the terrorist attacks of 9/11—the political responses available to these figures are hemmed in by specific generic horizons. There are tangible consequences, then, for framing presidents as unruly cowboys or toughened detectives. The fantasy structures that first make a president comprehensible to the general public go on to stipulate the scope of decision making once he or she enters office. In other words, the dictates of fictional formula come to drive the presidency, and not the other way around.

Popular formulas can precede political discourse, especially those formulas directed at juvenile males (storylines featuring cowboys, superheroes, or detectives). What has habitually attracted American audiences to the gunslinger or the private dick has also regularly dovetailed with what attracts them to the presidency. Arguably, American politics need not resign itself to such moribund plotlines. When authors graft their executives on formulas proven to enhance book sales, the fictional president rarely materializes as a meaningful character—that is, as a living, breathing entity worthy of being investigated, or adequately realized in conversation with a living, breathing society. POTUS instead manifests as a wooden dramatis personae. Today, the old pull of nationalist sentiment far less often dictates presentations of the presidency; in the twenty-first century, the Didactic Era is all but dead. For better or worse, the dime novel industry drew focus away from American history and politics proper, and it fundamentally altered how young men were asked to decipher concepts like public virtue or the common good. Buried beneath a surfeit of fragmented sensations and static set pieces, and designed to provoke bald emotions in an immature audience, the office and its holder have lost a tangible sense of character, personal as well as communal, as the expediency of marketable thrills has vaulted all other concerns. If contemporary readers are dissatisfied with the current state of presidential discourse, they could do worse than to interrogate the idea of the presidency vis-à-vis the prison-house of genre.

And yet, in another sense, the commander in chief is never exclusively a trope designated for child's play. These cheap thrills have worked in part because they effectively cater to political and aesthetic desires. As this chapter has shown, the president is not merely a pedagogical fixture, or an agent of the symbolic order that effortlessly re-enforces hegemonic ideals; instead, the president always already retains traces of excess, a propulsion toward pleasure—however perverse these pleasures may appear to be. Like the frontiersman or the private detective, the fictional president can embody the law while, at the same time (and this caveat remains crucial), sustaining a sense that the law never truly applies to him. Much more than a signpost for discursive restraint, the fictional presidency produces personal as well as political surpluses. Even as the presidents from books for boys teach young readers to respect authority, they spur audiences to feel more powerful by reveling in imaginary sites of release, such as the frontier wilderness or the murky margins of modernity. This dynamic demonstrates one of the greatest values of reading the chief magistrate in generic terms, that is, as a narrative pattern that generates crisis as well as resolution. "Generic conflict and resolution involve opposing systems of values and attitudes, *both of which* are deemed significant by (...) American culture" (Schatz 2009: 575, author's emphasis). Accordingly, one must revisit these moments to contemplate the complex interplay between genre, desire, and the presidency.

To put a finer point on it: one need not abolish fictionalized chief magistrates from the fantasy structures that organize American life, then or now. Rather, one ought to re-read the presidency as an ambivalent fiction that has managed to fuel the desires of a relatively broad coalition of readers. Without resigning themselves to the preservation of untenable aspects of books for boys—a lack of innovation; a toxic masculinity fueled by intolerance for racialized Others—or ignoring these restraints, and therefore overlooking how these texts channel the perceived power of the presidency into the hands of immature male readers, I wish to consider how one can *repurpose*, rather than reject outright, the iconography of the presidency. As the next chapter will illustrate in detail, if it ceases to be pleasurable to "read" the president, then the excitement behind a given candidacy will never translate into meaningful social change. Without question, the conduit that connects hagiographic executives to the excesses of presidential adventure remains a difficult one to navigate. While Woodworth's pedagogical president tarried with the *jouissance* of the open frontier, Alger depended on didacticism to render his titillating executive in a coherent (or, legitimate) manner. Having analyzed these tensions, let us push just a bit further: how can contemporary readers harness the political and aesthetic desires effectively cultivated by these fictional presidents to achieve more benevolent ends?

5

The President in Books for Girls

To an intimate degree, the obsession between an American voter and his presidential pick can resemble a fling with a dashing stranger, and the voter's subsequent devotion to this president in the face of adulterous impulses dovetails with the trajectory of an ideal marriage. One might therefore liken the relationships between voter and presidential love object to the plotlines peddled by popular romances. To attempt to draw such a link is to reconsider the correlation of politics and desire, or, even more significantly, politics and love. By placing America's affairs with its chief magistrates in dialogue with fictional executives that periodically pop up in popular romances, this chapter advances two related propositions: first, that contemporary discourse surrounding the presidency—especially on the left—generally lacks an appreciation for the invaluable part that *pleasure* plays within the political process; and second, that contemporary discourse surrounding the presidency rarely recognizes the demand for a conceptual bridge between the amorous excitement, or seductive thrills, of a given campaign and the monogamous endurance demanded by the resultant administration. The presidents of popular romance transpose, into a readerly register, a complex relay between political infatuation and the apogee of a governing regime. That is, these literary liaisons invite readers to contemplate how sexy campaign promises can be brought to fruition as sustainable policies—and why this kind of transition routinely fails.

Every so often, a romance features a female protagonist who falls, and sometimes learns to stay, in love with POTUS. These select titles are significant because it remains relatively unusual for American readers to contemplate their connection to the chief magistrate as an explicitly emotional bond. Contemporary conversations tend to consider the coupling between citizen and commander in chief as a hyper-rational one. In a manner that echoes a general disregard for the popular romance (especially among male readers), skeptics disregard a voter's passion for a president, as though the voter has inevitably been whipped up by fringe elements of society. At the same time, voters are asked to select their executive by sifting through a glut of data points—an enterprise that remains, to borrow Eva Illouz's phrase, both cold and intimate. In related ways, individuals increasingly select their lovers by swiping screens and relying on impersonal algorithms. Actors that prefer such cold intimacy to the unleashed cravings of politics contend that participants in the electoral system remain entirely too caught up in their own feelings, a dismissal that harkens back to the acerbic words of H.L. Mencken: "(The democratic voter's) amorous fancies are (. . .) immensely exaggerated . . . the sweet passion of love (. . .) is to him precisely what it is to a tom-cat" (Mencken 1926: 36). Mencken and his ilk have long castigated American democracy by describing it as mawkish. Against this critique, popular romances concerning love affairs with presidents demonstrate the correspondence of romance and public perceptions of POTUS as overlapping genres that negotiate a precarious line between desire and devotion. Laura Vivanco observes, "Romance novels have often been described as 'escapist' but romance readers cannot escape politics" (Vivanco 2016: 14). Nor, one might add, can politicos escape the romance.

By interrogating the presidents of popular romance, one simultaneously reevaluates overlooked political aspects of the genre. Myriad (male) readers have denigrated the romance "because its drama lacks relevance to male socialization patterns" (Mussell 1984: 16).[1] However, the works in question underscore how this unique kind of fantasy informs supposedly male socialization patterns. Indeed, as Kay Mussell makes clear, "Romances center on the problems of love, commitment, domesticity, and nurturing. These are values assigned by culture to female sensibility, and they are frequently neglected or devalued. But romances place these female values at the center of the fantasy" (59). In effect, the popular romances surveyed in this chapter revolve around values including love and commitment, domesticity and nurturing, and, in so doing, they reveal how so-called female concerns persist as the primary focal points of American politics. It is not that these values are supplemental to the fashioning of a political imaginary. Far from it. The texts that I will analyze show how concerns previously thought to belong exclusively to female readers exist at the very locus of America's most potent political fantasies. It is not unheard of to read the popular romance as a symptom of a political substratum, but it remains exceedingly unusual to read politics as the symptom of a libidinal fundament. Perhaps the time has come round at last to talk about American politics as personal affection, sexual lust, and enduring love.

---

[1]Carolyn Heilbrun writes, "Men, however, never troubled to read women. Even today, there are male scholars and writers who declare themselves incapable of such an effort, or disinclined to it" (n.p.).

For example, Katy Evans's *Mr. President* demonstrates how the life cycle of a presidency parallels the life cycle of a popular romance: the foreplay of a campaign as courtship; the surge of enthusiasm as a crowd looks for its representative (the crowd and representative as surrogates for individuals within an amatory coupling); the eventual ambivalence of the marriage pact.[2] The female protagonist becomes smitten with the presidency and she spends the duration of the text in pursuit of a man who pines for the highest office in the land: "Nothing was more exciting than meeting the *president*" (Evans 2016: 12, author's emphasis). But this heated story does not concern itself with a woman who wants to be held in check by a man—a reductive assumption about the popular romance held by many naysayers. Instead, like countless works within the tradition, Evans's fictional president proffers the transgressive thrill of female empowerment, this time via greater political engagement. The thrill does not erupt because a man saves a woman but because a fictional executive opens an imaginary space in which a woman can participate in the public square and openly declare her own wishes.[3] "Take steps in embracing your own political power," Evans's book pleads. The protagonist's intimate connection to the presidency spurs her to "want to do great things too"; accordingly, the man secures the heroine's fealty not when she recognizes his raw animal magnetism, but when he champions one of her ideas for his campaign (21). Underwhelmed by opinion polls and algorithmic relationships, she demands a president who will respond to his constituents, which is to say, an executive who will listen to her ideas and understand what she truly wants. In effect, the presidency stirs Evans' protagonist to make history and not to remain a passive object in a male-dominated game.[4] Evans's protagonist needs to lose control and take bigger risks, to chase that better feeling—the pleasure that comes from listening to what she fancies instead of being stifled by social expectations: "I cannot deny myself him" (184). In short, fictional presidents in the popular romance help

---

[2]Fannie Hurst's novel *A President is Born* (1928) figuratively connects the presidency and a blooming romance. The would-be president only recognizes the seeds of the presidency germinating within him after he falls for a young woman named Dora: "How suddenly and gloriously alive this future" (Hurst 1928: 400).

[3]Seminal critics of the popular romance have asserted the genre's transgressive potential. Janice Radway on romance reading as a radical act: "Interstices still exist within the social fabric where opposition is carried on by people who are not satisfied by their place within it or by the restricted material and emotional rewards that accompany it" (Radway 1991: 222). Tania Modleski on romance writing as a radical act: "Even the contemporary mass-produced narratives for women contain elements of protest and resistance underneath highly 'orthodox' plots" (Modleski 2007: 16).

[4]This phenomenon shows up in gay romance novels as well. David Levithan's 2006 text *Wide Awake* follows a young gay couple as their love blossoms in tandem with the rise of a gay president: "The electoral college was secure, and I was in love with a boy who was in love with me" (Levithan 2006: 3). The fight to elect a representative here synchronizes with romantic union: "Our pulses intermingled . . . we pursued happiness . . . I was a part of history" (220–1).

to overturn "impediments to love in the power relationships of a patriarchal society that devalues women's emotions and desires" (Mussell 1984: 69). These texts unveil, among targeted female readers in particular, a longing for more robust political stimulation: a hankering to take part in political struggles alongside a tacit acknowledgment that, although POTUS could never fully satisfy their cravings, disenfranchised women must nonetheless persist in fighting for their own pleasure as well as lasting happiness.

Moreover, in recognizing that, as much as she wants to please the president, her own yearnings remain equally valid, the protagonist of *Mr. President* highlights the distinctively democratic dimensions of countless popular romances. The rupture caused by a young woman's sudden attraction to a fabricated president reveals how imperfections in the current state of things are precisely what propels the subject's desire. To be political, that is, to be forever open to something new and more exciting, remains a messy business. In one of the text's more interesting asides, *Mr. President* includes a brief commentary upon Alexis de Tocqueville's *Democracy in America* (1835): "I love it because it's not about how perfect democracy is, but rather how imperfect it is" (Evans 2016: 237). As she realizes that her pleasure should not be secondary to the man's pleasure, and that her personal as well as political desires remain eternally unfinished things, the protagonist discovers the democratic dimension of her own love story.

Despite this uptick in democratic desire, though, an unresolved issue remains: the problem of consummation. The sought-after marriage plot threatens to leave the woman cooled off, unsexy, even melancholy. To wed the president, the protagonist must slide back into a corseted arrangement in which she remains maternal, aristocratic, and apolitical. At the end of *Mr. President*, the election results pour in and her lover has won, which ostensibly means that their thrilling affair has reached its terminus. Her lover's ascent to the role of chief magistrate marks a fundamental shift in his priorities and, at least in theory, a foreclosure of their secretive attraction to one another: a twilight of desire in a personal as well as political sense. "Love has no place in the White House" (299). The prevailing tension between fiery campaign and stable-yet-boring administration proves to be a crucial characteristic of the popular romance as well as American politics at large.

Blue Moods of Melancholy Marriage

In Rita Mae Brown's *Dolley* (1994), a schism separates illicit desire from duty—or, political passions from the status quo. Brown's protagonist Dolley Madison is caught between her undying love for her husband, President James Madison, and her avidity for a younger politico, and aspiring candidate for the presidency, Henry Clay. While her husband carries the heavy burden of leading the republic through the War of 1812, her devotee aspires to do things differently. For her part, Dolley attempts to balance her submissive role as wife to Madison with her tantalizing role as confidante and co-conspirator to Clay. Brown's love triangle reframes historical narratives surrounding the presidency: no longer fashioned exclusively as a mouthpiece for eternal principles—a relic of the Era of Good Feelings—the president must incite a woman's pleasure. In turn, following the Lacanian dictum that the subject should never give up on her desire, Dolley's relationship with the presidency allows her to re-politicize her subjectivity, which in term revives her bodily appetites. "The worst thing that can happen to love is habit," Srecko Horvat writes. "A truly revolutionary moment is like love; it is a crack in the world, in the usual running of things, in the dust that is layered all over in order to prevent anything new" (Horvat 2015: 4). Cue the lascivious Clay.

Clay and Dolley meet in a clandestine fashion to discuss America's political climate, a sequence of meetings that stirs in Dolley an ache to join the proverbial fray. Clay represents the vitalism of political wrangling; he initiates a lust in her for what has not yet been achieved —namely, a radical pining for female suffrage as well as more opportunities for women to be involved in American politics. Historically speaking, the War of 1812 was an opportunity for a second revolution, a chance for citizens to feel once more, or, for the first time, the heart flutterings of that seminal event. Along these lines, Dolley's flirtatious encounters with Clay prompt her to overcome her lethargy as housewife and First Lady, respectively, and to enjoy the rejuvenating effects of revolutionary fervor. Dolley confesses: "Thinking of the French revolution reminded me of taking tea with Henry Clay" (R. Brown 1994: 257). Tapping into the sexual energy of sedition, Dolley enters into dalliances with Clay to escape from the boredom of the "bourgeois concept of marriage" (115). She slips from the social contract solidified in the steadfast avatar of her husband—an unattractive yet morally upstanding leader aligned with the nation's legal apparatus, thanks in part to his authorship of some of the nation's founding documents. The American presidency starts with an insurgent encounter before drifting into a duty-bound version of itself.

Unlike Clay, Dolley's husband Madison is enfeebled and at times downright uninspiring. Brown's narrative unfavorably compares the cuckold Madison to George Washington: Dolley's famous rescue of Washington's portrait from a burning White House during the War of 1812 exacerbates the sense that Madison cannot quite measure up to the preeminent general. Madison stands "like a statue" in his social position, locked into the presidency, removed from the fires that first precipitated colonial rebellion (R. Brown 1994: 16). In other words, Madison—like a litany of leaders during the Era of Good Feelings—stands atop a lofty perch, recused from the political thrills that so flush Dolley's cheeks. Brown's Madison lacks passion; he is too "damned principled" to feel things deeply (223). The revolutionary spirit fades into inflexible restraint. As commander in chief, Madison demands sacrifice and obedience on the part of American citizens, but he has in the process forgotten the importance of pleasure. Set apart from her rapidly shrinking husband as well as the concept of bourgeois marriage that defines her personal as well as political parameters, Dolley keeps alive the flames of a revolutionary zeal that once compelled her fellow citizens to fall head over heels in love with their heady promises. Madison's conservative regime prefers the comforts of a general stasis. Yet "a 'zero risk' love is not love. Falling in love consists precisely in this contingency, in the fall itself" (Horvat 2015: 12). That is to say, apolitical love is not love at all.

Dolley nonetheless loves the chief magistrate. For all of Clay's ebullience, the would-be executive proves "incapable of deep love," and Dolley responds: "I remain bound to my husband . . . the Union will hold" (R. Brown 1994: 202–04, 171). Brown's novel clings to the notion that a subject's love of the president should supersede her desire for political intrigue. Eternal principles must win the day. Several factors explain this reactionary outcome. First, the novel's problematic conflation of militarism with politics; when he is thrust into battle, Madison becomes sexier: "He felt like fire, he felt so young" (277). Exhilarated by the antagonism of combat, the fictional Madison abandons the arch premise of consensus, and thus rekindles his wife's attraction toward him as well as the national essence that he represents. His wife positively glows: "No one's calling you an old man now" (318). This troubling treatment of militarism as a romantic spark resurfaces periodically in popular romance.[5] Second, Dolley's devotion to her husband may be written off as a byproduct of what some critics deride as the hidebound tendencies of the romance, since female protagonists within the genre reliably return, after heart-pounding escapades, to the palliative assurances of bourgeois marriage. Finally, Dolley remedies the initial split between political pleasure and organizational principle through an appeal to ambivalence. Brown's protagonist gets to be constructive and, at the same time, defensive—upholding, in prim and proper fashion, the status quo. Although Brown's president never relinquishes his *noblesse oblige*, he keeps (re)kindling a secret germ of transgressive potential: his veiled humor, his innate rebelliousness, and his "heritage of flames" (314). Through a good dose of magical thinking, Brown's text weds the pleasures and principles embodied in the presidency. It subsequently paves a path—a path that Alain Badiou would call a truth procedure—from the act of falling in love, catalyzed by a political and/or love event, and the deepening of that love, which occurs when the movement at last names its figurehead. "I tell (Madison) every day that I love him," Dolley declares. "In the beginning of our marriage he used to blush. I believe now that it fortifies him" (84).

---

[5]Jayashree Kamble argues that popular romance in the late twentieth century "carries an awareness of the militaristic fervor of the age," and it reveals the difficulty of combining "allegiance to nation" and "couplehood within the nuclear family" (Kamble 2012: 154–5). A fictional president smooths over such ideological tensions, since the presidency envelopes feelings associated with both nation and family.

But a key question remains: how does a political movement travel from youthful infatuation to convicted caring? In a democracy, a social order founded upon political wrangling and the allure of ceaseless change, defined by what one might call its evergreen inconstancy, how does an infatuated subject avoid falling out of love with the avatar of the ideal that once gripped her with such ferocity? Unmistaken melancholia pervades Dolley. The story is punctuated by fears that everything young America has built since the revolution will be taken away by the War of 1812: "I can bear anything, dear God, anything but the loss of my husband" (R. Brown 1994: 286). Between Madison's ever-visible mortality and the encroaching British forces, Brown's novel reflects a rapidly aging America, a republic that has lost its democratic vitality and no longer pursues greater pleasure but merely tries to conserve whatever vestiges of contentment it can salvage. As the Madison administration anxiously fans the nation's dying heritage of flames, readers find less and less to excite them, save Dolley's dalliances with Clay. Love and politics appear to be sorely in need of reinvention.

The morose Madison regime speaks forcefully to the condition of the contemporary left in America: a bloc that appears to have been caught in a loop of infatuation followed by deflated dreams. From their lust for Bill Clinton to Barack Obama to Joe Biden, many self-defined members of the left habitually express a hunger for change—but once the candidate enters office, many supporters almost immediately sink into a state of disappointment (for a multitude of reasons, including neglect by their romantic and/or political partner). Despondent, the aforementioned Democrat scrambles to hold onto the scraps of a revolution deferred. In terms familiar to readers of the popular romance, the bourgeois union, despite its assumed righteousness, ushers in only disaffection and regret. Walter Benjamin coined the term left-wing melancholia to describe this perpetual weakening of political passions: "What is left is the empty spaces where, in dusty heart-shaped velvet trays, the feelings—nature and love, enthusiasm and humility—once rested" (Benjamin 1994: 305). The pursuit of leftist pleasure eventually trails off into "wrathful disappointment" (W. Brown 1999: 22). That is to say, the yearning for a leftist candidate fades as the resultant administration offers middling compromises, incremental adjustments, and stern scolding for voters who are supposedly not doing enough to translate the aspirations of the campaign into real-world governance. In response to an ache for alternatives, leftist voters receive chilled demands for self-sacrifice as well as unappetizing commands to protect the letter of the law by taking the moral high road.[6] A similar blue

---

[6]Following Mark Fisher, one may consider the economic valence of this issue: "(Left-wing projects) are all inadequate and all for the same reason, over and over again, in that they don't take the desire of the capitalized seriously—they reject it and therefore keep re-inscribing moralism" (Fisher 2021: 204).

mood saturates *Dolley*. (This book's epilogue returns to the connection between presidents and melancholia, but in accordance with Sigmund Freud's more productive use of the term.)

Like *Dolley*, Ellen Feldman's historical romance *Lucy* (2003) highlights a love triangle to track a transition from passions surrounding a would-be president to the dying embers of administrative ennui. This time, a transgressive affair erupts between the charismatic Franklin Delano Roosevelt (FDR) and Lucy Mercer, whose magnetic attraction to FDR leaves her speechless. "How did I find the courage," Lucy asks herself, "or the audacity or the sheer recklessness to risk him?" (Feldman 2003: 7). Echoing Clay and Dolley, readers see the spark between FDR and Lucy lit during clandestine discussions of politics. From these intimate discussions, unusual for so-called proper women of the time, Lucy whirls uncontrollably into a torrid tryst that threatens to derail her amour's presidential aspirations. On the other side of this triangle, readers meet Eleanor, FDR's wife, who represents the organizational acumen and lofty principles of the coming Roosevelt administration. She proves to be "a stickler for facts," preaches self-discipline, and always goes high when opponents go low: "I admired her scruples. Who could not? But I *enjoyed* his stories" (35, emphasis mine). Just as the government cannot legislate sentiment by creating holidays like Mother's Day, Lucy refuses to forego her own pleasure in the face of social conventions and the domineering presence of a figure that the novel characterizes as a matriarchal killjoy. Simply put, Lucy will not submit to the matriarch's left-wing melancholia: "I was made for happiness, not sacrifice" (8). War once again plays a pivotal—and problematic—role in preserving desires political as well as personal; here, military conflict has a way of "unlacing restraints" (30). Against the apolitical beliefs of her social class and the respectable ethics of Eleanor, Lucy thirsts for a revolutionary desire that promotes risk and compels her to accept nothing less than delight. In a word, she will not follow Dolley into a blue mood. Neither Lucy nor the president is willing to ration their respective pleasures; they neither allow the heat of their initial affair to cool nor relinquish their ardent desires to the "heaviness of heart (that) derives from routine." They will not resign themselves to the "stuffiness" that occurs when "the juices (begin) to dry up in the body social" (Benjamin 1994: 305–06). Following Woodrow Wilson, who imperiled his hopes for the White House in the name of love, FDR and Lucy exemplify the fraught attachments that launch a presidency: "(Love) cannot be a defensive action simply to maintain the status quo . . . risk and adventure must be re-invented against safety and comfort" (Badiou 2012: 11).[7]

---

[7]Roland Barthes writes, "I cannot claim to think properly . . . I cannot hope to seize the concept of (love) except 'by the tail': by flashes, formulas, surprise of expression" (Barthes 2010: 59, author's emphasis).

But once FDR ascends to the highest office in the land, what will happen to the potency of this initial political and/or love event? Can desire survive in the wake of supposed fulfillment? Once the promise of change has gone from white-hot belief to prosaic certainty, will Lucy's lust for the president—the man as well as the myth—endure? Lucy's blind adoration for FDR undergoes a dramatic shift at the precise moment that FDR pivots from candidate to officeholder. Feldman's novel details the "orgy of recklessness" in the crowd that attends FDR's inauguration, revealing, it would seem, the dangerous undercurrents of incited political pleasure (Feldman 2003: 91). Just as Madison must avoid the fate of the hot-headed Clay, who will, Dolley acknowledges, never be president, FDR learns to tame the hedonistic impulses that his candidacy has inspired. He must establish decorum and compel his "childish" crowd to "suppress their excitement"—without, and this point cannot be overstated, losing their sense of pleasure in him (89). It is in the middle of his inauguration that FDR tells Lucy he loves her. But it is also during FDR's inauguration that Lucy loses her innocence and realizes that FDR cannot stand on his own due to his infection with polio. Will her crush dissipate as Lucy turns to penance over her choice of personal pleasure instead of principle? Or, will she follow the fictional Eleanor's lead, who "cannot live with a man who falls short of . . . perfection"? (158). The second half of Feldman's text threatens to sink into the melancholia that overwhelms *Dolley*. And yet somehow it never does.

A Lasting Love

In the first half of *Lucy*, the eponymous heroine, and the nation for which she acts as a stand-in, fall head over heels for FDR, "giddy with anticipation," eager to consummate the relationship and staggered by "the sheer impossibility of the event" that will launch FDR into prominence and voters into his metaphorical arms (Feldman 2003: 178). In the second half, Lucy's love evolves from youthful anticipation to durable union, which is to say, from political movement to functional regime: "Love is above all a construction that lasts. A tenacious adventure . . . real love is one that triumphs *lastingly*" (Badiou 2012: 32, emphasis mine). Horvat adds, "Revolution is not a one-night stand" (Horvat 2015: 9). To achieve a lasting love, though, the voter and the candidate must accept imperfection, even boredom, as part and parcel of the democratic relationship.[8] Let us examine,

---

[8]Slavoj Žižek insists that, although "democracy always entails (. . .) the rule of dull mediocrity, the only problem is that every attempt to elude this inherent risk and to restore 'real' democracy necessarily brings about its opposite—it ends in the abolition of democracy itself" (Žižek 2009: xxviii).

then, how *Lucy* bridges the divide between revolutionary courtship and the marital bliss of presidential administration.

While never swept under the rug, FDR's glaring imperfections neither deflate nor generate guilt at his political movement's initial "swooning" (Feldman 2003: 190); instead, his imperfections make him seem "hugely, gloriously human" (170). His admission of his own sickness makes him all the more appealing to Lucy as well as the public. For her part, rather than give up on POTUS once he has entered office, Lucy persists in her love for what he represents. She fans her heritage of flames without becoming desperate or defensive. Crucially, both FDR and Lucy strive to be the "equal" of their "lover's memory," as they recognize a need to re-ignite their love for one another so that the sun never fully sets on their entangled appetites (217). In her head, Lucy tells Eleanor: "Don't spoil his pleasure. Don't make yourself unhappy" (40). Lucy recognizes that pleasure is relational, not self-indulgent, and a partnership must keep the pursuit of gratification alive as its central pillar. Accordingly, in the latter half of the text, Lucy adjusts her expectations and transforms her bond with FDR "from random encounter to a construction that is resilient . . . in the case of love, you must, often very urgently, re-make your declaration" (Badiou 2012: 44, 51). Instead of lamenting the loss of a vibrant Roosevelt at the peak of his powers, or experiencing pangs of nostalgia for the unbridled lust of the initial encounter, Lucy will not be "beholden to certain long-held sentiments and objects"; rather, she holds to "the possibilities of political transformation in the present" (W. Brown 1999: 21). Sitting with FDR at the end of his term (and the end of his days), Lucy chooses happiness—for herself, for him, and for the larger political movement within which they find one another. At the close, the affair between Lucy and her president lasts not because of righteous proclamations or bids to conserve power, but because the two parties recognize an overriding need to provide each other with delectation. Personal desire must be fueled and fed anew, just as political commitments must be reinvented. Even in the face of grief, loss, and betrayal, Lucy maintains her investment in a pleasure that precedes, and then proceeds from, FDR's political program: "Only the knowledge of the happiness I gave him stifles . . . the howl of Eleanor's pain. Only the happiness" (290). Especially in an age of left-wing melancholia, in which party officials force voters to choose pragmatic arrangements over the pursuit of pleasure, the mature yet unsatiated love of Lucy and her commander in chief offers a useful lesson that can be applied to popular romance and political paradigms alike.

Sienna Snow's *Commander: The Politics of Love* unfolds along a parallel track. In the first section, the relationship between the female protagonist and the president involves a transactional arrangement that privileges power and money; in the second section, one filled with relentless sex scenes, the protagonist forfeits self-control and submits to the pursuit of pleasure alongside her well-endowed executive; in the third and final section, the protagonist at last confesses her love for the president and pledges fealty to him. Not a hasty synthesis, the ending of the novel submits that politics infused with love must stoke the pathos of participants and concomitantly coax that spark into an enduring flame: "We are as complicated as it gets, full of entanglements, need, and a binding history" (Snow 2018: 231). It is not that becoming more political precedes one's ability to fall in love, or that falling in love precedes a political reawakening; rather, these texts reveal how *love and politics are always already imbricated phenomena.*

Written around the same time as Feldman's novel, Susan Elizabeth Phillips's *First Lady* affirms the durable presidency as an analog for mature love. Following the death of the president, the First Lady flees from her patrician existence. In disguise, she meets up with a blue-collar man and his two children and, during a road trip through so-called flyover country, she rekindles her sexuality as well as her political vision. Their arrival in Iowa—the well-known site of the nation's first presidential caucus—marks her libidinal reawakening, in both a sexual and political sense. The romantic partners half-jokingly refer to Iowa as "The Land of Lust" (Phillips 2000: 173). Although the protagonist needs a detour to arouse her, *First Lady* ultimately returns to the White House—this time, with the protagonist herself having won the title of POTUS. She realizes that her partner's resistance to marriage and her resistance to the White House were synonymous. Having found their passion for one another, they can now enter into a lasting love, as a consensual regime that actually works. The newly empowered woman realizes that if she balances pleasure and familial devotion, she can discover happiness. To avoid left-wing melancholia, organizational politics must maintain a healthy degree of unfulfilled passion in tandem with principles of nurturance, self-sacrifice, and commitment: "I love you, I admire you, I lust after you, I adore you" (369). Jean-Luc Nancy could have been describing either love or democracy when he stated, "Love is impossible . . . at once the promise of completion—but a promise always disappearing—and the threat of decomposition, always imminent" (Nancy 1991: 93, 99). Like democratic politics, love is not about defeating the impossible in the name of an absolute; love and politics *are* the impossible. A desire for completion moves in tandem with the truth that the fires of revolution must be relit in perpetuity.

However, one must acknowledge essential differences between politics and love, because to conflate the two concepts overzealously leads to unsavory outcomes. Politics is by definition antagonistic. The erasure of this intrinsic contestability leads to authoritarian nightmares. One need only look at several recent examples for proof: Obama was depicted by many of his supporters as a savior, and this Cult of Personality inspired an affection that was not always fertile in terms of policy achievements; even though Donald Trump arguably did a better job of stoking the passions of his loyal followers than his opponents, the cultish reverence of his followers did not produce a healthy kind of love. To move a bit closer to the source, *Lucy* takes on a deeper resonance when one accounts for its unique cultural context: it was published in the immediate aftermath of an abuse of power by another charismatic president, Bill Clinton, in his sordid relationship with intern Monica Lewinsky—a real-world plot that uncomfortably echoed the outline of Feldman's novel. When one amalgamates love and politics, one engages in a "collective transfer of love to a political figure"—a fetish, in which the Two becomes One and therefore flattens the relationality, which is to say, the indispensable sense of difference, that makes political engagement so incendiary in the first place (Badiou 2012: 70). Indeed, *First Lady* problematically flattens its presidential love affair by celebrating "the whole unbelievable beauty of two people being one" (Phillips 2000: 370).

Yet Badiou would interject at this point that the question is not one of flesh-and-blood presidential politicking; it is primarily a question of aesthetics. Through the work of art, audiences can realize striking similarities between political revolution and private desires. These events remain interdependent. Philosophers including Jacques Rancière and Georges Didi-Huberman have discussed the sensuous quality of politics, arguing, in their respective manners, that the political event only becomes accessible to the public through the realm of the sensible. Didi-Huberman insists upon the importance of pathos in this process, since the sensible image forces spectators to combine thought with emotion: "Our senses (. . .) are *moved* by this rendering sensible: moved in the double sense of putting into emotion and putting into movement of thought" (Didi-Huberman 2016: 86, author's emphasis). Particularly in its treatment of the presidential love object, the popular romance invites its readers to make politics sensible, to give revolutionary impulses a distinctive shape. And this rendering sensible moves readers in visceral ways, through her very innervations. The presidents of the popular romance therefore reveal an intersection of the love event and the political event through art: a rendering sensible that improbably sustains bottomless passion and strict devotion, vitality as well as self-reflection.[9] In their depictions of the presidency, then, popular romances must navigate between the pathos of politics and the politics of pathos. These texts warn of a passion that becomes too political and a politics that becomes too passionate; in response, they imagine a politics that can sustain passion without sacrificing discipline, wisdom, or insight.

Importantly, to dismiss gullible readers of the popular romance as mistaking a fetish for the thing itself, of the unsophisticated merging of the Two into One, is to repeat the mistakes that many readers, especially

---

[9]Judith Butler instructs her subject "to become philosophical in and about one's passions . . . one lives (one's passions), and seeks to know them (. . .) by bringing one's questions into the practice of love itself" (Butler 2002: 65).

male ones, have made in addressing this highly influential genre. The *sui generis* formula of the popular romance provides a fictional interface with which readers might transpose their emotional needs into a political key and, concomitantly, transcribe their politics into a form that better speaks to their emotions. As Byung-Chul Han observes, "Political action occurs in a sphere that intersects with eros on manifold levels . . . love stories that unfold against the backdrop of political events point to this hidden connection" (Han 2017: 44). Fiction performs an indispensable part in helping readers to confront their own needs and wants on the political stage. "Popular romance represents many of our deepest fantasies, about social as well as individual satisfaction" (Radford 1986: 19). In these texts, audiences confront a tacit connection between seditious gratification and the emotional life of the female subject—a connection that renders sensible the dissatisfaction of legions of American women.

A prime example of this ongoing dissatisfaction, Mary Higgins Clark's first romance, *Mount Vernon Love Story* (1969) orbits around the theme of unrequited love: George Washington's unrealized desire for Sally Fairfax; his ungratified hunger for approval from his mother. Clark's love story does not concern itself with the union of the nation's first president and his wife but with Washington's idyllic quest to return to his beloved birthplace of Mount Vernon. Iterations of this impossible quest multiply as the text compares the Capitol, with its "half-completed buildings," to Washington's "symbol of promise," thereby positing the city's central figurations not as finished products but as a dream indefinitely deferred (Clark 2003: 245). For her part, Washington's spouse comprehends how her desire for her husband is maintained not by his presence, but by his never-ending absence: "If we were separated for a while, I think the reunion would be so wonderful" (207). Clark embedded the theme of unrequited love into the very structure of *Mount Vernon Love Story* as its narration oscillates between the story of Washington's life before his inauguration and the story of Washington following his departure from office. By shifting back and forth between pre- and post-presidency, Clark's novel renders POTUS as a missing love object, at once eagerly anticipated and nostalgically recalled. Ardor and melancholia somehow coexist. Popular romances that involve imagined presidents thus embrace the impossibility of their aims without losing a persistent push for shared pleasure. In this way, these overlooked works illuminate the stamina of a political love that can last thanks to its endless reinvention.

"They Are Not Mutually Exclusive"

To misread love is to misread politics—specifically when one fails to account for the complexities of desire. In the final pages of his book on democracy, Pierre Rosanvallon isolates romantic allegiance from political allegiance. According to Rosanvallon, an interpersonal romance involves commitments being tested daily, whereas political relationships are built on a ceaseless waiting game. Describing something akin to left-wing melancholia, Rosanvallon calls contemporary political attachments "perverse" because they oscillate between "an insatiable appetite for promises and a disenchanted turning away from politics" (Rosanvallon 2018: 267). Against such "chronic expectancy," he proposes what he calls a permanent democracy: a democracy that can "overcome" its problems, "realize" its potential, and "successfully avoid" the risk of mediocre outcomes (268). Rosanvallon's misreading of romance as a source of bottomless affirmation directly informs his need to cure what he denounces as the pathology of a political mode that makes too many promises—that is, the pathology of presidentialism.[10] One is reminded, however, by the thread which binds love to politics, that a love without promises deferred, with neither anticipation nor risk, is not love at all. Until readers recognize the need for a contentment that sustains a kernel of discontentment, they cannot hope to revamp their stagnating political project.

Let us close, then, by turning to Irving Stone, a mid-century American writer who made his career imagining a presidency that could hold in productive tension a longing for devotion (the utopian promise of marriage) with an unslaked thirst (the lust-filled drive behind courtship). Stone's historical novels concerning well-known executives borrow heavily from the popular romance, in that he structured his retellings of presidential narratives around the imperatives of the love story: the perspective of a long-suffering female protagonist; the courtship that parallels one's foray into the political arena; and the culminating marriage that somehow maintains the passion that first sparked the romance. To address the emotional demands of American government—namely, fidelity to a political cause in tandem with a recognition that dissatisfaction is the lifeblood of democracy—Stone relied upon the blueprint of the popular romance. Now, stagnating political actors in search of answers might draw their lifeblood from Stone.

In *Love is Eternal*, Stone infused politics with the stuff of romance (and vice versa). First, he likened the political engagement of a female protagonist to flirtation, passion, and unrequited love. Once more, Henry Clay plays the role of the rake. A smitten Mary Todd tells Clay: "If you were not already married, Mr. Clay, I would wait for you." And then, in a later exchange: "'I'm still waiting,' (Mary) replied, her eyes flashing mischievously, '. . . for you to be elected president'" (Stone 1954: 11–12). The ellipsis speaks volumes

---

[10]Rosanvallon periodically acknowledges a need for dissatisfaction: "Democracy consists fundamentally in the unremitting examination of its own indeterminacy" (Rosanvallon 2018: 236). To resist the urge to achieve transparency or a "cured" body politic, Rosanvallon might have attended to the role of aesthetics in conserving this unremitting examination of democracy's indeterminacy.

about the carryover between lust and presidential campaigning. Moreover, the would-be First Lady finds in her presidential amour a vehicle through which she can feel her political potency, overcome her disenfranchisement as a woman living in nineteenth-century America, and receive respect at last from a male authority figure. She feels flushed whenever surrounded by political intrigue, innervations that directly correlate with her developing sexual attractions. For Mary Todd, William Henry Harrison's election in 1840, a watershed moment in the politicization of American life in which an enormous wave of voters became interested in presidential contests, commences her seduction of Abraham Lincoln. The remaining events of the chief magistrate's biography dovetail with a marriage plot purloined from the popular romance: during the courtship phase of her life, Mary must choose between Stephen Douglas and Lincoln, just like the citizens of Illinois, and then the United States at large, need to pick a side. Stone's blurring of the personal love object with the presidential love object was consistent and thorough: "Why is it that you accept Mr. Lincoln for yourself as a leader of your party," Mary asks her sister, "But reject him to lead me . . . to happiness?" (105). Once more, the ellipsis speaks volumes, as Stone's reader recognizes how Americans are led to cultivate devotion to a president in ways that echo the emotional resonance of a marriage. Like any good marriage, an effective regime demands "stamina" (39). In the final stages of Stone's presidential romances, the First Lady usually learns—or, more accurately, reaffirms— that her hubby cannot possibly satisfy her every urge, in the same way that no electoral result could ever put an end to her yearning for political gamesmanship. Lincoln confesses, "In this troublesome world, we are never quite satisfied" (206). Mary laments, "Are we never to know fulfillment?" (283). When the president and his lover consummate their shared pursuit upon entering the White House, they do not enter into a state of perpetual pleasure; instead, Stone's presidential romances typically conclude with a lost election or a martyred spouse being killed off. Stone's presidency thus requires devotion and dissatisfaction in equal measure: "Life in the executive Mansion (is) something less than Utopia" (410). Although organizational politics cannot scratch the itch with a sense of finality, and although the struggle, the "agony," must continue, the commander in chief and his lover never cease to "passionately pursue" their joint goals (400). Stone's take-home message was a democratic one: a contention that love and politics contain within themselves the seeds of their own discontentment—and yet they never relinquish a drive for two parties to please one another. Stone's American presidency is forever, as well as forever born anew: "Therein lay the miracle of love, that it could eternally re-create itself" (150).

    Cut from similar cloth, Stone's *The President's Lady* focuses on the tumultuous love affair of Rachel and Andrew Jackson, recounting the scandal that trailed the Jackson marriage because Andrew married Rachel when she was still technically married to her former husband. The plot centers around

Rachel's desire to exit politics in the name of privacy, Andrew's drive to enter into politics and change the world, and the culminating election of Andrew to the highest office in the land: an event that holds in tension Rachel's unwavering devotion and Andrew's political proclivities. Like all of Stone's presidential romances, *The President's Lady* deploys the executive as a trope to suture the progressive stimuli of political wrangling with the conservative demand of a well-oiled regime.

Unsurprisingly, given the fact that the real-life Jackson was America's first populist president, Stone's Andrew is propelled by political possibilities. From the text's inception, Jackson likes "to graze danger," and he recognizes that a successful political career requires an embrace of risk (Stone 1951: 30). In his mind, love and politics necessitate boldness as well as defiance of the status quo. He refuses to allow the establishment, the elites that look down their noses, to stifle his passions: "We can't let that kind of thinking keep us from our love" (93). If one were to doubt the correlation between love and politics, one need only turn to the novel's conclusion, in which Rachel dies a martyr's death and the text supplants her feelings for Andrew with the ardor of the American people for its chosen commander in chief. A "mob of his followers" floods into the White House, "wanting to reach Andrew, to embrace him . . . these were the people; they had stood by him . . . he loved them, and would fight for him the rest of his days" (339). Meanwhile, Andrew proves himself to be the consummate politico—a gambler; a restless adventurer, unafraid of contestation, or, antagonism as a constitutional part of being human. All of his activities end up in political embroilments because he cannot avoid the tug of his heartstrings by factionalism. For Stone, to be political involves plunging recklessly into one's desires, settling for nothing less than pleasure, and demanding satisfaction (to borrow from the parlance used by Jackson as a professional duelist). Being in love requires a similar forfeiture of inhibition: "The important thing was to know the full extent of one's love and *to give oneself to it*" (148, emphasis mine).

Rachel nevertheless conceptualizes love—and politics, one must assume, since there can be no significant separation of the two—in an altogether different fashion than her husband. She claims that love must be a fortress. For her, love is about safety as well as stability. She begs Andrew, "All I want is to be secure in our love" (Stone 1951: 93). To avoid gossip, Rachel longs to retreat into their private fortress, Jackson's Tennessee manor the Hermitage. And one certainly cannot ignore outright these demands for routine, the calls for domestic tranquility that accompany any candidacy, for lover or president. One of the Jackson's family friends confides in her concerning Andrew's potential run for chief magistrate, "When a man rises that high he is freed from all petty bickerings, jealousies and quarrels" (271). Rachel too wishes for an end to politics, at which point Andrew would settle down: "Please let my husband find his fulfillment" (239). However, the termination of the marriage plot, which coincides, or is eclipsed by, the plot of Jackson's presidential campaigns, decidedly does not deliver total fulfillment. Naysayers continue to politicize her affair after Andrew's victory and at this point Rachel realizes that the antagonistic forces that drove Andrew to the highest office in the land will never cease. The marriage-election pact must maintain within itself a degree of restlessness that spurred the personal and/or political courtship from its inaugural event.

The President's Lady reveals how in the mutually entwined games of love and politics, there can be no end to desire—only a potential maturation, in which one glimpses the incommensurability between one's desire for permanent love and its climactic realization. That is, even if Andrew were capable of terminating the open-endedness that drives him and cease his politicking (a dubious proposition in its own right), he would simultaneously lose Rachel's love. "It was the same will to do things that made me fall in love with him," Rachel confesses. "And kept me in love with him always" (Stone 1951: 154). Falling in love with Andrew entailed "reaching out for love," or, taking bold risks and accepting the consequences, come hell or high water. To love Jackson meant choosing the road of "contention and strife" (208). It was the initial uncertainty that made her heart race. It was the unknowable, the transgressive, that drew her to him. Readers might surmise, then, that the couple celebrates its anniversary on the Fourth of July for reasons personal as well as political: Andrew and Rachel mark the durability of their love through a nod at the *antithesis* of durability— remainders of rebellion; the undoing of prior arrangements at a moment's notice via passionate plunges. This momentous date in American history symbolically weds their desires to their devotions. It signals a perpetual recommitment, or reinvention, of their love through repeated gestures at its chameleonic core. A glimmer of impossibility inspires their love—just as it continues to inspire American democracy.

Circular by design, Stone's historical romances are revolutions in multiple senses of the term. They tie into a knot the openness of the beginning with the resolution of an ending. In particular, Stone's presidential romances employ the metaphor of seasonality to combine the thrilling germination of a candidacy alongside the judicious harvest of an administration. "There was a time to cultivate one's fields . . . but there was also a time to be out in a man's world, fighting for the things one believed in" (Stone 1951: 145). Stone's romances thus hold in productive tension the heart-pounding variability of the start with the comforts of a lasting love, sealed by the affections of an elected president: "How surely the end was implicit in the beginning" (336).

Stone's *Those Who Love* returns to the concerns that he first sketched in *The President's Lady*. Once again, the novel tracks a young couple, Abigail and John Adams, from the radical ruptures of their early courtship to the fruition of a successful marriage/presidency. This time, the female protagonist is the equal of her husband in her investment in the enthralling aspects of political participation. A suffragist, Abigail is driven by political action at a constitutional level. Her grandfather comments, "I've always maintained that man is a political animal. Can it be that woman is too?" (Stone 1965: 37). Abigail's excitement stems from listening to the revolutionary chatter of John's companions; the sweet nothings that John and his lover whisper to one another remain insurrectionary in nature. "My love life will never be dull," she gushes, and the same can be said of her lover, the second president of the United States: "This is politics . . . there's high color in your cheeks. You're like a man rescued from ennui, willing to be thrown into the arena" (93, 141). Abigail's passion for political contestation cannot be isolated from her desire for her amour. Her appetite for open-endedness in the body politic informs her own bodily needs. When a friend contrasts the coming revolution with kissing Abigail, John slyly comments: "They are not mutually exclusive" (163). Against the illusion that their ascent to the presidency would end their passion, they recognize right away that a triumphant romance, like a triumphant candidacy, must not squelch the pursuit of pleasure in its shift from courtship to conclusion. A family friend cautions, "After marriage you must never let your passion for each other die" (59). Stone highlighted the libidinous impulses of presidential politics as well as how a presidential narrative could be grafted onto a love story for the betterment of both.

Stone's historical romances improbably manage to keep passion alive: "Their pleasure in each other remained unslaked" (Stone 1965: 58). These texts pull off the feat because their protagonists ultimately acknowledge the impossibility of their aims. Abigail says to John, "I never imagined you were perfect" (71). Abigail accepts disappointment from the beginning of their romantic and political journey, and so she remains prepared to leave her fantasies partially unfulfilled. Still, this resignation never slides into outright melancholia because she recognizes the peril of love/politics without unslaked gratification: "If I did not contest every step of the way with John, and suffer so intensely over his causes . . . if I could be detached: loving, sympathetic, but without involvement, would my love be more idyllic, more romantic?" Her answer comes without hesitation: "Non-involvement would mean the loss of love" (207–08). Although she understands the old pull of an uninvolved, apolitical kind of love, the perfect kind that one finds in fairy tales, she also comprehends that such a love remains idyllic, or, fundamentally unrealizable. Love demands an active cause; it longs for greater intensity and yearns for a return to incompleteness to (re)activate one's activism. Democracy is a highly variable thing, ever-changing, and so Abigail's love for the husband-president must involve periodic reinvention—a wiser knowledge of the unrealizability of her relationship, seasoned with a willingness to slip in and out of the throes of passion.

Those Who Love again turns to the metaphor of seasons to convey its picture of a well-rounded love. Stone composed one of his most lyrical passages on this theme:

It was one of life's gifts, this tender and profoundly stirring physical passion which each night swept them far out to sea on the hurricane that engulfed them; and then, the storm spent, allowed them to drift slowly, gently, back to shore, to the protected cove where they could lie quietly at anchor, falling asleep in each other's arms. (Stone 1965: 80)

The terminus—the presidency, a position upon which the second half of the novel expounds at length—must restore the seductive aperture: the opening through which the female protagonist as well as the reader first trespassed. After all, a democratic courtship depends upon an interminable array of suitors. *Those Who Love* closes with Adams leaving office: "The face of the father would change. The face of the ideal, never" (647). In this pregnant moment, a so-called Founding Father relinquishes his throne and reopens the possibility of a still more stimulating affair to come. Concurrently, the ideal remains, and so Stone's reader anchors himself, through a sort of devoted marital pact, to the lasting value embodied in the chief magistrate. In the closing line, Abigail's mind races back to one of the earliest scenes in the novel: "He had held out both arms to her, an open book in each hand. And her life had begun" (647). An open book and open arms: the exhilaration of a nascent love; a beginning that endures throughout one's life, until its very end. The presidency: a long series of passionate trysts atop the sturdy foundation of friendship. "This was the opposite of blind love," Abigail sighs. "It was love with a compass . . . the mature acceptance of the imperfectability of man" (57). The presidency: a friendship punctuated by the impossible.[11] One returns full circle, then, to the questions posed at the start of this chapter—can an executive light the proverbial furnace, and keep the fires lit, without turning the minds of his supporters into uncritical mush? Can supporters of POTUS avoid falling into left-wing melancholia and cling to idealism even after they have become conscious of the starry-eyed spell? If one listens to untold readers of the popular romance, the answer would be a resounding yes.

   The fictional presidency is not a blind beacon of fulfillment, destined to leave readers disappointed; rather, the presidential love object encourages readers to refine their understanding of the political aspects that undergird American love stories—and, perhaps more importantly, the libidinal aspects that undergird American politics. A fictional president does not foreclose the reader's desires, but fosters them and, ideally, assists her in achieving a higher degree of contentment by grasping the nature of her desire. That is to say, audiences learn to love the presidency not in spite of its imperfections,

---

[11]Jacques Derrida writes: "To think friendship with an open heart—that is, to think it as close as possible to its opposite—one must perhaps be able to think the perhaps, which is to say that one must be able to say it and to make of it, in saying it, an event" (Derrida 1997: 30).

but *because of them*. René Char once described "the fulfilled love of desire remaining desire" (qtd. in Nancy 1991: 87). The popular romance regularly treats the president as an object-cause of desire—not as a panacea or hegemonic tool—and so it recognizes, however unconsciously, the transgressive, messy, and downright romantic undercarriage of American democracy: its injunction to throw caution to the wind; its compulsion to fan the heritage of flames; its imperative to believe in a lasting love without the accompanying delusions of an unimpeachable mate, or a political representative free from contradiction.

6

Hamlin Garland, Ulysses S. Grant, and the Tortured Heart of American Realism

American realism reveals its most enduring tensions through its frequent representations of the presidency. Indeed, by examining depictions of POTUS from a broad range of realists during the second half of the nineteenth century, one starts to see more clearly the fortunes and failures of this literary movement, its ascent into prominence as well as its eventual slide into relative obscurity. A foremost realist of the period, Hamlin Garland tried his hand at creating one such presidential portrait with *Ulysses S. Grant: His Life and Character* (1898)—a partially fictionalized biography that employs the figure of the executive to re-articulate Garland's basic aesthetic principles. Although a mostly uneven effort, Garland's treatment of Grant's life warrants careful scrutiny, since its very unevenness reflects a writer as well as a dominant literary mode at a crossroads.

Upon first reading, *Ulysses* stands out as a quintessentially realist text. Raymond Williams offers a working definition of literary realism: fiction focused on "an ordinary, contemporary, everyday reality, as opposed to traditionally heroic, romantic, or legendary subjects" (Williams 2001: 300). Correspondingly, Garland's pseudo-biography at times dismantles Grant as a heroic or legendary subject in favor of a more ordinary portrayal of the man himself (whatever that means). Garland's text elsewhere underscores how the world went back to normal not long after Lincoln's death: "So in the nation at large the business and necessary daily duties of men, interrupted for a moment, resumed their course as a great river rolls on over a sunken ship. Lincoln, who seemed so colossal, so necessary, ceased to be a moving factor in the affairs of state" (Garland 2015: 316). *Ulysses* therefore reduces the titanic Lincoln to a mostly inconsequential germ in the grand scheme of human progress, a reduction that would have resonated with Garland's fellow realists. Later, the text asks its readers to share the perspective of Grant's hometown neighbors who, on the mighty General's return following the Civil War, seem nonplussed by all of the pomp and circumstance. Because of their down-to-earth temperament, the townsfolk do not "stand in awe of princes and potentates of any sort." They instead make their indifference quite clear: "Grant, in his dusty hat and cockle-bur-decorated trousers, was not imposing to them" (341). In one sense, then, Garland's *Ulysses* is a realist work because it does not put much stock in run-of-the-mill hagiography.

Yet the publication date of Garland's book on Grant corresponds precisely with a pivot point in the author's career as well as in the life cycle of American realism. Keith Newlin notes that in the mid-1890s Garland shifted away from his earlier experiments in realism. Some of his critics have surmised that Garland made this pivot for purely financial motives, as the well seemed to be running dry on marketable realism and he was nothing if not an opportunist.[1] Other detractors have referred to this junction as precipitating an inexplicable drop-off in Garland's career—a long, painful decline into irrelevance.[2] Charles Miller views the back half of Garland's career as a barometer for the shifting winds of American realism at large. In his initial output, the unsparing Garland established the roots of naturalism and, in so doing, he anticipated later writers like Willa Cather, much to the chagrin of the leading realist, William Dean Howells, who described Garland's "youthful" texts as a bit too unforgiving and grim. Yet from the mid-1890s onward, Garland yielded "to the advice of genteel editors" and entered into a sixteen-year "flirtation with romantic fiction" of the most conventional sort (Miller 1966: 125–26).[3] Caught at the close of the century between too-real and not-real-enough, Garland suffered a fate that many

---

[1] In his critique, Bernard Duffey writes: "(Garland) sold his Western, reformist, and realistic birthright to produce the long series of inanities" (Duffey 1953: 69). But, for Duffey at least, Garland was always already a sell-out, willing to shift genres for the highest bidder: "Garland's commitment to a sentimentalized and quaint local color as his best literary hope was made at the outset of his career" (72). James Koerner counters that Garland cannot be dismissed so easily as a mere opportunist, and that the evolution of the author's style stems from a sincere shift in beliefs. See Koerner (1954).

[2] Donald Pizer remarks, "An excessive number of studies have been devoted primarily to accounting for (Garland's) decline" (Pizer 1967: 45).

[3] In his afterward to *Main-Travelled Roads*, Mark Schorer downplays Garland's role in the germination of naturalism, since Garland refused to accept brutality or selfishness as essential "parts of human nature" (Schorer 1962: 261). Instead, Schorer contends, Garland displayed a strong "sentimentalizing strain," one that reveals a romanticism that has been there since the beginning: "When things aren't how (Garland) wants them to be, he makes them so" (265). Joseph McCullough seconds this assessment: because of his sentimentalizing strain, "Garland's apparent 'decline from realism' . . . was not so sudden or so inconsistent as it appears on the surface" (36).

of his fellow realists also endured: a tortured position between the radical, on a futile hunt for unvarnished authenticity, and the genteel custodian of middle-class bourgeois values. To read the two halves of Garland's career as a strict binary, however, would be an error; his initial realism harbored bourgeois ideals, just as his later romances preserved the drive to uncover something truer, if unflattering, about the human condition. Composed at the most consequential moment of his career, *Ulysses* reveals an author, and a larger aesthetic impulse, at a major impasse. The pseudo-biography declares all idols to be false (or crumbling, to use his preferred term)—but it simultaneously idolizes Grant, the so-called greatest of common men. Garland's treatment of the president unveils the realist paradox of idolizing anti-idolatry.

That is to say, Garland's confused vision highlights a conundrum at the heart of realism as well as late nineteenth-century discourse surrounding the highest office in the land. The chief magistrate theoretically aspires to embody the American people because to embody the people, a fiction as potent as the presidency itself, is to tap into what is supposedly real, that which ineffective politicians could never access. To become president requires exposing the artifice of one's competitor(s) as well as the preceding officeholder; at the same time, to ascend to the presidency requires establishing oneself as a fetish, an idol to be venerated with little critical thought. The American executive exists as an icon and iconoclast, all at once. Many realists similarly struggled in their prose between the impulse to break down the established order and the impetus to unlock, and then maintain, a permanent essence that they declared to be "reality." Of course, more often than not, the realist's concept of reality correlated with a genteel tradition—a sense of what was decent, natural, and true, but which remained, in fact, as arbitrary as the falsities that realists elsewhere claimed to debunk. Realists and their imaginary presidents drifted back and forth between realism and romance, caught in a whirlpool with few signs of escape.

President Grant provided ideal fodder for a realist-cum-romancer like Garland because the former president's life story took many unexpected twists and turns.[4] Born to a lowly tanner, and never a truly wealthy man, Grant was a member of the unpolished part of the population—a peasantry that supposedly spoke to something real, an American *vox populi*, or, folklife. Although he ascended to the status of cult hero, Grant remained all-too-human thanks to his life-long addictions and his financial woes. After his triumphs in the Civil War, he stood atop the mountain of celebrity, but he never fully overcame his dread of public speaking. Grant was continuously built up and just as habitually torn down, by himself as well as others, and

---

[4]This correlation may help to explain why Garland "maintained to the end of his life that (*Ulysses*) was one of his best books" (McCullough 1978: 24).

these internal fluctuations resonated with Garland at a time in which the writer was himself idling at a monumental intersection. Garland's *Ulysses* thus marks a restiveness within realism as well as a restiveness within popular presentations of the presidency.

The Covert Romance of American Realism

To unpack the bond between realists and semi-fictional depictions of the commander in chief, one ought to begin by acknowledging the strong political undercurrents of realism in America, particularly for writers like Garland. Mark Twain, an occasional realist, hints at the political dimensions of realism in *The Adventures of Huckleberry Finn*. The reader encounters a steamboat named "Walter Scott," crippled in the middle of a river. Twain's text openly derides romanticism with the name of the boat—Scott was, after all, one of the romance's main progenitors—in arguably the book's most gripping, or most "realistic," moment. For Twain, Scott and the romantics were partially responsible for the Civil War because romanticism was intimately wed to feudalism. The aristocratic South promoted phony facades to cover up the gruesomeness of its social structure; realists meanwhile sought to unmask these hidden evils. Many realists petitioned for a robust democracy that would be rooted in commonalities among all people as well as a rejection of foggy claims of inheritance in favor of enhanced self-reliance. When realists advocated for a national literature driven by competition instead of prestige, they did so in terms that were understood to be acutely political, especially in the wake of the Civil War and at the dawning of the Progressive Era.

According to Alfred Kazin, Garland, "the bandmaster of realism," chose realism as his style of choice "to open the common mind to vistas of nationalism, freedom, and democracy." The political possibilities of realism were not of secondary interest to Garland; no, politics constituted realism "at its most primary level": "In (Garland's) mind realism was not a literary counterpart of Populism; it actually was Populism" (Kazin 1942: 37). Like Howells, Garland—in theory, if always not in practice—saw his realist texts as a leveling force, one capable of appealing to the commoner and deflating elitists. For Garland, Kazin argues, "realism stood for 'progress'; romanticism—how much of a romanticist Garland was himself he never knew—for reaction; realism signified democracy, romanticism aristocracy" (37). Garland's politicized realism would have synergized nicely with the public character of Grant: a self-defined man of the people that never quite fit in at the soiree; a commoner who ostensibly fought against the turpitude of Southern peerage. But Kazin notes that Garland slid readily into romantic prose after the mid-1890s, at which point the author's supposedly principled stand started to look suspiciously like a marketing stratagem. In fact, from the very first stage of his career, Garland's works displayed romantic undercurrents, including an excessive reliance upon the orderliness and predictability of the cosmos. Like Howells, he "resorted often to 'romance' to preserve the moral assurances of his 'realism'" (Trachtenberg 2007: 192). The figure of Grant coalesced rather seamlessly with Garland's romantic inclinations, since the author read Grant as a man of destiny with an unwavering moral compass.

Garland was hardly the only realist to gravitate toward the presidency. If he were the only one, his story would be an interesting but relatively minor footnote in America's literary history. Instead, *Ulysses* can be seen as indicative of a much larger trend among America's men of letters, ranging from Howells to Wolcott Balestier to Jacob Riis.[5] Howells, for instance, was commissioned to write two presidential biographies, one for his wife's cousin, Rutherford B. Hayes, and one for Abraham Lincoln, widely cited as the best campaign biography and a text that was so interesting to Lincoln that Honest Abe borrowed it from the Library of Congress and composed extensive marginalia in the weeks leading up to his assassination. Far from being tangential to his foundational works of realism, presidential biographies allowed Howells to explore the tenets of this fledgling movement, and to do so in a fashion that remained expressly political in nature. Later, another realist-cum-romancer, Balestier, citing Howells as his paramount influence, composed a campaign biography for presidential candidate James G. Blaine, in which he expounded upon one of Blaine's recent publications by cataloguing as well as championing their uniquely realist qualities.[6] Time and time again, then, major realists returned to the presidency to articulate their aesthetic agenda in a way that would resonate with audiences as being politically engaged. However, to represent the presidency remained a route replete with traps. After all, the office is draped with the trappings of aristocracy: a lone figure, elevated above the crowd, innately qualified to command. Howells and Balestier romanticized their chosen subject, even as they longed to infuse him with a so-called democratic spirit. In precisely this fashion, Garland's *Ulysses* confirms the tortured heart of American realism.

But before one can move into a detailed analysis of Garland's book on Grant, one must account for the internal frictions of American realism. Alan Trachtenberg, for one, affirms the argument that American realism

---

[5] I have charted this trend elsewhere in greater detail: see Blouin (2021).

[6] Wolcott Balestier wrote of a book published by presidential candidate James Blaine, "(Blaine) makes his point squarely and enforces it fully, but he does not enforce it too far; the finger is laid upon the spring with a firm touch, is held a moment, and at the delicate instant, which is neither too soon nor too late, is withdrawn. This modest quality of style, which is neither brilliant nor engaging, and takes no eye because the essence of its being is retirement, makes above all its imposing sister qualities, easy reading ... the style of the volume is, however, something more than easy to read. It can be stately upon occasion. But the occasions are sparingly chosen, and in the midst of its fluency it seldom fails of a kind of dignity" (Balestier 2017: 201).

was driven primarily by politics: "The literary battle lines were drawn
. . . on a distinct political terrain. Realism represented nothing less than the
extension of democracy into the precincts of fiction" (Trachtenberg 2007:
184). Concomitantly, though, Trachtenberg argues that realists periodically
retreated into a romantic faith in stable, unmoving truths, as when Howells
contended that "real life, in America at least, was at bottom truly governed
by a moral universe," a position echoed by Garland's texts on multiple
occasions. Like Howells, Garland preserved a metaphysical core on which
to ground his vision of reality. Even as realists like Garland claimed to
pursue an unrefined, untreated exposition of an American bedrock, they
simultaneously drew from idealistic, at times downright utopian, sources.
Their chief magistrates dance on a fault line: in the popular imagination,
each president must catalyze a new reality and typify their *zeitgeist* by
defying outdated regimes of truth—a sense of reality that no longer holds
at the outcropping of every subsequent regime. Yet each POTUS must also
install him or herself as a permanent fixture in place of a passing reality:
a mighty icon meant to put to rest forever the debates of the day and
thus terminate the democratic exercise. Through the image of a president,
realists could tap into something much more real and, concurrently, much
less so. Put differently, in the hands of American realists, the iconoclastic
icon of the commander in chief expressed a steady appetite for political
deconstruction in tension with a persistent impulse to erect deathless
moral constructs.

According to Warner Berthoff, Garland perpetuated this unsettled practice
to an extraordinary degree. "Embracing the cause of realism," Berthoff
observes, "was much like joining an insurgent campaign in American
politics. You committed yourself to a radical attack upon existing offenses,
to honesty and a clean sweep, to partisan feelings of evangelistic intensity"
(Berthoff 1965: 2). However, Berthoff does not find such evangelistic
intensity to be nearly as cutting edge as one might assume because, in
truth, "the old and clouded Romantic commandments to originality and
sincerity were redefined and restored to use" (43). In other words, Berthoff
demonstrates how realists like Garland adopted a posture of radicality that
was undermined by their dependence upon familiar patterns, borrowed in
part from the annals of romanticism. Garland believed that the world was
always progressing in the right direction, that mankind was good by design,
and that the mystical notion of common-ness was a crucial pillar for the
righteous American society to come. In effect, "Garland showed how the
liberating standard of realism could relapse into nothing more than a new
way of raising the old sentimental-utilitarian test of value" (135). Insurgent
one moment, nostalgic the next, Garland endowed his conflicted realism
with a presidential form.

Amy Kaplan, whose groundbreaking study of American realism
demonstrates the conservative underpinnings of an ostensibly progressive

style, muses, "Is realism part of a broader cultural effort to fix and control a coherent representation of a social reality that seems increasingly inaccessible, fragmented, and beyond control?" (Kaplan 1992: 8) Faced with the explosive effects of industrialism, many American realists gave shape to a coherent society by reinserting comforts from days gone by. According to Kaplan, realists like Garland imagined resolutions to modern conflicts by positing a logical, highly predictable social order. But, unlike Berthoff, Kaplan does not dismiss Garland's unevenness as the signature of a would-be romantic; rather, she draws out his unevenness as evidence of the intriguing aspects of American realism itself. "Realists draw boundaries," she acknowledges, even as they "explore their limits" (11). Complicated texts like *Ulysses* necessitate competing modes of representation, which is to say, they shatter the status quo even as they maintain recognizable touchstones to orient a subject supposedly drowning in the frenzies of contemporary existence. In Garland's variation, the figure of the executive improbably encompasses these competing modes. For Garland, Grant's presidency invited readers to undermine the political idols that held them enthralled without, and this caveat remains indispensable, committing to unadulterated iconoclasm.

Of note, Garland's pseudo-biography was not his first attempt to use Grant's persona to articulate the scope of his realist enterprise. He employed Grant in an earlier short story, "Up the Coulee: A Story of Wisconsin," from the collection *Main-Travelled Roads*. "Up the Coulee" presents two brothers as a strict dichotomy: Howard McLane, a New York actor that forsakes his rural roots in favor of a cosmopolitan existence, and Grant, the morose younger brother that stays on the family homestead to assist their parents. The story ties the character of Grant to the former president when Howard gifts to his brother General Grant's autobiography, because the General is "his namesake" (Garland 1891: 80). Furthermore, most of the fictionalized Grant's attributes align with the life of the former president, as evidenced by Garland's reuse of descriptors from "Up the Coulee" in *Ulysses*: Grant from "Up the Coulee" likes to "talk politics" and his "brutally bald words" thrill audiences; this Grant remains the powerful silent type, with an intense reticence and a reluctance to indulge himself in anything; considering his brother, Howard remarks: "How inexorable that face!" (Garland 1891: 86, 79). In *Ulysses*, Garland would again emphasize Grant's taciturn personality as well as the inexorability of his stony facial features; he recorded how Grant's body was "scarred with wrinkles that had histories, like saber cuts on a veteran, the record of his battles" (Garland 2015: 97). Grant proved so vital to Garland's evolving aesthetic sensibilities, that is, that the author employed the presidential character on at least two separate occasions.

Indeed, "Up the Coulee" enunciates the tortured heart of realism that later materializes in *Ulysses*. The melancholy essence of the agrarian Grant—his hardened features; his hopelessness—is meant to startle Garland's reader and push her to question the morality of a system that exploits its farmers.

The presence of Garland's stand-in for the commander in chief is meant to help democratize his audience. And yet, against the fanciness and aloofness of his urban brother, Grant cuts the figure of a tragic hero, perfected by the absence of pretense. In a manner typical of Garland's preliminary works, the story oscillates between pastoral romance, nostalgic as well as tragic, and the stark horrors of realism.[7] Grant stands out because his spirit remains "magically, mystically beautiful over all this squalor and toil and bitterness" (Garland 1891: 78). In other words, Garland's fictional universe is comprised of toil as well as triumph: a dynamic effectively conveyed via images of the reform-minded president Grant. President Grant exudes sadness and the constancy of loss because of his imperfections; he is not only a totem of progress but also a reminder of American promises that remain stubbornly unfulfilled. Yet even as the figure of Grant recalls what Garland described, in the dedication of *Main-Travelled Roads*, as the "toil and deprivation" of rural America, his fictionalized president conveys the silent heroism that Garland said his parents possessed in ample measure. In these instances, Garland's president transcends his meager circumstances to offer audiences a beacon of hope. The dueling forces in "Up the Coulee" appear to be more inconsistent than conciliatory, as when the story cannot decide whether it wants its downtrodden rustics to join the long march of civilization, or whether it wants to preserve them as permanent outliers, enshrined as a diasporic community that must forever persist in its worthy struggle.[8] While the story's young people "were hungry for the world, for art," the premise that Garland's tale could resolve this struggle only leads its readers back to the fantasy of a democracy that could reach its terminus, akin to Howard's utopian vision of his hometown, soaked in "old-time charm" and impossible delusions of prelapsarian return (Garland 1891: 85, 55). Ultimately, the melancholy figure of the president allowed Garland to hold these competing social forces in tension: to edify the intrinsic excellence of the assumed march of American progress while exhibiting a degree of incompleteness, one that defines the democratic project and its constitutional thirst for reform (in short, its political character). In Garland's estimation, the idea of the presidency can encourage the audiences of his realist tracts to

---

[7]Readers may recall the prelude to *The Americans*, in which Henry James stated: "The balloon of experience is in fact of course tied to the earth, and under that necessity we swing, thanks to a rope of remarkable length, in the more or less commodious car of the imagination; but it is by the rope we know where we are, and from the moment that cable is cut we are at large and unrelated: we only swing apart from the globe-though remaining as exhilarated, naturally, as we like, especially when all goes well. The art of the romancer is, 'for the fun of it,' insidiously to cut the cable, to cut it without our detecting him" (James 2017: xvii).

[8]In his analysis of Garland's novel *A Spoil of Office*, Walter F. Taylor describes Garland's style during this period as "a *mélange* of ill-assimilated elements, which are all of them promising in themselves, but which are not fused by the author's imagination into an artistically effective whole" (Taylor 1985: 171, author's emphasis).

balance fashionable demands for political reform with an underlying need to maintain reassuring romances from the genteel canon.

An Erratic Portrait of the President

Claude Simpson summarizes the deadlock of Garland's literary career at the moment in which *Ulysses* was published: "Just how one may infuse the ideal with the real without becoming visionary and often over-optimistic is not clear" (Simpson 1941: 234).[9] First-time readers of *Ulysses* will no doubt notice an utter lack of clarity in Garland's portrait of the former POTUS. The reader may account for this unevenness in part by attending to the history of the book's publication: it involved numerous editorial disagreements between editor and author, and it was initially sold piecemeal in segments to *McClure's* rather than being released as a single, coherent work. Nevertheless, I would once more argue that the erratic quality of *Ulysses* more substantively stems from a writer—and a literary movement— stuck at a crossroads. Caught between realism and romance, reform and resignation, Garland's pseudo-biography represents a wide array of social as well as stylistic changes that were taking hold during the literary life of the Progressive Era. *Ulysses* illuminates why Garland was "a spokesman for (the) disintegrating movement" of American realism (Taylor 1985: 175).

During the decade leading up to the publication of *Ulysses*, Garland moved to Boston to attempt to carve out a place for himself among the so-called Boston Brahmin, but he wound up cultivating his own eclectic literary style. While in Boston, he studied the works of Hippolyte Taine and Herbert Spencer, two of the leading thinkers in the study of human evolution. Garland came to believe that society was evolving in a very specific fashion, and he desired "to understand not only how evolutionary and biological processes in nature led from simple to complex forms but also how these processes could be applied to society" (McCullough 1978: 15). On the one hand, Garland's evolutionary roadmap exemplified the realist project because it relied upon science—or at least, scientism—instead of mythological fables concerning the invisible nature of things. Garland feigned objectivity in a manner that catered to realist sensibilities. Furthermore, his evolutionary roadmap privileged heterogeneity above homogeneity; evolution required endless variation and, the logic went, individual liberty. Subsequently, Garland portrayed American society through what he called a "Veritist" lens: to glimpse the inner workings of modern life, with its complexity

---

[9]Lewis O. Saum, for one, does not see Garland's stories as depictions of the unrelenting futility of the West. Instead, he believes that "Garland passes basically optimistic judgments" (Saum 1972: 589).

and its regional differences, was to glimpse the steady development of mankind. Yet Garland's Spencerian approach carried with it many of the same inconsistencies that we have already seen. Thanks to his reliance upon what Donald Pizer calls romantic individualism, Garland's interpretation of America's trajectory still revolved around romantic ideals.[10]

Garland's lone work of literary criticism, *Crumbling Idols*, conveys the friction between realism and romance via its muddled Spencerian ethos.[11] This text explains the evolution away from feudalism, the "dying echoes of Romance," through a celebration of regional literature, which he claims to be the enduring staple of an American realist tradition (Garland 1894: 4). Garland's prose glides lightly, if a bit awkwardly, across the story of American history, seizing on the politics of the Civil War to legitimize Garland's aesthetic preferences (and vice versa). For Garland's narrator, the dying South exemplifies "conventional and highly wrought romanticism against the swiftly-spreading democratic idea of equality" (59). Garland's realist agenda shines through as the text attempts "to embody the present in the finest form with the highest sincerity and with the frankest truthfulness" (44). But one must pause on Garland's use of the phrase "finest form": was Garland recording the brutal truth of democracy's spread—or was he merely promoting a different kind of romance, a story that remained as conventional as it was fantastic? "Into every novel which had a core of realistic problems," Simpson contends, "Garland put a conventional romance" (Simpson 1941: 232). The inconsistencies of Garland's venture into literary criticism surface in passages such as the following, meant to lionize local color: "This literature will not deal with crime and abnormalities, nor with deceased persons. It will deal, I believe, with the wholesome love of honest men for honest women, with the heroism of labor, the comradeship of men,—a drama of average types of character, infinitely varied, but always characteristic" (Garland 2015: 25).[12] Although he clung to the heterogeneous variations that compelled his evolutionary plots, Garland nonetheless maintained a handful of immoveable elements: wholesomeness, heroism, fraternal bonds, and the bourgeois concept of character. That is, although Garland claimed to

---

[10]For Pizer's extended argument, see Pizer (1958).

[11]It is worth noting that, like Garland in *Ulysses*, Herbert Spencer himself presented his argument in a dialectical fashion that did not *resist* confusion but rather *embraced* it. In the final line of *First Principles*, Spencer asserted: "(Man) will see that though the relation of subject and object renders necessary to us these antithetical conceptions of Spirit and Matter; the one is no less than the other to be regarded as but a sign of the Unknown Reality which underlies both" (Spencer 1860: 499).

[12]Other passages sweep into even wilder sentimentalism, like when Garland describes the potential of Veritism: "It will have the perfume of the orange and lemon trees, the purple dapple of spicy pepper-tree fruit, the grace of drooping, fern-like acacia leaves" (Garland 1894: 86). In moments such as this one, it remains difficult for readers to miss the romanticism that undergirds Garland's realist project.

be stripping away the falsities of romanticized American myths, particularly in the South, he nonetheless championed hegemonic norms. Unlike many of the naturalists to come, he refused to acknowledge the unsightly, grotesque aspects of America's evolution, or to consider the possibility that the nation could ever falter in its pursuits.

With his account of Grant's life, Garland continued to oscillate between realism and romance. Early in *Ulysses*, a phrenologist visits the titular character's hometown to deliver prophetic information. The inclusion of this scene may not surprise readers familiar with the fact that Garland was a well-known advocate for spiritualism and the occult. Yet Garland also infused this moment with tensity: when the phrenologist declares to Ulysses's father that his son is a "child of destiny," the reader is likely meant to share in the tittering of the townsfolk and to revel in the narrator's mocking of poor Jesse Grant as simple-minded (Garland 2015: 11). However, Jesse believes what the phrenologist says about his son, and then the young Grant, of course, goes on to prove the prophecy correct. Is social evolution, then, a scientific/ spiritual certainty, or a powerful fantasy that pushes its believers to dream ever bigger? Is American progress quantifiable, mythological, or somehow both at the same time? Equal parts salt of the earth and everlasting marble, Garland's president presents Manifest Destiny as a joke as well as a reality of the highest order.

The inconsistency of Garland's view of social evolution reached a fever pitch in his depictions of Grant during the General's service in the Mexican War. From one perspective, these scenes remain the most "realistic" in the entire text, as they disenchant readers of any delusions that the conflict with Mexico was noble or righteous. Garland's narrator freely admits America's greed as well as its barbarous behavior during combat: "No excuses can be made to cover that. The war was questionable" (89, 103). When compared with other depictions of the war with Mexico in presidential biographies of the nineteenth century—most notably, Nathaniel Hawthorne's flattering treatment of Franklin Pierce's infamous participation in the war—Garland's description of these battles was quite critical. That is, his critique to a significant degree countered the presumed propulsion of Manifest Destiny by exposing its design as excessively romantic. However, from another vantage point, *Ulysses* insistently frames the Mexican people as somehow "less evolved" than Americans; unlike the United States, the text pontificates, Mexico remains "organically weak" because it is not yet a cogent "organism" (97–98). With its heavy reliance upon Spencerian jargon, *Ulysses* transforms Mexico into an exotic, pre-modern dreamscape that has never moved past the age of Cortez. On the one side, Garland's book exposes Manifest Destiny as a ruse perpetrated by petty politicians like General Scott, Grant's commanding officer: "(Scott) felt, as did all his men, no doubt, the Manifest Destiny of the American States behind him" (92). Garland showed Grant's superior Scott to be exploiting the war for his political power; in this instance, the narrator cuts the grandeur of America's imperial might down to size. But the text also gilds Manifest Destiny with a romantic revelry regarding commoners: "(Grant) came to believe also in the destiny of the American republic. A very inconsiderable but valuable man was this lieutenant busily bringing the wagon-train forward, and growing a red beard" (92). Grant's innate commonness—his propensity for menial labor; the comically unimportant growth of his facial hair—does not always function as a tool with which readers might deconstruct Manifest Destiny. Quite the opposite: in Garland's account, Grant's authentic presence imbues Manifest Destiny with its vitality. In other words, Garland inflated America's imperial might through a reevaluation of Grant's smallness and a suggestion that everyday people, not the gentry, drive the nation's expansion. Garland's realism shifts into romance—and then back again.

Is Grant inherently presidential, or only randomly so? Is the presidency preordained, the byproduct of luck, or worse, a system rigged to favor some individuals over others? One might recall how the farming system of "Up the Coulee" relegates the boy named after Grant to a diminutive status. In one scene from *Ulysses*, Grant shows "the metal of his *inherited* nature"; in the next moment, Grant rails against aristocracy and the idea that a hard-working man should inherit anything (Garland 2015: 105, emphasis mine). On one page, "Society is an organism, history the story of its development," and Grant's rise is driven by an "elemental force" (379, 393); on the very next page, however, Garland's narrator bemoans greatness as a social prison—an endless trial in the public eye. Grant desires to be ordinary again because commonness is where true freedom resides.

Along these same lines, one might ask if Garland wanted his rustic characters to enter into the march of progress—to be elevated by the metaphysics of civilization—or if he held that civilization should go back and learn something from the hardened heroes of the untamed West. To an extent, *Ulysses* appears eager for the civilizing process to encompass far-flung farmlands: "The souls of these people were without color of art or charm of poesy. Intelligence they had, and probity and power, but not grace. However, each year liberalized them appreciably" (Garland 2015: 19–20). *Ulysses* ostensibly acknowledges that the agrarian communities of America remain undeveloped and in need of artistic growth. But the narrative immediately reverses this presumed flow of things by musing that the seed of genius in untapped locals should be used to fertilize the rest of the nation. So which is it: will so-called civilized forces liberalize innocent yeomen, or will these covert polymaths emancipate east coast elites? Garland's characterization of Grant's in-laws further accentuates these internal vacillations. Mr. Dent stands out—or, more accurately, blends in—as a "plain, inexpressive youth, quite commonplace"; Mrs. Dent, in contrast, effuses "a certain refinement, as well as capacity" (59). For his part, the omnipresent president Grant maintains a vital tension between art and artlessness. He is equal parts loquacious and laconic, a denizen of the finer things and a paralyzed public speaker, a propagandist of peace and a prototypical berserker whose value to society becomes obvious only during times of war. Simply put, Garland's schizophrenic portrayal of the president reveals a realist-cum-romantic at war with himself.

Garland's portrayal of Grant complicates the reader's presumed grasp of American history. Both masculine and feminine, in the problematic terms of the day, Grant embodies the nation as a City on the Hill as well as a crude, sanguinary entity. During the military conflict, Grant becomes, "for the time, something superhuman" (Garland 2015: 213). He stands above the fray as a hero for the ages, the devotional centerpiece of a warrior cult. However, Grant is only a cultish icon "for a time" (186). That is to say, Grant cannot escape from the prison of his moment, and he reveals the ugly cost of his enormous popularity. The narrative at one point forces its reader to become disenchanted with its main subject by veering off into a tangent on the heroism of a forgotten soldier: "General Grant was not in command at that moment; Sergeant Reese was" (278). Wary of hyperbole and jingoism, Garland's narrator sporadically insists upon dismantling the mythologized Grant and the violent posture that the presumably great man assumes. If Grant is an immortal hero, why did Garland comment so relentlessly upon the lack of "military zeal" in Grant's personality (66)? And why did Garland so often retreat into proclamations of peace rather than revel, like other pseudo-biographers, in the president's feats of strength? Garland's reader is left decidedly on the fence when she hears that "the insistent snarl of the drum . . . had its beautiful side, too" (50). The reader's emotional response to Garland's text may match the emotional composite of Grant. "He never became soured or embittered," the prose declares in a fit of positivity, yet "his face was almost grave, almost sad" (287, 324).

Said another way, *Ulysses* is a confused text that reflects its confused author. When Garland wrote that Grant "subscribed to no creed, but he had an unspeakable faith in the integrity of the universe," he could have well been referring to the stalemate within his development as a writer (Garland 2015: 522). From the heights of America's grandest fairytales to the pits of its deepest shames, Garland's book on Grant remains an acutely discordant one.[13] According to Garland's critics, these incongruities reveal an author abandoning the initial tenets of realism in favor of maudlin Western romances—a charge exacerbated by the dismissive perception,

---

[13]Garland parallels the nation's fate with the fate of his protagonist: "In calling these 'years of failure,' it must be remembered that the whole nation was in unstable equilibrium . . . the impending struggle between North and South made all business uncertain and fitful" (Garland 2015: 138).

held by many of his naysayers, that the Grant book is nothing more than shameless hagiography. But when readers examine the erratic contours of *Ulysses*, they cannot ignore the tortured heart of Garland's realism. It is important to remember, after all, that Garland turned to a story about the American presidency at the same moment that he was privately re-evaluating the inconsistencies of his work and the work of his contemporaries.

An Impossible Balance

What denigrators widely consider to be the greatest weakness of *Ulysses* should actually be considered the book's greatest strength: the text's tenuous balance between romance and realism advances in a dialectical fashion and, as a result, it underscores a compelling dynamism, reflected in American aesthetics as well as American politics. *Ulysses* conveys a necessarily messy articulation of the presidency, and so Garland managed to capture a fundamental aspect of POTUS in the popular imagination by treating the chief magistrate as an idol while simultaneously goading readers into iconoclasm. The dialectic of *Ulysses* speaks to a restless democratic consciousness that cannot be stilled by any imposition of partisan portraiture.

As Raymond Williams argues, much of what passed for realism in the late nineteenth century merely required opening one's eyes to see a "common world," that is, "a simple recording process," undertaken by a "passive observer" (Williams 2001: 314). But Williams insists that realism is much more than detached, clinical observation; in its more engaging moments, it provides a "living tension" (315). The *sui generis* form of literary realism preserves the meeting place of toil and transcendence. It sustains the imbroglio of the world as one wishes it could be versus the world as it really is. Therefore, *Ulysses* should be read as tracking the spirited ways in which the American public has rejected as well as redeemed its political representatives.

Garland's depiction of Grant moves dialectically. As we have already seen, the war with Mexico proves to be "the most romantic and the most unjust war" (Garland 2015: 108). The life of the common soldier "had its sunny days as well as its cold, gray, hopeless ones" (136). Although these frictions signal a profound contradiction, they also enable readers to confront living tensions, which is to say, tensions which reveal something essential about the unsettled aspects of American life. When Grant meets Lincoln, Garland's narrator describes the mood of the meeting as "far from the esthetic, the superfine, the scholarly." Nevertheless, this meeting stands out as "one of the supremist moments of our history" (258). In these moments, Garland interplayed greatness with commonness through gestures at how Americans labor in the primordial clay as well as erect marble mausoleums for their deceased chief magistrates.

Garland's president walks an exceedingly thin line between heroism and the ordinary, and he does so in a paradoxical fashion: "(Grant) would not have been human had not some feeling of foreordination assumed possession of him" (Garland 2015: 237). Grant occasionally believes himself to be a man of destiny, but this sensation of supremacy—of Manifest Destinies, personal as well as political—simultaneously grounds him, since his superhuman qualities are precisely what make him invaluably human in the first place. Later, Garland's text teases out this concept a bit more: "Had (Grant) been slain with Abraham Lincoln, he would have been a myth, a mysterious, epic figure like Charlemagne. Now here he was before them, just as unassuming" (337). Interestingly, even as Garland the romantic found occasion to draw parallels between Lincoln and Grant, Garland the realist rejected these parallels to remind his readers of Grant's underlying humanity. President Grant is made to be more significant than Lincoln because we know Grant as a mortal man, not merely a hero. Similarly, Grant conjures images of the General's Greco-Roman namesake; like the mythological Ulysses, Grant wants badly to return home after his endless battles—but what does "home" really mean here? Like that mammoth victor of old, Grant does not know what to do when he returns, and his climactic domestication weakens his principle identity as an adventurer. But regardless of this dismal prospect, he persists in his pursuit of home. It appears as though war is the only thing that gives Grant purpose—yet he loudly pines for peace. Peace eventually dwarfs the legend and thrusts him back into oblivion: a state that he, like Garland's assumed reader, both desires and fears. Grant is dreadful *and* divine.

Because Garland's narrator does not shy away from the personal faults of his subject, his portrayal wavers between rags-to-riches tale and conventional hagiography. Grant rises to fame during the Mexican War, leaving behind the abject poverty of his childhood (or so the story goes); after the conflict ends, Grant spirals into alcoholism and poverty; the Civil War again catapults Grant back into the national spotlight; after the combat, he plummets into financial ruin. In effect, Garland's narrative lifts Garland, drops him, and then picks him up again. *Ulysses* moves from "the eager, erect, hopeful, and ambitious youth" to an older veteran, "looking fagged out, lonesome, poor, and dejected" (Garland 2015: 167). These shifts occur like clockwork: one instant, Grant is a man with "no ambition"; an instant later, he stands before Garland's audience as a reticent, self-controlled man with absolute command over the plotting of his life (142). Again, critics have derided Garland for his asymmetrical characterization of Grant, but when placed into conversation with the unsettled state of American realism at the *fin de siècle*, the utter slipperiness of Garland's prose starts to communicate something of greater significance: "Nothing in human history surpasses the vivid contrast between the arrival of the penniless and despondent ex-captain in 1854, and the return of General Grant, whose fame had gone around the world . . . he was considered a bit of human driftwood. Now no cannon was loud enough of mouth to bid him welcome" (325). In Kaplan's terms, the living tension of American realism demonstrates that it is only in constant dialogue with the romance that realists can define themselves. Writers like Garland residually affirmed this living tension through their accounts of the presidency.

The hero returns home in the final section of *Ulysses* only to find himself a villain. Like Howells in *The Rise of Silas Lapham*, Garland reversed a dominant plotline in fiction from that era: Grant's fall from grace in society's eyes marks his ascent into a stronger moral position. At the same time, faced with deification, Grant loses himself in his own romance, and he must somehow claw his way back to reality without abandoning his unimpeachable character—that is, the romance that supposedly made him worthy of study. Like Howells and Balestier, Garland turned to the executive as an excuse to play with these conceptual thrusts and parries.

One of the book's closing chapters conflates presidential identity, replete with ritualistic iconography, and the brand new world of speculative finance. Through a conflation of iconography and finance, the last segment of the text offers a metacommentary upon the act of exploiting a president's image to achieve one's ends: the very enterprise in which Garland remained so thoroughly engrossed. "It was a time of 'boom': that should be remembered. Speculation was universal . . . men were prepared to believe any sort of romance which concerned itself with railways or buildings . . . a fairy-tale of speculation" (Garland 2015: 490). On the one hand, Garland utilized the figure of Grant to critique the excesses of the Gilded Age by focusing upon the story of Grant's failed endeavors on Wall Street. Grant's shady business partner capitalizes upon a naïve Grant by utilizing the former president's name recognition "to induce others to invest in doubtful speculations" (501). On the other hand, by poetically weaving the loss of Grant's trophies with the booms and busts of an incipient financial sector, *Ulysses* provides a subtle critique of the business of presidential biography. Mirroring Garland, Grant too must learn an invaluable lesson concerning the speculative nature of presidential branding. He emerges from this catastrophic period with a much deeper appreciation for the enormous costs of becoming an American idol.

From popular brand to bankruptcy, Garland's reader tracks a series of presidential booms and busts. For example, *Ulysses* breaks down its mythological subject throughout the closing pages by revealing an all-too-human figure engaged in a painful confrontation with mortality. "Had he died at the end of the war (Grant) would have been a mighty hero, but the *man* would have been unknown" (Garland 2015: 520, author's emphasis). In excruciating detail, Garland's narrator records Grant's final days as the once-proud General grows smaller and smaller: "His illness brought out the purely human side of a great historical character" (510). However, readers cannot have one without the other, that is, an idol without a man. Grant's status as presidential icon renders his weakened state all the more palpable; his frailties and imperfections only give greater potency to Grant's final elevated status as a mortal being. First, "no waking and no warmth come to the great commander, lying so small and weak beneath his coverlet"; then, "the pomp and pageantry of the funeral which followed surpassed anything ever seen in America . . . the majestic marble mausoleum" (524). Garland here followed in the footsteps of his predecessors Hawthorne and Howells, two men equally invested in the presidency as a tool with which to straddle the line between mud and marble, between clear-eyed realist and hopeless romantic.

Perhaps most importantly, Garland's Grant maintains a complicated relationship with the realm of aesthetics. Garland's Grant initially defines himself as "a great lover of good novels" (Garland 2015: 48). Throughout *Ulysses*, the fictionalized Grant acts as a mouthpiece for civilization proper. However, he just as regularly appears to be the avatar for a rugged, so-called manly lifestyle that reserves no time for frivolous things like literature.[14] He does not "discuss books or religion or art," indeed, he establishes his public persona against such cultural preoccupations: "He was absolutely non-aesthetic. In his world the word 'art' had very little meaning; of painting, sculpture, he knew nothing . . . he did not cultivate the society of writers or scholars . . . (he had) little tolerance for the finer qualities of life . . . he read for information—to obtain light on the subject in hand" (152, 399–400). Garland's text underscores the thorny relationship of the would-be realist to the world of aesthetics through Grant's confused rhetorical style. Although Grant proves to be a realist *par excellence* due to his "simplicity and lack of display," he simultaneously touches upon universal meanings that can apparently be shared with everyone—an assumed romantic essence, waiting to be unearthed and evangelized (396). Because Grant employs "plain Anglo-Saxon speech, without oaths or abridgment," Garland's narrator can praise the president's lack of persuasive capability. The narrator petitions Americans to evaluate the merit of individuals with alternative criteria, such as the ability to load logs, to do "good work" on the homestead, and to obey one's parents (206, 22–23). Later, though, the reader finds Grant to be quite talkative: Grant reveals himself to be an ideal communicator who "seemed to have no secrets" and, as a result, "everyone knew exactly what the president meant; he had intended to express, not conceal, his ideas" (455, 389). Garland's chief magistrate thus encapsulates the allure of an

---

[14]In reference to Howells, Michael Davitt Bell observes a widespread effort among realists "to ally realism with the concerns of 'ordinary'—that is, non-'artistic'—people" (Bell 1993: 31). Garland's portrayal of Grant shares a similarly paradoxical approach to aesthetics, or the division between what Bell calls the "man," the one who evades "the sin of art in order to secure genteel cultural respectability," and the "artist," the individual who wishes to use art to make meaningful contributions to American life (35).

almost wordless mode of communication. His stony face invites ungrounded flights of fancy, even as his voice and potent gaze offer a shortcut to total understanding.

A reflection upon the realist movement serves as the closing salvo of *Ulysses*. In the final pages, readers, at last, leave Grant's bedside and follow a funeral march to his mausoleum, as Garland awkwardly—or, I would counter, deftly—swerves from superhuman to human and then superhuman once more. The author grants his reader no solace. Like the president's old acquaintances, Garland's readers stumble on a familiar icon stripped of artifice, so unassuming, so "plain and neighborly," that they depart from his graveside with an inevitable "sense of disappointment, not to say bewilderment." Garland's readers too may have "better enjoyed the deep thunder of a martial voice" (291–92). Following a related script, Grant uncovers the key to his humanity by turning at the terminus of his days to the act of writing. After the fields of politics and military and financial speculation have let him down, he decides to become a writer of his life. Writing offers nothing less than his salvation.[15] In its closing moments, Garland's account celebrates the redemptive potential of autobiography. Garland may have dwelt at such length upon Grant's epic struggle to compose his memoir because Garland too was in the process of learning how this kind of heroic effort, that is, the act of life writing, could still be a revelatory one: "By writing so often about writers, realists explore both the social construction of their own roles and their implication in constructing the reality their novels represent" (Kaplan 1992: 14). Through his commentary on Grant's trials as a would-be writer, of both self and nation, Garland's text gestures at how writing can give form to one's innate nobility as well as the nobility of humanity at large. Yet the writer must relearn, in perpetuity, that such a utopian visage remains eternally incomplete. To pursue truth in writing, as in politics, demands endless revision. It means eternally grasping for better words—the curse of democracy and realism proper. The tortured heart of American realism as it materialized in Grant's biography inspired Garland to explore the fruits of self-actualization alongside the utter impossibility of such a harvest. *Ulysses* closes with a profound meditation upon the crucial entanglement of realism, romance, and a democracy engaged in the Sisyphean struggle of fashioning its political imagination from fictionalized accounts of the presidency.

---

[15]Garland had to write in the "rapidly changing milieu" of the 1890s; departing from his reform-centered works of the past, he felt—not unlike the character of Grant—as though he had to realize his aims "not as a social prophet, but simply as a man" (Taylor 1985: 176).

7

Gore Vidal and the Performative Presidency

Gore Vidal regularly concerned himself with the American presidency. It has been said that Vidal acted as the president's "most devoted literary antagonist" (McCann 2008: 8). The presidency was forever on Vidal's mind in part because he was raised in a prominent political family and later cavorted, and then crossed swords, with the likes of John F. Kennedy (he shared a stepfather with Kennedy's wife, Jacqueline Bouvier). Furthermore, Vidal grew up under the tutelage of his grandfather, T. P. Gore, a well-known Senator from Oklahoma defeated in the 1936 presidential primary, and Vidal's father served as the director of Air Commerce under the Franklin Delano Roosevelt administration. Vidal also counted among distant cousins Jimmy Carter and would-be president Al Gore. Vidal himself ran unsuccessfully for Congress in 1960 and the Senate in 1982, and he harbored life-long fantasies of serving as POTUS. "I might have been president," he mused. "My grandfather used to say I'd live in the White House one day" (qtd. in Parini 135). It comes as little surprise, then, that much of Vidal's output returns obsessively to the imperial presidency.[1] As a playwright, political prognosticator, and peddler of popular prose, Vidal presented the American presidency as a prison as well as a postmodern trope. He examined the fetishization of the office by interchangeably worrying over the tyrannical tendencies of American culture and, paradoxically, highlighting the impotence of America's primary avatar due to its status as a marketable image, churned out by mass media machinery. Through his interrogation of

---

[1] Don Fletcher and Kate Feros summarize, "Born in 1925 into one of America's prominent political families, Vidal has maintained a love/hate relationship with the establishment throughout his life" (Fletcher and Feros 2000: 134).

the presidency as a performance, Vidal lionized as well as lamented its place in the American imagination—a conflicted position that reveals a great deal concerning the nation's unsettled relationship to its own democratic practices.

Even when he appeared to be tackling other topics, Vidal was frequently talking about POTUS. The presidency provided Vidal with the most fertile ground upon which to posit his existential concerns regarding power, publicity, and populism. Vidal did not mince words: the president is an "awful title" upheld by "that peculiarly American religion, President-worship" (Vidal 1977a: 176). According to Vidal, chief magistrates from the beginning of the country's history have been drawn magnetically toward despotism. Because cynicism ran deep for Vidal, he viewed the presidency as the primary symptom of a failed social experiment. To understand America's (d)evolution from Republic to Empire, readers could do much worse—or so Vidal contended—than to scrutinize Article II of the Constitution and its establishment of the presidency, which he declared to be the Achilles heel of the entire enterprise. That is, if the political profile of the republic ever held merit, it has long since disappeared, thanks to the development of the imperial presidency. According to Vidal, America's intrinsic shortcomings— its imperial lust; its abject plasticity—can be traced back to the nation's poorly conceived devotion to its commander in chief.

To prove his thesis, Vidal created a veritable palimpsest of American presidents with rulers from the ancient world. He declared FDR to be "our Augustus" and equated Harry Truman with Tiberius (Vidal 2002: 43). By overlaying portraits of previous presidents atop Roman emperors, Vidal achieved two things: first, he cultivated fear of "imperial momentum . . . out of control," which is to say, he instilled anxiety in his readers regarding "imperial, presidential vanity" (55, 61); second, and often in tension with his first point, he undermined the presidency as a mindless echo chamber in which recycled presidential images play on an endless loop. For Vidal, the television age transformed presidents into "two-dimensional figures on a screen—in a sense, captives of the empire they created" (48). Vidal's fictionalized presidents therefore achieved dueling ends: they convinced audiences of the enduring entropy behind world history and they equipped witty gadflies with a finely tuned capacity to recognize the presidency as a marketing ploy. On the one hand, Vidal wrote: "The bright brazen thread of tyranny was woven into the respectable flannel of a virtuous mercantile republic"; on the other hand, he admitted: "The American empire is governed not from the Oval Office but from the White House TV studio, from which His Imperial Majesty is beamed into every home and heart" (14, 5). Ronald Reagan quite effectively served Vidal's disparate purposes, since Reagan can be deposited as a former actor merely "going through the motions of being an emperor," as well as a tyrant in the mold of Caligula that ought to conjure unspeakable horror for any lover of liberty (70). For every ignorant and powerless president, Vidal posited a Goliath to strike terror in the reader's heart. Vidal's internally conflicted presidents embody the dreadful consolidation of power that accompanies empire-building and, at the same moment, "bread and circus" stuff—empty distraction and zero-calorie fodder (75).

In addition to his fascination with Rome and the classics, fostered in part by his prep school experience at Exeter as well as his years living in Italy, another crucial aspect of Vidal's POTUS palimpsest is the all-important, and woefully under-analyzed, influence of William Shakespeare. Vidal habitually viewed the American presidency through a Shakespearean lens—that is, he refracted his historical accounts of the presidency through the prism of Shakespeare's plays. As audiences will recall, Shakespeare ruminated extensively upon the trappings of absolute power in tandem with his case that all of the world is a stage. With near monomania, Vidal focused upon a Shakespearean push and pull of power as it pressed in upon the presidency; in turn, Vidal's executives reveal themselves to be fetishes on the world stage, stand-ins for a potency that is always already absent.

Along these lines, one cannot discuss Vidal's chief magistrates without at least gesturing at his most famous literary creation, *Myra Breckenridge*, a controversial novel concerned with the perversity of power. Vidal's titular character possesses a "tyrannical lust" as well as an "imperial gaze," and her need to dominate others culminates in one of the most disturbing scenes in twentieth-century American fiction, in which Myra rapes a young man (Vidal 2019: 15, 39). Yet as she commands others, Myra also wants to be desired, and so she cultivates an aloof, enigmatic persona, or "a mystery to be plumbed" (177). At first, she bolsters Vidal's critique of the corrosive presidency by underscoring its drive to mastery: "What, finally, are human relations but the desire in each of us to exercise absolute power over others?" (34). As in Ovid's *Metamorphoses,* a text that heavily inspired Shakespeare as well as Vidal, the propulsion to empire mirrors the grotesque act of bodily invasion (more specifically, the act of rape). At the same time, Vidal's *femme fatale* connects power to a hyper-simulated media landscape, exposing how the executive becomes yet another circulating image. "The only thing we can ever know for certain is skin," Myra points out. "Stardom is everything" (165, 128). A figure that undergoes a tremendous amount of plastic surgery, and consistently changes her personality based on fashionable Hollywood films, the Ovidian Myra remains all-powerful and, at the same time, utterly devoid of substance. Like Vidal's Janus-faced president, she positions herself as both legend and fetish. James Tatum astutely observes, "The political fictions of *Lincoln* and the outrageous burlesque of American sexuality in *Myra Breckenridge* are two side of the same erotic coin" (Tatum 1992: 216).

Through his dissections of politics and performativity, Vidal called for public intellectuals to cultivate the position of a perpetual outsider. In their unique ways, Ovid, Shakespeare, and Vidal each critiqued humanity's imperial drive by cultivating a sense of detachment from existing institutions. Said another way, Vidal's protagonists are characterized by a cleverer-than-thou sensibility that allows them to reject the allure of dominion over others. However, as the final section of this chapter illustrates, the potential cost of Vidal's foreclosure of fictionalized presidents in this manner is a widespread propensity for shallow individualism and a diminishing faith in the democratic process. For instance, Vidal's critical posture blurs the line between resisting Donald Trump's unique brand of performativity and embracing a self-same cynicism. Various critics note that Vidal's work can come across as elitist: superficially democratic but quite cautious when it comes to the suggestion that American voters should have a bigger say in their shared governance. Vidal's proto-fictive presidents—as omnipotent as they are impotent—ultimately complicate America's attitudes toward its democratic imperatives.

The Shakespearean President

Vidal's affection for Shakespeare has been well-documented. Beyond his young yearnings to play Puck in a *Midsummer Night's Dream*, Vidal boasted that he "managed to read all of Shakespeare before (he) was sixteen" (Vidal 1992: 13). Indeed, classical allusions pepper Vidal's prose. His historical novel *Lincoln* refers to Shakespeare more than any of his other publications. Despite its effusive gestures at the Bard, however, *Lincoln* does not receive much praise as a literary exercise. In fact, Roy Basler lambasts *Lincoln* as "among the worst novels I have ever read"; he finds it to be "exaggerated" and "only twenty-five percent historical" (Basler 1985: 10, 15). Tabling the questionable assumption that a historical novel must adhere to certain pre-existing standards of fidelity, critics dwelling upon Vidal's portrait of Honest Abe as out of proportion with "the facts" have overlooked the specific literary underpinnings of this work.[2] Harold Bloom departed from the critical consensus in a pregnant, if under-developed, aside: "Vidal's Lincoln is Shakespearean" (Bloom 1992: 226). As Bloom provocatively proposed, *Lincoln* remains above all else a novel that wishes to explore the American presidency through a Shakespearean lens. One cannot fully grasp the meaning of Vidal's *Lincoln* if she does not first address the influence of the Bard of Avon.

Generally speaking, *Lincoln* demonstrates a Shakespearean dependence upon the larger framework of tragedy. Readers of course know from the

---

[2]Most critics prefer to read Vidal in a strictly non-literary sense. Joyce Carol Oates has described Vidal's *Lincoln* as "workmanlike," claiming that he subordinated "the usual role of the novelist to the role of the historian-biographer" (Oates 1984: 36–37).

beginning of the text that Lincoln is destined to die, and so they must watch
helplessly as the fate of POTUS unfolds. Upon his arrival in Washington,
D.C., Lincoln spots "a large crane (that) was silhouetted against the sky
like a gallows" (Vidal 1984: 5). Equal parts prophetic and fatalistic, the
events of *Lincoln* fit within Shakespeare's tragic mold, as Honest Abe
perceives himself to be a ship tossed around by circumstances beyond his
control.

Some of Vidal's Shakespearean references are broadcast in bold letters,
such as his allusions to *Julius Caesar*, *King Lear*, and *Richard III*—all plays
concerned with the corrosive allure of power. For instance, *Lincoln* points to
Julius Caesar when it ruminates on the "death of tyrants" (Vidal 1984: 614).
Elsewhere, the novel gestures at *King Lear* by describing one powerbroker's
"Lear-wild hair" and worrying over how Lincoln's second term would
involve the president being "corrupted by youthful flatterers" (606, 587).
Vidal emphasized particular relationships and themes recycled from the
Bard: calling upon Lear, Vidal's novel tracks an egomaniacal presidential
candidate, Salmon P. Chase, who must come to terms with being "erased, as
it were, from power," in the company of a sympathetic daughter (Kate Chase
as Cordelia) that he initially tries to "sell off" for his advantage, but who
proves highly loyal to him in the long run (541). Moreover, Vidal layered
the character of Chase atop Shakespeare's Gloucester in a power-driven
vision of history by labeling Lincoln's main competitor, like Gloucester, "old
and blind, with only a loyal daughter to look after him" (231). Although
it is Gloucester's son Edgar that attends to Gloucester, the parallel remains
difficult to miss. Following Shakespearean patterns, Vidal's *Lincoln* depicts
conniving politicos as they face their impending irrelevancy as well as the
utter disappointment of achieving absolute power (this time, in the form of
the American presidency).

Vidal also conveyed his ambiguous relationship with Lincoln by
presenting the sixteenth president in a tortured light alongside Prince
Hamlet. Lincoln too remains unsure of his ambition to be king; he wrings
his hands when others dive into action. To underscore this intertextuality,
Vidal had Lincoln's Secretary of State William H. Seward describe Lincoln
as a "presidential Hamlet" due to his "*non*-execution of the office" (Vidal
1984: 103, author's emphasis). Like Hamlet, the exceedingly witty Honest
Abe ascertains the truth by thrusting enemies like Chase into uncomfortable
situations to expose their malicious intent. Arguably, no one in Shakespeare's
corpus exudes wit like Hamlet, and Vidal's Lincoln follows suit. Lincoln
lays ingenious traps and masterfully controls the course of events without
outwardly signaling his own plots. And in line with Hamlet, Lincoln
knows how to deploy a performance to "catch the conscience" of those
opponents who seek to dethrone him. His rhetorical skills are unrivaled
as he effortlessly capitalizes upon semantic tricks to confound opponents.
The president's admirers reflect upon Lincoln's adroit maneuvering and

celebrate his remarkable political craftsmanship. Whether this skill set can be considered positive or negative remains an open question, since Vidal both loathes Lincoln the would-be despot and admires the man's "ideal meanderings," which is to say, his "highly meaningful evasions and delicate avoidances . . . feints and parries" (608, 611). Students of *Hamlet* will recognize immediately its titular character's frustrating yet admirable characteristics in the eponymous hero of *Lincoln*. Plagued by ghosts as well as bad dreams, the president's only course of action is to delay the inevitability of his death.

Although a ubiquitous uneasiness with power defines Shakespeare's tragic heroes, not all of Vidal's powerbrokers are as redeemable as young Hamlet. An association with profound consequences, *Macbeth* remains the most logical precursor to Vidal's *Lincoln*. Through allusions to the violent King Macbeth—doubtful at times, certainly, but a far blunter instrument than Hamlet (Macbeth conducts himself as a former general and, thus, he proves to be more temperamentally aligned with Ulysses S. Grant)— Vidal rejected the presidency as a disease of the body politic. In his *Lincoln*, Vidal married the acerbic shrewdness of Hamlet, with the pubescent prince's disinterest in power, to Macbeth's carnal cravings for dominion. By shaping Lincoln in this light, Vidal redeemed what he viewed to be the best attributes of the republic—intellectual disengagement from petty politics— while recalling America's repellant imperial tendencies. Equal parts Hamlet and Macbeth, Vidal's Lincoln both transcends the highest office through ironic detachment and finds himself subsumed by America's larger drive to empire.

A berserker Hamlet, Shakespeare's Macbeth endlessly equivocates. He never feels at ease in his ascent to the throne, instead worrying that he will be outed as the wrong man for the job: "Those he commands move only in command, nothing in love. Now does he feel his title hang loose about him, like a giant's robe upon a dwarfish thief" (V.3, lines 19–22). Although the troops love Lincoln, for reasons that his opponents and allies can never quite sort out, Honest Abe feels similarly out of place in his newfound role as American despot. Like Macbeth, Lincoln enters into a deeply flawed structural apparatus, consumed by expectations, compelled to declare himself "exceptional" and commit atrocities. Likewise, *Macbeth* depicts the monarchy as a cyclical phenomenon that propels even the most honest of men to murder in the name of achieving, and then maintaining, personal control. In the same manner that King Duncan exploits Macbeth, Malcolm exploits Macduff. "Bearlike," the Scottish king muses, "I must fight the course" (Shakespeare 2003: V.7, line 2). For Shakespeare as well as Vidal, then, the issue is not the individual man but *the nature of the office*. Lincoln describes the presidency as a prison: "There is nothing left of me. But there is still the president. He must be allowed to finish the work that he has been chosen to do" (Vidal 1984: 568–69). Shifting into an alienated, third-person voice, Lincoln understands his position of power as being thrust upon him rather than freely chosen.[3]

Vidal channeled Shakespeare to track the consumptive influence of power and, in turn, to interrogate the intrinsic flaws of the American presidency. With their toxic ambition, power-seekers fester in the shadowy corners of *Macbeth* as well as *Lincoln*. Just as Shakespeare's political tragedy features a range of militant figures with "daggers for smiles," Vidal's novel portrays a gloomy, foreboding Washington in which future presidents vie with one another for the American throne (Shakespeare 2003: II.1, line 141). With one eye forever cast over his shoulder, Lincoln—like Macbeth—must anxiously keep his guard up, since even his closest allies are eager to advance at the Scottish monarch's expense. "It is a terrible thing," Honest Abe admits, "When this presidential bug starts to gnaw at a man" (Vidal 1984: 509). To ascend to the highest office in the land necessitates an unhealthy degree of anxiety concerning potential usurpers. Exhausted, Lincoln resembles the weary Macbeth, who at long last discovers kingship to be a tremendous burden: "Now I am cabined, cribbed, confined, bound into saucy doubts and fears" (Shakespeare 2003: III.4, lines 25–26).

Perhaps the clearest bridge between *Macbeth* and *Lincoln*, though, is their shared focus on ambitious females behind the throne, including Lady Macbeth, Kate Chase, and Mary Lincoln. In a problematic fashion, these determined women manifest the terrible cost of power. Kings and presidents alike project the brutal demands of their public positions onto unsavory female accomplices. Mary Todd, for one, reveals the position of king and president to be synonymous through her title as "the Republic Queen"—an amalgam that prompts one observer to comment, "She is going to be a very royal First Lady" (Vidal 1984: 302). Lady Macbeth, meanwhile, establishes a blueprint for the *femme fatales* of *Lincoln*. Frustrated with her husband's dallying, Lady Macbeth bursts out: "Unsex me here, and fill me, from the crown to the toe, top-full of direst cruelty" (Shakespeare 2003: I.5, Lines 42–43). The female characters of Vidal's text echo the Scottish queen—from Mrs. Surratt, a "good woman (who) thought only of murder," to Mrs. Grant, who appears to be measuring the drapes of the White House upon her visit (Vidal 1984: 18). For her part, Kate Chase remains singularly dedicated to gaining presidential power for her father. Presenting her "regal self," she at one point sits in the "presidential rocker" at Ford Theater in a figurative (and foreshadowing) attempt to hold court over the stage below (466–69).

---

[3]*Macbeth* and *Lincoln* each contemplate how to break out of this systemic crisis: *Macbeth* elevates Malcolm to the status of "good king" precisely because he remains wary of the monarchy: "Had I pow'r, I should pour the sweet milk of concord into hell, uproar the universal peace, confound all unity on earth" (Shakespeare 2003: IV.3, lines 97–100). In *Lincoln*, Seward muses over a similar conundrum: "How does such a sovereign lay down his scepter?" (Vidal 1984: 460, author's emphasis).

Indeed, in Vidal's hands, Mary Todd manifests as a near carbon copy of Lady Macbeth: she worries over Lincoln's perceived lack of gumption; horrific dreams haunt her; and she appears to go insane as the result of her involvement in her husband's ascent. These overzealous women signify the imperial lust with which conflicted male protagonists must do battle. Wrapped in dreams and delusions, these *femme fatales* manifest the gloomy unconscious of Vidal's POTUS.

To accentuate this thin line between conscious and unconscious presidential longings, Vidal drew from another Shakespeare play, this time a comedy: *A Midsummer Night's Dream*. Shakespeare's comedy famously exposes how difficult it can be for subjects to delineate reality from dreams. This difficulty remains especially applicable in the realm of presidential politics, an arena in which—or so Vidal has claimed—outward expressions rarely signify, with any accuracy, the cavernous depths that they conceal. Many characters in *Lincoln* move about Vidal's figurative stage as if in a trance, or "a fever dream" (Vidal 1984: 220). Dreams can be prophetic, like the foreboding dreams of Mary Todd and Lincoln, or they can unveil latent feelings of guilt. Lincoln spends much of the novel explaining his dreams to people in hopes of accessing the truth within himself. In these moments, Vidal scaffolded *Lincoln* on a Freudian framework to juxtapose a superficial reality with a teeming undercurrent, which is to say, the secrets of an unconscious that could only be plumbed through back channels and secret alleyways.[4] Lincoln thus hovers in a liminal space between truths that go unsaid and lies that he and others must spread to achieve their political goals. "I dream so much these days that it is hard for me to tell sometimes what is real and what is not . . . all this great trouble, that will pass now the way a dream does when you wake at last, from a long night's sleep" (634). Put a bit differently, like *Midsummer*, Vidal's text toys with the boundary between the president's everyday life and the implicit political plotlines that run beneath the surface. The novel posits the presidency as a psychoanalytical barrier that must be overcome if readers are to comprehend what is "really happening." For chief magistrates, reality becomes the dream and, as we shall see in the next section, the lie becomes the truth. Lincoln's uniqueness—and part of what redeems him, as opposed to, say, some of the modern presidents to whom Vidal turns elsewhere—resides in his ability to navigate this hinterland and make sense of it all, "like a man in a dream" who skillfully tracks the interplay between his political unconscious and his self-deception (490). Yet this uncommon ability remains precarious at best.

---

[4]Vidal himself might have rejected this reading. He has remarked, "Freud was a Viennese quack" (qtd. in Parini 2015: 252). However, just because Vidal would likely not accept this connection does not mean that the influence was not present. Vidal made a habit of denying influences that clearly existed throughout his corpus.

Against the portrait of the executive as a stoic, Vidal's Lincoln moves back and forth between dream and reality, between what Edgar Allan Poe would have called "horrible sanity" and redemptive bouts of madness. Vidal's novel acknowledges its debt to Shakespeare's proto-Freudian qualities when an advisor to Lincoln reminds the president that dreams are prominent features of Shakespeare's works. By highlighting the fitful fantasies of Lady Macbeth as well as the permeable partitions that divide *Midsummer*, Vidal depicted the presidency as a false façade that only occasionally exposes the inner truth of individuals condemned to occupy the office.

A binary between the latent and manifest content of POTUS appears in its most Shakespearean guise in Vidal's commentary on the nature of performance. Again, Shakespeare declared all of the world to be a stage. One might also recall Puck's closing remarks from *Midsummer*: "If we shadows have offended, think but this, and all is mended—that you have but slumbered here while these visions did appear" (Shakespeare 2004: V.1, lines 417–19). Breaking the fourth wall, Puck addresses the audience directly for the first time—as a character? As the actor that plays Puck?—and, in so doing, he raises questions about the spectator's position vis-à-vis the play itself. Like Lincoln, Vidal's readers are left to ask themselves: are we external to the play, and observing it from a detached box above the stage, or are we within the play, consumed by it and only at the very last moment aware of our compromised status as engrossed dreamers? The presidency leaves Lincoln the man in murky territory, unable to distinguish between when he is playing a political part and when he is "being himself." This tactic further underscores Vidal's Shakespearean inheritance.[5] By treating the play as the thing, Vidal called into question America's political machinery; in his works, the presidency becomes nothing more (or less) than artful misdirection, designed to divert the audience's attention from a sinister underbelly.

The third act of *Lincoln* turns pointedly to this issue of performativity. Conveniently enough, Lincoln's real assassins were historically embedded in the theatrical world—John Wilkes Booth was a popular actor, and his sidekick an aspiring one—and, as Vidal's novel painstakingly emphasizes, Lincoln's demise took place in the liminal space between stage and spectator (a blurry divide through which the murderous actor bound). In addition, Vidal occasionally reduced Lincoln to a masked player standing upon a rostrum. By setting up a barrier to Lincoln's thoughts—the novel's free indirect discourse notably never enters into the stream of the chief magistrate's consciousness—Vidal presented POTUS as an enigmatic icon: "How little anyone really knew about this new president" (Vidal 1984: 40). Lincoln plays the bumpkin when necessary, even as he weaves tangled

---

[5] "Shakespeare conceived of the imaginative creation (the play) as related to the real world much as dream was related to the play-world" (Mandel 1973: 66).

webs to capture others through the deliberate and delicate art of flattery. He therefore cuts a composite figure comprised of countless Shakespearean characters, a point that the text overtly states: "(Lincoln) acted Shakespeare rather more subtly than most actors" (526).[6] To comprehend the genius of the president, Vidal's reader must somehow separate the performance from the thing itself: "The face was noble; the character was not" (159).

Still, Lincoln's inability to relate to his audience perhaps rescues him from being diminished to mere performance. Since the presidency never quite suits him, Vidal's audience can maintain an enduring hope that Lincoln may yet be redeemed. In its allusions to *Hamlet*, Vidal's text proves mostly smitten with its protagonist because, thanks to Lincoln's discomfort with his ascent, Honest Abe manages to operate at an arm's length from the presidency. He wears his royal garb like an ill-fitting garment, and thus, he never quite fits into his powerful role: "Lincoln was, as always, disheveled" (Vidal 1984: 565). Nonetheless, the gravitational pull of performativity remains daunting: "Even Seward had difficulty separating the practical if evasive and timorous politician from the national icon that Lincoln and his friends had so carefully constructed" (232). Lincoln is always at risk of losing control over his identity and being transformed into a mere icon, one sickeningly circulated by the media.

In sum, through his extensive references to Shakespeare, Vidal depicted the presidency as a hyper-performative blight on American life. *Lincoln* is a story of vacuity, empty-headed consumerism, and the unclear demarcations that are meant to separate American politics from the frivolous world of fashion. Vidal's text satirizes the popularity of a certain type of beard that Lincoln grows, while it dwells at length on Chase's "unrelenting awareness of the importance of the appearance of things" (92). According to Vidal, presidential appearance outstrips substance. The play is, in fact, the thing— and there may be nothing else. While *Lincoln* highlights the power of a fetishized sovereign (the novel's tragic face), it simultaneously exposes the superficiality of the fetish (the novel's comedic undercurrent). For Vidal, the American executive is only ever another player strutting about the globe's proscenium.

Staging POTUS

Although I hesitate to dwell for too long in the sixteenth century, we simply cannot comprehend Vidal's works concerning the presidency without a passing familiarity with Niccolo Machiavelli. Near the close of Vidal's book

[6]Vidal did not invent the Lincoln/Shakespeare alignment out of whole cloth. The historical Lincoln memorized soliloquies from *Hamlet*. See Anderegg (2015).

on Honest Abe, "(Lincoln) was now beginning to behave like Machiavelli" (Vidal 1984: 579–80). In *The Prince*, the Italian thinker expounded upon the notion that to govern others is to perform, which is to say, for a leader to maintain his power involves prioritizing appearances over substance. In truth, to keep up appearances *is* the substance of politics proper. While previous commentaries on the art of governance sustained the illusion that being in charge involves sincerely held beliefs and a consistent agenda, Machiavelli was one of the first figures to extrapolate that a commander must divorce the performance of power from a solemn investment in authenticity or truth-telling. Machiavelli wrote, "A wise ruler cannot and should not keep his word when it would be to his disadvantage to do so . . . one's spirit should be calculated in such a way that one can, if need be, turn one's back on these qualities and become the opposite" (Machiavelli 2007: 68–69). With this sentiment at the front of our minds, let us turn to Vidal's work as a playwright, in which he developed further the Shakespearean dimensions of the presidency by commenting upon its heightened performativity.

Vidal's Lincoln transitions from storyteller to the story as his life becomes fodder for myth-making.[7] Vidal used the ongoing commodification of the Founding Fathers to attack the uber-mediation of POTUS in the twentieth century. As the stuff of legend, Lincoln presumably serves as the nation incarnate; at the same time, the coherence of this icon proves to be a trick. Lincoln's image is a gimmick, an inflated signifier divorced from a real human being.[8] Hyperbolic depictions of the president maintain an impression of national unity—but only, Vidal insisted, if the audience suspends critical thought and fails to interrogate their performative nature. "The close connection between politics and the media in a democracy has remained one of the central tenets of (Vidal's) polemics" (Peterfy 2000: 203). While a Shakespearean president like Lincoln can ostensibly salvage some semblance of dignity through his associations with theater, a supposedly more dignified venue than, say, television, or through his associations with Shakespeare as a keystone of Western Culture with a capital "C," Vidal's highly performative presidents lose their assumed dignity as they sink into the position of "mindless cue-card readers," eager to "preside over our bright noisy terminus" (Vidal 1993: 737). But Vidal's dismissal of the modern media and the dupes that uncritically consume it was more complex than it may initially seem to be. After all, Vidal himself spent a tremendous amount of his professional life situated in front of a television camera. He initially conceived of *Lincoln* as a television broadcast, and the pressures of the medium significantly influenced his approach to Lincoln's pseudo-

---

[7]For a sustained study on how the Lincoln myth came into existence, see Horrocks (2014).
[8]According to Brian J. Snee, Vidal attempted to separate Lincoln "from the myths that have clouded the minds of Americans" (Snee 2016: 124).

biography.[9] Consequently, one must not lose sight of Vidal's ambivalent treatment of television: he both loathed its tendency to numb the mind and, concurrently, capitalized on its plasticity. Not unlike many of his contemporaries—or Shakespeare, as we have already seen—Vidal framed the sovereign's power as enchanting but devoid of solidity.

The author relentlessly degraded the superficiality of today's chief magistrates. In a pregnant aside, Vidal revealed that one of his extended meditations on Hollywood was really just a diatribe against President George H. W. Bush. Raised backstage, as it were, within a political family, the elder Bush finds it easier to take "for granted the old saw that the show must go on than to grasp what the show is all about" (Vidal 1992: 57). In Machiavellian terms, Bush lacks political principles "other than how to master the stage-business necessary for him to take the temporary lead in a play he knows by heart but has not, perhaps, taken to heart" (59). Performative presidents invariably consider the fate of their nation to be "as unreal as a play" (61). Too egomaniacal to comprehend their limited purpose in the overall scheme of things, Vidal's executives rekindle Caesar's self-declared status as a living god while bypassing Lear's revelation that he is but a mere mortal.[10] The presidential performer longs for nothing more than to hold the audience's attention as spellbinder. In sum, Vidal's narrowing of American politics to yet another branch of show business underscores the fatuousness of the contemporary presidency.

Vidal's most critically successful play, *The Best Man* presents the presidency as being irrevocably ruined by the mass media apparatus. It depicts the office and its holder as floating signifiers meant for easy consumption. Vidal's opening description of the set provides clues as to what the audience should expect from the play: "Dominating the living room, stage left," he commented, "is a television set." In other words, the prop that most "dominates" the audience's attention is an object designed to deliver superficial spectacles to the masses. Shortly thereafter, Vidal's play confirms the ethos behind this prominent centerpiece: "Since one hotel suite is apt to look very like another, this same set could be used for the opposition's suite" (Vidal 1998: 7). By rendering the hotel rooms of the dueling politicians to be essentially the same, and suggesting that one set could effortlessly replace the other with only minor alterations, Vidal underscored his message that the presidency is only ever a simulation. In effect, Vidal's America interchanges one president for another, with little shift in substance. *The Best Man* tells

---

[9]"Working out the historical materials for television," Marcie Frank remarks, "allowed Vidal to develop many of the features that he used to organize *Lincoln*" (Frank 2005: 50).

[10]In *Julius Caesar*, the emperor proclaims, "I am constant as the North Star" (Shakespeare 2004: III.1, line 66). Meanwhile, in *King Lear*, the unloved king says of his former flatterers, "They are not men o' their words; they told me I was everything. 'Tis a lie. I am not ague-proof" (Shakespeare 2004: IV.6, lines 122–24).

the tale of William Russell, a thinly veiled stand-in for real-life candidate Adlai Stevenson, and Joe Cantwell, a Nixonian figure, as the two men battle during a heated convention for key endorsements in their pursuit of the presidency. Russell never quite fits into his role as a politician; instead, he feels himself vanishing, as calculating politicos transform him into a caricature of himself. Sounding a good deal like Lincoln, he laments: "I look to remind myself I really exist. One needs constant proofs" (11). Vidal's audiences can never be sure of the distinction between political deception and truth. Or, more to the point, Vidal's audiences realize that deception *is* truth—and that the impression of truth is always already a deception. A Machiavellian logic holds firm.

Vidal's play denigrates the highest office in the land by presenting presidential candidates as grist for what is now commonly referred to as the infotainment mill. Russell's estranged wife tells him in a private moment, "This is the first time you've touched me when there wasn't a camera" (Vidal 1998: 43). Even Vidal's heroic candidate cannot escape the trap of a presidency that transforms everyone that it touches into a parody of himself. The play likens Russell's nemesis, Cantwell, to a television performer that acts like a pitchman by selling himself as well as party doctrine to an illiterate audience. As his name implies, he delivers political cant well. Echoing Vidal's account of Bush, Cantwell pontificates and panders but he does not appear to have any moral reason for running for office: "You're so busy trying to win you never stop to figure out *what* it is you're winning" (66, author's emphasis). *The Best Man* foreshadows a period in which it has become increasingly difficult to separate the staged, canned patter of politicians from the reality beneath. Beyond fooling uncritical spectators, what good is this sort of presidency, anyway? Vidal predicted an attention economy in which one's puissance would be based almost exclusively upon one's ability to hold an audience's attention for as long as possible—a reality confirmed by the Twitter-centered presidency of Donald Trump, whose undeniable skill at commanding the spotlight first catapulted him into the role of commander in chief.

An Evening with Richard Nixon extends this conversation into more experimental territory. Although the play's unsuccessful run ended at two weeks, it remains representative of themes that preoccupied Vidal throughout his career. The play commissions George Washington to narrate Nixon's life alongside Nixon's predecessors, John F. Kennedy and Dwight D. Eisenhower. Nixon mostly speaks in his own words, as Vidal's play recycles direct quotations from the president himself. In effect, Nixon appears in several senses to be automated: he must speak lines that have been scripted for him. He serves as a mere prop. Washington announces at the open, "I'm afraid I haven't read the script yet, but it says here that we'll be doing Mr. Nixon in *depth*." To which Kennedy quips, "You won't drown" (Vidal 1972: 5, author's emphasis). In addition to his curtailment down to a soundbite,

Nixon mechanically obeys the dictates of the playwright, as the play compels Nixon to perform "as Nixon"—a twisted experience that Jean Baudrillard would have described as hyperreal. As Kennedy and Eisenhower travel back and forth between the diegetic and nondiegetic regions of the stage, becoming part of the play's reality and then providing metacommentary from the wings, they wear masks of themselves, exacerbating tensions between the presidency as mere mask or scripted lines and the so-called real presidency, which presumably exists outside of the simulation. "(Nixon) turned his campaign over to a New York advertising agency . . . this time the product was going to be packaged properly" (88). David Greenberg observes of the Nixonian paradigm, "Politics has come to be seen as an illusion, a superficial contest of images, that, like the pseudo-event, has no intrinsic meaning" (Greenberg 2003: xxiii). After spending "twenty-two and a half million dollars on television," Vidal's spectator watches as Nixon "is painted and aimed at the camera" (Vidal 1972: 91, 103).

In a Shakespearean mode reclaimed to reflect the dawning of postmodern reality, *Evening* probes into a schism between screens and unmediated truth. Vidal's biographer Jay Parini rightly observes, "Gore anticipates the postmodern turn" (Parini 2015: 162). Because Nixon is "programmed to say only what he has actually said over the years," he remains imprisoned behind his own words (Vidal 1972: 11). In effect, Nixon's presumed truth acts as a barrier because he can only speak in phrases employed to achieve certain political outcomes. Deception comprises Nixon's truth. Interestingly enough, Vidal's play reflects what it presumes to be the genuine truth onto a television screen positioned behind the stage: a screen that purportedly shows the audience what is actually happening, beyond the superficial rhetoric of the president—student protests; covert government bombings; the deadly costs of Nixon's policies. *An Evening* thus reverses the assumed flow of things by projecting the truth onto screens and, concurrently, revealing the truth—Nixon himself, "in his own words"—to be nothing more than a screen meant to block out what is real. What appears to be inauthentic reveals itself to be authentic (and vice versa). Because he remains shrouded in fabrication, Washington cannily observes to Kennedy and Eisenhower that Nixon proves "more naked than the rest of you" (115). That is, unlike his predecessors, "Tricky Dick" need not wear a mask *because he is all mask*. "The Nixon mask is powerful because it is redundant. The mask of a man who seemed to be wearing a mask already" (Greenberg 2003: xvi). Unlike Vidal's Lincoln, a man who uses his wit to evade being consumed completely by his office, Vidal's Nixon exists as a potent symptom of the hyper-mediated age. The Machiavellian Nixon remains nothing more or less than his political performance. For Vidal, there was a deeper existential truth to be begrudgingly admired here, because Nixon—not unlike Myra Breckenridge—capitalizes upon the nascent postmodern condition in a manner that his spectators have yet to comprehend, let alone deploy to their advantage.

"Lonely Decomposition"

Even as Vidal discredited mediated images of the president, he insisted upon preserving a better, somehow more real presidency, lurking in the recesses of America's post-lapsarian present. Vidal wrote of Washington: "Plainly, the father of his country knew best, but his intransigent sons ignored him" (Vidal 2004: 98). In Vidal's version of things, Washington as well as the other Founding Fathers at least on occasion transcended the performative aspects of the office and thus retained a degree of authenticity. Mesmerized by Washington's "majestic presence," Vidal periodically stripped away the political nature of the first president and left only a mythical essence, which he positioned in contrast to the derivate personas of mid-century officeholders like Kennedy or Nixon (19). Although Vidal submitted POTUS as incriminating evidence of America's deficiencies, he nonetheless pushed his reader to study the so-called better presidents.[11] Vidal's presidents are pristine origin points, nefarious agents of social devolution, and the political equivalent of cheap products peddled to a pitiful populace—all at once. Significantly, this complex constellation of meanings defines not only Vidal's vision of the chief magistrate, but broader presidential narratives that permeate present-day American discourse. Simply put, Vidal uncloaked America's uneasy relationship with its democratic imperatives.

According to Heather Neilson, Vidal dwelt on "the ignorable pseudo-historiography of a fetishizing vision" (Neilson 1997: 31). And yet he also disarmed the more disturbing dimensions of this fetishizing vision by sustaining faith in a metaphysical constant, an invisible essence, beneath the executive's title. He confessed that Washington was both the nation's first president *and* its first millionaire. Is the presidency a sign of recent entropy in the United States—or a birth defect that first appeared with Article II of the Constitution? Most importantly for the purposes of this book, can Vidal's readers reconcile these competing visions of the presidency—the real with the hyperreal? *An Evening* choreographs this conundrum for audiences through the incessant masking/unmasking of its myriad presidents. Vidal's spectator watches as the mythologized president dons a mask for the public, and then glimpses the real president, unmasked and purportedly speaking truth from the wings. For his part, Washington functions as a wellspring of truth, undermining Nixon's rhetoric with his unpolished utterances. By surrounding him with contemporary chief magistrates that plagiarize one another in a postmodern loop, Vidal endowed Washington with genuine power. Unlike Nixon, Vidal's Washington is not pre-

---

[11]Vidal argued that "certainly no reality intrudes on our presidential elections. They are simply fast-moving fictions. Empty of content at a cognitive level but, at a visceral level, very powerful indeed" (Vidal 1992: 32). Vidal's presidents are both empty and powerful.

programmed; he speaks from the heart. Or at least, so it would seem. *An Evening* does not always slide into such romantic adoration. Elsewhere, the nation's emeritus executive declares of the play, "Nothing is invented," and then quickly admits, "That line was invented" (Vidal 1972: 8–9). Occasionally undermining Washington's status as truth-teller, Vidal's play invites audiences to question which of its lines are simulated, including lines spoken by its presumably unimpeachable overseer. In another instance, the first president acknowledges his limited function in the story: "Orders are orders" (6). But who precisely gives orders to the play's, and the nation's, preeminent emcee? Vidal? A divine authority? This realization that Washington obeys directives from elsewhere undercuts the play's premise that the primary POTUS exists somehow above and beyond its confines: Washington too proves to be constructed, invented, and manipulated. At the opening, a stentorian voice asks who cut down the cherry tree, inviting the audience to recall the myth established by Parson Weems of the first president as a habitual truth-teller. Importantly, Washington-the-narrator does not respond with an admission of culpability; instead, he answers, "Later, Father" (3). His evasive response signals two things: first, that the presidency must be interrogated on psychoanalytical grounds, since many of these imperial hang-ups stem from "daddy issues"; second, and even more profoundly, *An Evening* cannot segregate the presidential real from the presidential fetish. When the curtain falls, and the play issues the question about the cherry tree once more, Vidal's multiple presidents join together in a farcical jig. The audience is left to wonder: does a real president exist anywhere, within or without the play's parameters? Or is it all deception? The play only delays and defers: "Later, Father."

One way for audiences to address this persistent evasion is to interrogate Vidal's understanding of democracy, that most loaded of terms. As we have seen, Vidal's texts fear a pair of evils: the undiscerning electorate as well as the unresponsive tyrant. These so-called duel evils, which will be unpacked in greater length in the following chapter, reflect an impasse in Vidal's visions of the presidency, an impasse between a democratic imperative that he did not trust and a despotic turn that he declared to be utterly ruinous.[12] On the one side, Vidal denounced authoritarians of every ilk; on the other side, he depicted the American public in equally unflattering terms: "Ten seated dummies on a trolley. They are faceless; above them a sign says: 'The American People'" (Vidal 1972: 21). Throughout *An Evening*, the American people come and go, fickle and indecisive, a byproduct of the nation's unreflective mode of consumption. Vidal elaborated upon "that somber, all-confining

---

[12]Jay Parini marks in Vidal "a disconnect between his democratic impulses and his need to enjoy the pleasures that came with wealth and connections . . . (Vidal is) a kind of socialist Tory, a snob who nevertheless objected to people in power" (Parini 2015: 58–59, 82).

Bastille known as the consumer society," before declaring to the consumers in question: "This bad society is what you dumb bastards deserve" (Vidal 1977b: 284–85). Jacques Rancière argues that, since the raging 1960s, anti-democratic voices like Vidal's have commonly complained about out-of-control consumerism in an attempt to rein in the purportedly out-of-control demands of the *demos*. In effect, as democratic voters clamor to have their demands met—civil rights; greater distribution of wealth—elitists have portrayed a witless consumer society in an attempt to dial back a perceived rise in democratic engagement. According to figures like Vidal, the same consumer that reads calorie-free tabloid magazines should not be trusted to make decisions in the voting booth. These sentiments materialize in *The Best Man* when Vidal's mouthpiece comments: "Life is not a popularity contest; neither is politics. The important thing for any government is educating the people about issues, not following the ups and downs of popular opinion." He continues, "A president should ignore (the people's) opinion and try to convince (the people) that his way is the right way" (Vidal 1998: 9–10). Vidal's ideal president, then, acts like Plato's philosopher-king, on a futile quest to return to the proverbial cave and rescue the hapless citizens of the republic.[13] When Vidal distinguished popularity contests from politics, he forced his audience to ponder what democracy would mean, exactly, without popular input. Isn't democracy another name for "the ups and downs of popular opinion"? At the same time, *The Best Man* worries over presidents that do not heed the public and harbor "some ideal goal for society" (33). The tyrant and the throng pose similar threats.

Just what is this strange presidency, removed in equal measure from democracy as well as despotism? Perhaps unsurprisingly, *The Best Man* gestures once more at *Hamlet* to articulate the impasse. Although Russell resists being defined as a man of inaction ("I am not Prince Hamlet," he groans), he nevertheless ends up making "a lot of fine speeches" rather than engaging in the political process (Vidal 1998: 23). Like Shakespeare's brooding Prince, Vidal's ideal president succumbs to the blessed "angel of grayness" (78). The play concludes with Russell refusing to do what he needs to do to attain the presidency. He opts to retreat to the moral high ground rather than lower himself to the crass demands of a consumer society. The title of the play underscores this reversal: the best man is perhaps unexpectedly the man who *loses* the election; the best sort of president is the one who rejects the presidency. Vidal wished for his special sort of man to occupy a liminal space, at arm's remove from both the mountebank and the masses. From Vidal's perch, "Democratization and demagogy belong together"

---

[13]Ray Lewis White writes, "The civilized man must, as Vidal demonstrates, be mentor to his uncivilized brothers" (White 1968: 132).

(Weber 1994: 220). *The Best Man* prioritizes wit and waywardness over political participation.[14]

Lincoln reaches the same conclusion as *The Best Man*: one can achieve the exceptional status of worthy president only by destroying one's claim to the title. To avoid becoming a full despot, Vidal's Lincoln abdicates the throne: "(Lincoln) willed his own murder as a form of atonement for the great and terrible thing that he had done" (Vidal 1984: 657). In other words, Vidal's political president dies so that the mythical president might endure.[15] Vidal's texts thus dispossess the presidency of its democratic baggage and, in the process, offer forth a sort of anti-presidency.

A critique of Vidal's vision of the president readily dovetails with broader critiques of postmodern thought. Vidal's audience must question his role as a detached observer who denied the public dimensions of the office. Like many of the voices that would follow him, Vidal expressed skepticism concerning power, metanarratives, and the homogeneity of consumer culture, and he championed an improbable position outside of the apparatus. But politicians are not simply flaneurs; by their constitution, they must operate in dialogue with the public. Contra such collectivist underpinnings, Tatum highlights Vidal's "ironic mode," with which the author perpetually dissented from societal expectations (Tatum 1992: 201). While Vidal's ironic mode may be understandable in characters such as Breckenridge, it may strike audiences as rather problematic when applied to the presidency, since the presidency must by definition respond to the demands of the *demos*. That is to say, to remove the president's indebtedness to popular opinion is to remove, simultaneously, the office's *raison d'etre*. Vidal's ideal presidents resemble his brand of public intellectual: a prototype for the type of political prognosticator popularized in his wake. Lincoln's poetic atonement upholds what one might describe as Vidal's doctrine of the gadfly. This doctrine of the gadfly promoted something like what H.L. Mencken, that great cynic of American democracy, called "prophylactic remoteness" (Mencken 1926: 169). Or, as Vidal's occasional ally Norman Mailer posited, "(Vidal's) heroes are hermetically sealed in upon themselves . . . nothing dramatic passes between them and other persons in the novel . . . (Vidal offered) a study of lonely decomposition" (Mailer 2014: 295).

In conclusion, Vidal paradoxically cast the so-called real president—the Founding Father, memorialized in the proverbial lost republic—into the dusky margins, while deconstructing the presidential icon as a simulated prison, designed to capture the American imagination. To follow Vidal's lead

---

[14]Elizabeth Dipple denounces Vidal as an "intemperate anti-academic," suggesting that his elitism leaves him perpetually disassociated from a like-minded community (Dipple 2021: 2).

[15]Dana Nelson writes, "Ever since the office was invented, presidents have been appealing to how it serves as a symbol of national strength and domestic unity (. . .) to claim more powers for the office than those it was explicitly granted by the Constitution" (Nelson 2008: 3).

is to refuse to accept a living president; subsequently, sympathetic readers lose sight of politics as a collective enterprise. In place of an inherently tyrannical presidency, one is led by Vidal to view politics as pure punditry, peddled by passive elites. Vidal's increasingly cynical audience members might even resign themselves to the limitations imposed upon them by an excessively performative presidency, under the tutelage of figures that Vidal would elsewhere lampoon with relish (like Nixon or, one must assume, Trump). Vidal's fictional presidents therefore reveal how the promise of shared governance has devolved over the last fifty years into so many soundbites, staged by anti-presidents in rapid retreat from public life.

8

The Imperial Presidents
of American Literature

Imperial presidents loom large in America's political imagination. For example, Ralph Ellison bookended his epic *Invisible Man* with the formidable presence of Mr. Norton, a presidential figure likened by a group of wise-cracking veterans to Thomas Jefferson, who impersonally presides over the narrator's *Bildungsroman* by imposing his own singular vision for the narrator's life. At the same mid-century moment in which Ellison depicted Norton, critics were defining the imperial presidency as a dramatic expansion of executive powers in response to pressures of the Cold War era (although, as we shall see, the imperial presidency was not exclusively a twentieth-century invention).[1] Given contemporary conversations surrounding the limits of presidential authority under executives including Richard Nixon, Lyndon B. Johnson, George W. Bush, and Donald Trump, the time has come for literary critics to consider the imperial presidents that populate the pages of American prose, and to ask how these characters reflect an evolving relationship between readers and POTUS.

If one concedes that the imperial presidency sets the calendar of contemporary American politics, it becomes incumbent upon readers to

---

[1]The real-world implications of this construct remain the subject of continued debate. On the one hand, critics of the unitary executive theory—a theory which promotes the logic of an imperial presidency—decry the degree to which this theory "gives intellectual substance and legitimacy to a potentially dangerous accumulation of presidential power" (Crouch et al. 2020: 151). Other critics reject this assumption on the basis that every president remains constrained by a power even greater than Congress: American voters. Dino Christenson and Douglas Kriner counter, "Presidents are significantly more constrained than often supposed . . . public opinion—not formal checks by Congress and the courts—serves as the primary check on the unilateral executive" (Christenson and Kriner 2020: 7–8).

analyze in greater detail how fiction has transposed this reality into broader public awareness. That is, readers must ponder how representations of the imperial executive render the expansion of presidential power generally palatable, or at least tacitly acceptable, to a vast coalition of individuals. However, embedded within this story of conformity is a kernel of something beyond it: a necessary fissure in the foundation upon which the entire edifice stands. The novels under review demonstrate how the fantasy structure of the imperial presidency is driven not by a promise of disciplinary wholeness, but by its very opposite.

On first blush, the imperial presidents of American fiction demonstrate the dreadful consequences of an individual with too much authority running roughshod over the populace. Norton foists upon Ellison's mouthpiece a grand metaphysical narrative—a lodestar to guide his personal aspirations; a fundamental ordering principle. Indeed, in Ellison's account, the imperial presidency serves as a sort of categorical imperative, or foundational premise, that guides a subject's "proper" behavior. Although popularly considered to be a kind of cudgel, narratives like *Invisible Man* demonstrate how the executive actually manifests his power in subtle ways, weaving into the innermost private lives of citizens. These tales contend that the concept of the commander in chief orients American lives by congealing history into a coherent narrative, inspiring or repelling certain attitudes, and evincing otherwise unspeakable desires. As such, the imperial president embodies, in Richard Hofstadter's terms, the paranoid style of American politics. Like the tip of a massive iceberg, the presence of an imperial president appears to confirm the existence of a "gigantic yet subtle machinery" (Hofstadter 2008: 29). He emerges as an "amoral superman: sinister, ubiquitous, powerful, cruel, sensual, luxury-loving"; he "wills, indeed, he manufactures, the mechanism of history itself" (31–32). Texts that consider imperial presidents regularly goad readers into reacting against an appalling state apparatus, personified by an all-powerful executive.

Yet, as Hofstadter notes, one can also read the subject's projection of this supremely effective enemy as an ideal: that is, the fictional president offers a dominant entity with which the relatively powerless reader might identify to experience a degree of separation from her otherwise vulnerable lot. In the face of an ever-swelling bureaucratic apparatus, voters might gravitate toward the fantasy of a solitary man who could be held accountable for global ills. Imperial presidents reflect "a desire for simplification" (Rosavallon 2018: 105). Even as the presidential Norton dictates the decision-making process of Ellison's narrator, *Invisible Man* channels the reader's gaze through Norton's eyes, down on an unruly electorate—a mob that either too rashly submits to a manipulative leader, or implodes in fits of seditious fury. Paradoxically, then, one of the emotions spurred by fiction's imperial presidents is *a distaste for democracy*. When a reader (temporarily) shares Norton's gaze and feels his repugnance at the thought of a mob, that reader identifies with a lofty, solitary position that encourages her to push back against the premise of democracy. Although many of the authors considered in this chapter present politicians with autocratic tendencies as a bitter pill to swallow, they simultaneously describe the scourge of the imperial presidency as a byproduct of too much democratic engagement, akin to a Caesarist or Napoleonic monarchy. After all, was it not a needy, gluttonous, and irresponsible electorate that elected the monster in the first place? Plato's claim that democracy inevitably degenerates into tyranny, at last, proves true. Through a compulsion to condescension, readers occasionally adopt the perspective of an authoritarian lording over the people ("the people" being an equally influential political fiction). The tacit assumption here is that the American people get precisely what they deserve. A good number of these books—including, at times, *Invisible Man*—advocate for a less democratic society: an apolitical community in which self-indulgent, irascible voters should no longer be permitted to govern themselves. By surveying chief magistrates portrayed by the likes of John Dos Passos and Sinclair Lewis, Stephen King and Philip Roth, this chapter unpacks the contradictory impulses of the imperial president as a construct through which audiences reject as well as embrace authoritarian impulses.

Said another way, iterations of the imperial presidency manifest what Jacques Rancière describes as the doubleness of contemporary democracy. Let us start with the more visible side of the equation. A domineering POTUS instigates resistance to state power, which is to say, protests by the individual against the despot that treads on him. The imperial president represents an oppressive apparatus that denies the autonomy of its citizens. At the same time, Rancière unveils a figurative alliance between the reader and an oppressive apparatus in which the reader is encouraged to feel hatred for the democratic order. Supporting Rancière's thesis, the texts that this chapter analyzes occasionally equate "bad democracy" with "young consumer(s) drunk with equality"—a crude synthesis, in the political imaginary, of "consumerism, equality, democracy and immaturity" (Rancière 2014: 26–27). For Rancière, the fate of democracy has suffered because specific actors continue to pass off the bitter fruits of capitalism as the outcome of too much democracy, especially in the wake of the 1960s and the New Left. In its recent villainous turn, the word democracy comes to signify the unreasonable demands of an ungrateful rabble. The unruly crowds of *Invisible Man* confirm this association. Through their doubleness, the books considered in this chapter deny readers firm footing in their alignment with the perspective of either the authoritarian or the people. Tyrannical overreach triggers a desire for less centralized governance; less centralized governance triggers a desire for tyrannical overreach. Caught between the chief magistrate as organizing principle and the organized masses, characters like Ellison's narrator must follow a lonely middle path—a well-marked route that leads readers into embracing bourgeois individualism (the principal norm of mid-century America). Novels like *Invisible Man* spend an inordinate amount of time tracking groups that consolidate power at the expense of the individual.

At stake in this reading is a more refined sense of the paradoxes inherent to American democracy. Alexis de Tocqueville has observed, "Democratic nations often hate those in whose hands the central power is vested, but they always love that power itself" (De Tocqueville 1840: 315). James A. Morone unpacks this paradox a bit further: "At the heart of American politics lies a dread and a yearning. The dread is notorious. Americans fear public power as a threat to liberty . . . the yearning is an alternative faith in direct, communal democracy" (Morone 1998: 1). Like Tocqueville, Morone contends that many Americans fear collective power while concomitantly thirsting for it. He describes a widespread belief in the imagined people as well as a refusal to embrace direct democracy via denunciations of the demonized crowd, with its inability to rule over itself. In strange ways, then, fictionalized presidents trigger a refusal of democratic intervention as well as an urgent need for populist personifications. Reception of these presidential icons remains deeply unsettled.

Consequently, the works in question force readers to interrogate the explanatory limits of power as a totalizing schema.[2] To treat the concept of the imperial president as a straightforward hegemonic tool is to flatten a complex interaction between reader and text. After refuting the stand-in for the imperial president (Norton), as well as alternative social arrangements that ostensibly reflect the will of the people (such as the Marxist Brotherhood), Ellison's narrator becomes frightened by the allure of centralized power. Said another way, the narrator fears ideology as a singular idea that purportedly explains every event in history. In Ellison's account, the despot parallels the activist. Ideologues multiply. The narrator confesses his greatest anxiety that he too will wind up speaking at a "lower frequency" on behalf of the reader, thereby maintaining the figurative and literal power grid into which he has been plugged (Ellison 1995: 581). He realizes that, as an omniscient narrator, he too might be acting as an imperial presence in the lives of his readers. *Invisible Man* ultimately contends that its reader should move outside of the unilateral vision that the presidential Norton has thrust upon her, into a place of invisibility. Such a place of invisibility—an anti-foundationalist position that exists, somehow, beyond the demands of modern power schemas, conveniently captured in the avatar of an imperial president—serves as an invaluable chasm in a range of fictional works from the second half of the twentieth century. These alluring sites of aesthetic

---

[2]Accordingly, the subgenre of books about the imperial presidency comes into frequent contact with the specter of Michel Foucault, who spent his career identifying the permutations of an ever-expanding power structure.

and political rupture reveal imaginary executives to be much more than static pillars within a sprawling disciplinary network, erected to promote unthinking compliance. By rejecting the monad as well as the multitude, novels concerning imperial presidents tarry around a constitutional void, one that marks both the limit of organizational politics and an opening for unheralded possibilities.

An American Paradox

Let us begin by pointing to a major nineteenth-century precedent to this phenomenon, Nathaniel Beverley Tucker's *The Partisan Leader: A Tale of the Future*. Tucker's *Partisan* reminds us that American literature has long maintained an interest in what has been perceived to be the imperial drive behind the U.S. presidency. Tucker, an author praised by the likes of Edgar Allan Poe, is best known due to his self-defined defense of state's rights and his presage of the Civil War. *Partisan* anticipates a Southern rebellion against the overreach of a Federalist despot. Set in the year 1849 at the start of Van Buren's imaginary fourth term, and published in 1836 as a tool with which to dissuade readers from voting the real-life Van Buren into office, Tucker's text tracks the reign of a president that disrespects the sanctity of local government. At the same time, *Partisan* laments the political gamesmanship of Van Buren and his followers—the partisanship derided by Tucker's title— and it therefore rejects the open-endedness of political participation in favor of aristocrats with intrinsic nobility, born and bred as "gentlemen" in the American South. Much of the novel's handwringing about Van Buren stems from Van Buren's perceived politicization of the presidency, especially in the wake of the Jacksonian moment—that is, the manner in which Van Buren and his followers "unapologetically and proudly celebrated the introduction of the competitive ethic into the councils of government" (Ketcham 1984: 144). At least as early as 1836, American literature grappled with the dueling impulses associated with an imperial presidency: a longing for greater political engagement by the people alongside a creeping dread of such engagement because, or so the naysayers would claim, this level of engagement could give rise to a dictator.

In this way, Tucker spoke to specific anxieties that accompanied the evolution of the presidency at the twilight of the so-called Era of Good Feelings. Early American executives served as cogs in a vast spoils system in which states did the "real governing" and the national government remained "highly specialized" (Lowi 1985: 27). With its reliance upon patronage, the U.S. political machine traditionally depended on regional government, with its smaller web of *quid pro quo* arrangements, whereas POTUS remained a largely symbolic figure—a puissant symbol, certainly, but not an actor with very much impact on the day-to-day running of the affairs of state. From

1804 until the start of the Civil War, American presidents were significantly indebted to the patronage parties that dictated presidential selection, initially via the King Caucus and then through horse-trading at brokered party conventions. The endurance of this system explains the dominance of the Congress as well as the most forgettable faces of the presidency during the first half of the nineteenth century. Presidents during the Era of Good Feelings were mostly safe candidates, handpicked by powerful elites. It was only with the exceptional demands placed upon Abraham Lincoln in 1860— and, as we shall see in the next section, the exceptional demands placed upon Franklin Delano Roosevelt (FDR) during the Great Depression— that those seemingly innocuous executives, vetted by redoubtable patrons, became a thing of the past. Although firmly situated within a system of elitist control, and perpetuating its basic assumptions, Tucker's dystopian novel nonetheless worries over what it views as the impending rule of an unyielding president.

Tucker was not the only cultural commentator of the early nineteenth century to anticipate the coming of an imperial presidency; his voice joined a growing chorus that understood the commander in chief, for better or worse, to be on a one-way track to dominance over America's political imagination. Early Americans appeared torn on the scope of the office, its dangers as well as its potential. "The revolutionary spirit tended to be hostile to prerogative," Michael McConnell remarks. "Many of the abuses denounced in the Declaration of Independence involved royal prerogative." But, he adds, "by the time of the Convention (. . .) some Americans (often called 'high-toned') had come to the conclusion that weak executives and legislatures were a curse" (McConnell 2020: 27). Against Federalist ferment on behalf of a better-endowed executive, prominent Americans increasingly worried about imperial drift. Benjamin Franklin bemoaned, "The executive will be always increasing here, as elsewhere, till it ends in a monarchy" (qtd. in Madison 1836: 154). Patrick Henry added, "Your president may easily become king" (qtd. in Tyler 1899: 328). Tucker's *Partisan* confirms these suspicions by dismissing high-toned emboldeners of an unchecked president and reverting to a so-called revolutionary spirit, one hostile to the idea of presidential prerogative. In a word, Tucker crafted the caricature of a four-term president to inspire his readers to be wary of tyrants.

By 1836, the drift into an imperial presidency was indeed well underway. Arthur Schlesinger, Jr. characterizes Andrew Jackson, who interchangeably triggered a fear of the mob and a fear of the despot, as the first president to expand dramatically the borders of presidential authority. First as a general and then as a president, Jackson initiated "defensive wars" by preemptively declaring military crises to enable the executive to operate in exceptional ways and therefore meet what he deemed to be exceptional demands. "If the president had exclusive and conclusive authority to define emergencies and circumstances," Schlesinger ponders, "Who then could gainsay his findings of 'imminent' danger?" (Schlesinger 2004: 36). For Tucker, Van Buren's subsequent rise to power foretold the building up of Jacksonian momentum and the dismantlement of America's republican values.

Yet one must not lose sight of the fact that Tucker's *Partisan* was forged from the fires of a gradual dissolution that led to Civil War. That is, the novel assumes the merit of hierarchies maintained by slave-owning Southern states, and so even as the text ostensibly petitions for "more democracy" with which to overthrow a tyrant, it paradoxically blames democracy for the book's predicament by valorizing autocrats. Put differently, *Partisan* laments the inertia that pulls democracy ever closer to self-imposed authoritarianism while concurrently clashing against clarion calls for a democratic revival. The book is a symptom as well as a critique of the Jacksonian moment. Democracy serves as both poison and antidote: a bizarre bromide that comprises the combustible construct of the imperial presidency, then as well as now.

On the one hand, Tucker's Van Buren controls a "great consolidated empire," thereby serving as a caricature against which Tucker could promote greater political participation by the people (Tucker 2015: 60). A bit awkwardly, since Tucker's protagonists are Southern aristocrats, Van Buren appears to be the unsavory epitome of a feudal society: "The wily president deemed it a needless waste of patronage to buy what was his by hereditary title" (80). Van Buren surrounds himself with sycophants and obsequious yes-men; bedecked in dazzling jewels and compared to Louis XI, he fosters courtly intrigue from a state of courtly repose. Tucker's imperial president closely resembles a European royal due to his "lazy and peevish" mannerisms as well as his "careless" conduct, his "folly, vanity, (and) indiscretion" (304). Tucker's cartoonish Van Buren even models one of the earliest villainous laughs in American culture: "The smile soon became a quiet laugh, which increased in violence" (149). The text cries out for readerly rebellion.

On the other hand, Tucker's Van Buren reflects a toxic political culture comprised of calculating politicos. For Tucker, the problem was not so much that Van Buren denied democracy and championed monarchy, but that the chief magistrate encouraged *competition*. For example, Tucker's tale takes Van Buren to task for manipulating one of his followers into "elbow(ing) the duke from his place of precedence" (Tucker 2015: 131). The author reserved his harshest criticism of his American tyrant for the final pages, in which he labeled Van Buren a "crafty politician" (353). Although Tucker aimed much of his novel's vitriol at the so-called presidential throne, the text appears most disconcerted by a rise in political gamesmanship—or, to put a finer point on it, an increase in politics proper, because gamesmanship is, after all, the *sine qua non* of politics. While Tucker's politicos depend upon unsavory Machiavellian tactics to govern, his Southern heroes do not change "in any dress, in any company, under any circumstances" (314). The Southern gentleman's fixed essence seemingly trumps the chameleonic character of the partisan. Tucker's protagonist does not hunger for a rise in rank; instead, he exudes contentment with the status quo. Even though this complacency may have struck Tucker's reader as preferable to the sinister cunning of the hyper-political Van Buren, the rejection of political engagement in *Partisan* simultaneously downgrades the importance of the voting public. Despite its apparent appeal for democratic revivalism, the text also demands a restoration of what it deems to be the established order—namely, Southern feudalism.

Tucker's paradoxical construct of the presidency instigates revolt and, at the same time, it undermines the premise of democracy by casting doubt upon the people as well as the process that elected a leviathan. Tucker's unflattering depiction of Van Buren remains inconsistent on a variety of fronts: most glaringly, the novel's presumably noble protagonists justify the institution of slavery on grounds that are eerily similar to the grounds upon which the character Van Buren bases his own unsavory dominion. How can Tucker's reader be expected to root against an oppressive tyrant while cheering on slave owners? Tucker's depiction of Southern gentlemen unconsciously blends with the text's critique of Van Buren by preserving a feudal logic. And this paradoxical arrangement sets the stage for future representations of the imperial president—stories that condemn consolidated control even as they lament a diffusion of centralized power. This paradox would be revived a century later with the ascent of fictionalized chief magistrates for whom Tucker's Van Buren serves as a grim harbinger.

The Fascists Within

Between the Great Depression and the Second World War, Americans witnessed the rise of a profoundly empowered executive. Franklin Delano Roosevelt deployed the president's Committee on Administrative Management as well as the First and Second War Powers Act to redefine the scope of the modern presidency, positioning himself as a bureaucratic overseer and laying the groundwork for imperial presidencies to come.[3] This expansion of centralized power was tangibly felt at all levels of society, from the halls of Congress to the radios in private living rooms that broadcast the president's Fireside Chats: "After Roosevelt, the presidency became

---

[3]On FDR's role in America's transition into imperial presidencies, Theodore Lowi notes, "The formalization of the presidency as the center of *management* preceded the explicit theory of presidential power and presidential centricity that came to be recognized in the 1950s" (Lowi 1985: 55, author's emphasis).

part of the daily world of the populace" (Kuklick 1988: 49). Once again, popular perceptions of the Roosevelt presidency adopted a Janus face: some Americans feared an unchecked commander in chief; other Americans saw Roosevelt as the inevitable result of an untrained and overzealous electorate. Mainstream discourse occasionally depicted FDR as the head of "a secretive cabal" with an insatiable "appetite for power." Concomitantly, authors undercut this ostensibly despotic ruler by portraying FDR as "an instrument (. . .) of popular will" that, *precisely because of his incredible popularity*, remained suspect, even "illegitimate" (McCann 2008: 6). In a range of fictional treatments of the president, dueling energies persist—the urge to topple would-be dictators in tension with the urge to install a dictator against a surge of unruly citizens demanding satisfaction. Gore Vidal reflects these competing urges in a letter to his grandfather, a life-long critic of Roosevelt, following Roosevelt's demise: "The king is dead—long live the president" (qtd. in Parini 2015: 46).

Set in the bucolic hollers of Vermont, Sinclair Lewis's *It Can't Happen Here* chronicles the ascent of president Buzz Windrip through the eyes of a defiant liberal named Doremus Jessup. Lewis's novel argues that America could quite easily find itself under the thumb of a martinet. Anticipating authoritarian personalities like Nixon or Trump, Lewis's misguided voters mistake Windrip for a "Strong Man" who will "really *run* the country and make it efficient and prosperous again" (Lewis 2014: 18, author's emphasis). In a totalitarian fashion, Windrip has no real agenda or policy platform for governance; he instead preys on the passions of the people to secure his personal power. He utilizes the fury of spiteful laborers abandoned by the American establishment to harass, intimidate, and intern individuals who dissent. Jessup slowly realizes that his approach to politics—to stand at a degree of removal and declare a pox on all of the houses, in the manner of a meek liberal—does not measure up to the demands of his moment. Friends and family laugh at his name, referring to him as a "door mouse." The Windrip regime eventually locks Jessup away in a camp. Although Lewis certainly mocked the meekness of Jessup, he nonetheless upheld the small-town editor's maxim that humor is what "makes life tolerable" by satirizing everyone: the self-serious fascists, the middling liberals, as well as the empty-headed citizenry of small-town Vermont (356). By ridiculing the death of politics under authoritarian oppression as well as the excess of politics under the hysterical sway of the people, *It Can't Happen Here* leaves its reader with virtually nowhere to go: "(Jessup) must remain alone, a 'Liberal,' scored by all of the noisier prophets . . . no matter which brand of tyranny should finally dominate" (359).

Lewis's work lambasts President Windrip not so much for his sinister methods, but because he dares to have any plan whatsoever. According to *It Can't Happen Here*, to engage in social planning invariably means seeking to start "a new paradise on earth" (Lewis 2014: 134). The text contrasts

Windrip's ideas for total reform with the platform of his Republican opponent, who admits that he does not work miracles, that "we live in the United States of America and not on a highway to Utopia," and that his Republican brand of "realism" will never be as "exhilarating" as the grand designs of Windrip (33). Fed up with authoritarians of all stripes, Jessup screams: "There is no Solution! There will never be a state of society anything like perfect!" (112). Lewis therefore skewered the imperial presidency to reject the entire premise of collective governance. By painting with its broad satirical brush, *It Can't Happen Here* exposes the promises of democracy to be futile from the first. As Lewis's narrative bundles all types of managerial leadership with fascism, the receptive reader of *It Can't Happen Here* will wind up deeply alienated from her community. What hope remains for government of any kind?

Lewis's POTUS proves innately despotic, driven compulsively toward imperial conclusions. In the eyes of its critics, the imperial presidency is a redundant term because the concept of the presidency remains intrinsically imperialistic. Citizens have no choice but to define the nation's executive as imperial because the role requires an endless acquisition of power and results in inevitable overreach.[4] Edmund Randolph, governor of Virginia, once described the American president as "the fetus of monarchy," and indeed, the office has been widely viewed as drifting toward tyranny ever since (qtd. in Conway 1889: 90). "Some say Windrip is crude," Lewis's novel remarks. "Well, so were Lincoln and Jackson" (Lewis 2014: 237). American presidents always succumb to authoritarian creep, the story goes; it is wired into the DNA of the job. To want to be president implies a desire to dominate mankind, history, and knowledge itself. Of the utmost significance, Jessup transposes this characteristic of the presidency into his everyday life as he too longs to harness the illusion of presidential power to exert control over his surroundings. Even though he despises Windrip, Jessup still relies on the iconography of the presidency to make sense of his chaotic world. He needs to align himself with an ideology, or, a single idea that explains everything. He realizes, albeit too late, that the explanatory narrative of POTUS is his biggest crutch, and that his whole damnable life has been "predicated on the privilege of planning" (105).

It Can't Happen Here treats the imperial presidency not only as a source of abuse but as an organizing principle, which is to say, as a conceptual tool with which the state purportedly promotes order, stability, and meaning. The imperial president embodies the state's disciplinary power grid, which

---

4Dana Nelson writes, "Ever since the office was invented, presidents have been appealing to how it serves as a symbol of national strength and domestic unity, and to its function as a focal point for foreign policy, to claim more power for the office than those it was explicitly granted by the Constitution" (Nelson 2008: 3).

hinders Jessup from thriving. If he wishes to adapt or grow, Jessup must somehow flee from strictures associated with the presidency. Lewis's presidency is not merely part of the novel's *diegesis*, then; it structures the entire narrative via the prison of Jessup's quotidian environment. Jessup's office remains replete with presidential memorabilia, like a patriotic portrait of McKinley and a fake newspaper announcing Lincoln's death. Readers spot many other presidential relics, including "the complete works of Thomas Jefferson, (Jessup's) chief hero" as well as "a signed photograph of Theodore Roosevelt" (Lewis 2014: 22–23). Moreover, Lewis's text situates the epicenter of Jessup's professional life on President Street, surrounded by "Chester Arthur, red-brick prissiness" (166). *It Can't Happen Here* thus situates its protagonist within a presidential paradigm by planting him firmly within a constellation of reference points that lead back to the core concept of the American executive. Ensconced in presidential lore, Jessup's movements within, and attitudes toward, the world unconsciously obeys the neat-and-tidy logic of the presidency. The subsequent corruption of the office by Windrip—or, perhaps, Windrip's exposure of the office's inherent corruption—sends shock waves into a thoroughly habituated populace. Suddenly, for Jessup, "it seemed impossible now to know anything for sure" (106). By throwing its comfortable liberal into the unknown, *It Can't Happen Here* interpolates its reader into rebellion against a presidency that has imperialized American experience at the most fundamental level imaginable: wall decorations that dictate the parameters of small-town America; pieces of infrastructure that train citizens to comingle the allure of social planning, the inner workings of their habitus, and the overarching concept of the presidency.

But even as it instigates distaste for the imperial presidency, Lewis's novel concurrently rejects the democratic antidote. The text declares that Windrip would never have risen to power without the assistance of a witless public. Lewis's story comments extensively upon how the masses harbor unrealistic expectations of what government can accomplish. With the emergence of Windrip, the *demos* expose its hideous inclinations: "Itching, indigesting, aspiring" (Lewis 2014: 151). Imagined fascist leaders manifest an ugliness within the American citizenry—the dismal impulse to aspire, to demand a better world. Unlike the pragmatic Republican or the isolated liberal, who represent "integrity and reason," the gullible crowds of *It Can't Happen Here* cannot overcome "frisky emotions" (85). In turn, the populist Windrip exploits his crowd by encouraging them to tilt at "windmills" (72). "Be selfish," he tells his followers. "Vote for the one man that's willing to give you something" (89). So what can the reader do with the relentlessly satirical *It Can't Happen Here*? Because Jessup believes in neither "a dictatorship of the bankers and utility owners" nor a "dictatorship of the proletariat," and because he rejects the authoritarian as well as the committed voter, Lewis's proposed solution seems to be total estrangement from one's community (310). To run off like Jessup and wait for something else to happen.

The imperial president of Lewis's fiction serves as a useful avatar for the conflicted perspective of self-described mob psychologists. Concerned with the rise in what George Orwell would later call groupthink—and, one must add, the swelling power of labor unions—mob psychologists rose to prominence in the early twentieth century by prognosticating upon the nature of ominous crowds. With his acerbic wit, H. L. Mencken chastised the *vox populi* and lambasted democratic man as completely untrustworthy. Elsewhere, a favorite writer of the hyper-managerial Theodore Roosevelt, Gustave Le Bon depicted the crowd as a contagion: an assembly of barbarians in desperate need of discipline. Yet, importantly, these mob psychologists often shifted their gaze to the imperial president to direct their vitriol at a solid, sensible form. After denouncing the mob, Le Bon turned on the mob's leader, who was supposedly "recruited from the ranks of those morbidly nervous, excitable, half-deranged persons who are bordering on madness" (Le Bon 2002: 73). The crowd, Le Bon posited, both requires a master and, paradoxically, proves incapable of selecting one responsibly. The democratic paradox becomes acute, painful, and even suicidal. Mencken labeled presidents like Woodrow Wilson as unprincipled mountebanks that advanced their careers by listening to the "murmurs of popular clamor" (Mencken 1926: 108). And "what are the sources of that power? They lie, obviously, in the gross weaknesses and knaveries of the common people" (109). Born from the mob, leaders cannot transcend the crowd's depravities; a self-defeating duality spins madly on. "There is, first, the mob . . . there is, second, the camorra of self-seeking minorities (and) rival rogues" (79). The word "camorra" means mob, of course, and so Mencken was implying that there is literally nothing outside of the mob. Voters deserve what they produce; leaders are never more than a lowly sum of their parts. Like the character of Jessup, mob psychologists stand solitary, awaiting (impossible) alternatives.

As one can see, Lewis was not the only thinker dancing along this fault line in the first half of the twentieth century. Dos Passos, author of the *U.S.A.* trilogy, grew quite reactionary in his later years, as he too wrestled with the paradoxes of an imperial presidency. In his novel *The Grand Design*, Dos Passos roasted Roosevelt and the overly ambitious New Dealers. Concurrently, though, he doubted the capacity of the electorate to issue reasonable verdicts, and so his novel avers that the imperial presidency is the inexorable outcome of an under-regulated democracy.

Dos Passos depicted FDR, the patrician president, as an arch aristocrat—an overbearing overlord with haughty mannerisms. He identified FDR with the president's elegant cigarette-holder: a totem of his feudal leanings. *The Grand Design* opens at FDR's inauguration: "The smooth broad-shouldered figure confident and tall of the president newly elected (with) the headmaster's admonishing voice" (Dos Passos 1949: 4). The story presents Roosevelt as both "smooth" and "condescending," a man who preaches, manipulates, and looks down his nose at the rubes that voted for him. Characters pass by the White House and imagine the resident despot decked out in his luxury suite: "The White House looked as peaceful as some forgotten old plantation mansion deep in the South" (65). Reviving Tucker's proto-imperial presidency, Dos Passos's narrative portrays Roosevelt as a thoroughly undemocratic charlatan, barricaded in his retreat as an obvious heir to the royal succession of Jackson-Van Buren, a duo referenced by Dos Passos's text on several occasions. *The Grand Design* attacks the presidency as a "mighty institution" that invariably installs a "Caesar" (369, 310). Dos Passos dismissed the economic boom that stemmed from the New Deal by stressing in its place a "presidential boom": the endless expanse of presidential influence into every corner of the U.S. government (146).

A bit derivative, Dos Passos tread on relatively familiar territory in his lampoon of FDR's hyper-bureaucratic presidency. For example, in a characteristically heavy-handed moment, the novel's protagonist Paul almost ruins his family by having an extramarital affair with his secretary, whom he nicknames Facts and Figures in a rather superficial critique of Roosevelt's bureaucratic sensibilities. According to Dos Passos's vision, each New Dealer yearns to become president. The author responded by compelling his readers to question the merits of the presidency itself.

On the other hand, *The Grand Design* portrays Roosevelt as the byproduct of an unrestrained democracy, which is to say, it frames FDR as the effect of an *excess* of democracy, instead of, say, treating social problems as a sign of an insufficiently egalitarian government. "When the Government steps in to put people on their feet . . . I don't see how it can result in anything but *more politics*" (Dos Passos 1949: 246–47, emphasis mine). As the text worries over "more politics," Dos Passos's readers might pause to ask: how is it exactly that the solution to presidential overreach could be *less* politics? The story unflatteringly portrays voters that ushered Roosevelt into office four times: "The American people have got to be told what to think" (202). By narrative's end, the protagonist loses all faith in government—a shift that leads not to revolt or reform, but to resignation. As inactive as Jessup, Dos Passos's protagonist rejoins "the multifarious public," putting on a military uniform to "just lay back and take orders" (432, 438). Although Dos Passos actively goaded his reader into challenging a centralized power, his effort culminated in a conviction that the electorate should never again be trusted with control over its fate. That is to say, even as Dos Passos longed to renew the democratic apparatus against an ostensibly dictatorial FDR, he did so in a desultory manner, deeming the possibility of the common man's triumph over elites to be a grotesque proposition indeed. The author reserved for himself a secluded place in the imagination of his readers, set apart from the masses as well as their unworthy leaders: a fantastical station, forever occupied by what Mencken deemed to be "a special sort of man" (Mencken 1926: 158).

Prophets of a Post-Imperial Presidency

The high-water mark of the imperial presidency was the mid-century presidencies of Johnson and Nixon. These administrations ushered in a sort of presidential mystique: "By the 1970s the title commander in chief had acquired almost a sacramental aura, translating its holder from worldly matters into an ineffable realm of higher duty" (Schlesinger 2004: 177, 188). This presidential mystique took center stage against the backdrop of the conflict in Vietnam, during which imperial presidents unilaterally bypassed Congressional and judicial restraints to strike against a perceived communist threat. Johnson himself succinctly summarized the development: "There is only one that has been chosen by the American people to decide" (Johnson 1966: n.p.). On the home front, Nixon imagined himself to be an overseer of the economy, posturing as supreme executive and, as such, displaying even greater imperial cravings than his predecessors. Subsequent depictions of Nixon in popular culture have presented a solipsistic tyrant, antagonistic with the press and quick to stymie calls for transparency.[5] Critiquing presidential overreach, Stephen King composed a tract concerning the post-imperial presidency, *The Dead Zone*: a representative text from the post-Watergate era that seeks to exorcise the Nixonian monster from under America's collective bed.

The Dead Zone obsesses over American presidents; indeed, it appears intent on redefining the limits of the office—or, more broadly, centralized power of any sort.[6] Congress passed a series of acts designed to rein in the executive branch following Nixon's fall: the War Power Resolution (1973), the Hughes-Ryan Amendment (1974), and the Presidential Records Act (1978). All of these initiatives were designed to dial back the power of an unchecked executive. Consequently, president Gerald Ford, hot on the heels of Nixon's departure, bewailed what he perceived to be a pendulum

---

[5]Critics point to LBJ's Tonkin Golf Resolution, which gave a veritable blank check for presidents in war time, and Nixon's support for the coup of Salvador Allende in Chile as signs of an imperial presidency flexing its newfound muscles. Yet at the same time, many public intellectuals favored the emergence of a stronger presidency. See, for instance, Clinton Rossiter's *The American Presidency*, Richard Neustadt's *Presidential Power*, or James MacGregor Burns's *Presidential Government*.

[6]King returns to this theme in *11/22/63*, a novel concerning the assassination of John F. Kennedy and the gross overreach of a man who thinks he can control time, and *Under the Dome*, a novel that focuses upon a stand-in for president George W. Bush who declares a state of emergency in order to exercise his executive prerogative. For detailed analyses of these texts, see Blouin (2021).

swing too far in the opposite direction. America has shifted too dramatically from an "imperial" presidency, he complained, to an "imperiled" presidency (Hunter 1978: 22). Caught in this historical eddy, King's *The Dead Zone* follows two star-fated men, a Nixonian politician named Greg Stillson and his would-be assassin, a psychic named John Smith. The novel chronicles the corrosion of the presidency as it interrogates the wisdom of imbuing the office with inflated significance. By the conclusion of *The Dead Zone*, King has gleefully confirmed Ford's suspicions that the presidency is indeed imperiled; however, like Lewis and Dos Passos before him, King rejected shared governance as utopian and destined to fail, thus leaving his readers without meaningful democratic alternatives.

Stillson unveils the imperial presidency to be a ticking time bomb. At the beginning of *The Dead Zone*, readers witness Stillson's savage murder of an innocent dog, and from that point forward, they can only wait as he slouches like some rough beast toward the highest office in the land. Marching down pathways paved by earlier executives, he initially promises, like Lewis's Windrip, to use his exceptional status to bypass checks and balances in the name of more direct reforms. The dupes of King's novel interchangeably describe the populist Stillson as a "square shooter," "a man," and "an exception to the rule" (King 1979: 363). When Johnny meets Stillson, he confirms the attendant danger: this power-hungry monster will stop at nothing until he becomes president. While Stillson views himself as destined "for greatness," readers recognize from the start that greatness in Stillson's case means violent, unrelenting domination (8). As Stillson claws his way up the social hierarchy, he cultivates "gestapo tactics" to cement a fascist hold (174). Echoing *It Can't Happen Here*, King's text illustrates how it is not only *likely* that America will succumb to authoritarian rule— it is *inevitable*.[7] The beginning of King's book spells out the trajectory of the imperial presidency by comparing the conflict in Vietnam to a "bad hotdog" that Johnson fed to the American public. After the public got sick of tainted meat, Nixon came along and "cured" the nation by feeding them "even more hotdogs" (47). In short, *The Dead Zone* positions Stillson as next in line in a long, deadly succession of imperial presidents. To counter this compulsive behavior, King featured a Vietnamese refugee named Ngo Phat, a gardener who plants the idea of assassinating Stillson in Johnny's mind. This relatively minor character plays an oversized role by conveying to King's reader the self-destructive tendencies of POTUS. It is the continual overreach of chief magistrates, from Johnson to Nixon to Stillson, that triggers a fierce backlash—in this case, a Vietnamese refugee who heralds

---

[7]King's text renders the connection to Lewis's novel explicit, arguing that the imperial president had been looming large "ever since Sinclair Lewis had been crying woe and doom and beware the fascist state in America" (King 1979: 326).

the merits of political assassination after witnessing American abuses on his native soil.[8] The antagonist's name evokes a forsaken pregnancy: the arrival of a still son, whose advent underscores a tragic coda to the failed gestation of American history. Stillson's ignoble end, in which he attempts to use a child as a human shield to protect himself, illuminates how America's presidential lineage no longer produces healthy progeny.

Although the rise and fall of Stillson parallels the rise and fall of America's imperial presidency, *The Dead Zone* draws an even more intriguing parallel between Nixon and its protagonist. Because he can tell the future, Smith doubles as an extraordinary political prognosticator. Without a doubt, his name—the epitome of the quotidian—identifies how Johnny Smith is very much not identical to Stillson, which is to say, his supreme ordinariness, as opposed to a thirst for endless power, saves Smith from a Nixonian fate. But Smith's name also connects him to another historical figure: captain John Smith of Virginia settlement fame, a man with serious imperial appetites. In a word, even as he resists the siren call of presidential power, Smith unconsciously follows in the footsteps of Nixon, like some somnambulist unaware of the invisible forces that propel him. From one of its opening scenes in which the reader spots in Johnny's apartment a poster of Nixon selling used cars, Smith's parallel of Nixon runs barely below the surface. For instance, the car crash that nearly kills Johnny occurs at the precise moment that the driver vents to Johnny about his son's disrespect of "Tricky Dick"; Johnny's subsequent coma, in which he enters into a sort of limbo state, figuratively as well as literally parallels Nixon's holding pattern in Vietnam; upon waking, Johnny's first question involves the re-election of Nixon, as it dawns on him that he has missed "some great and fundamental upheaval in American politics" (King 1979: 119). During his rehabilitation, Johnny reads *All the President's Men*, Bob Woodward and Carl Bernstein's well-known book concerning the Watergate scandal. Shortly after his release from the hospital, he is assaulted by journalists that want to "have a swing" at him, in parallel with Nixon's antagonism with the media, conjured in Nixon's famous line, upon losing to John F. Kennedy, that the media will no longer have him to kick around: "An unhappy reporter will be your enemy. Nixon made them unhappy and they tore him to pieces." Johnny mirrors the disgraced president to such an extent that he feels compelled to over-compensate by declaring: "I'm not Nixon" (153). In sum, Johnny's private journey—his costly seizure of power and control; his perceived abuse at the hands of the press; his redemption when he decides to reject mastery in favor of ordinariness—follows the cyclical turns of the imperial presidency. By the close of the novel, Johnny has descended so far from the Nixonian heights that nearly destroyed him that he comments on how he cannot believe Nixon was ever president.

---

[8]For more on Stephen King's connection to Vietnam, see Magistrale and Blouin (2020).

And yet, like the other texts considered in this chapter, *The Dead Zone* does not counter the proposed despotism of Stillson with a stronger devotion to democracy; rather, the novel worries that the imperial presidency depends upon the will of the people, and so the feckless masses must not be trusted to resolve the issue. Put differently, because Stillson was "the people's choice," King's narrative dwells at length upon gullible, vindictive audiences (King 1979: 310). In King's fictional universe, American voters are rarely to be trusted. His narratives point to small, incremental changes made by likable elites, like the centrist Chadsworth or the husband of Johnny's ex-girlfriend, a Republican politician—men who neither harbor utopian sentiments nor strive to make meaningful social changes. If American democracy breeds irrationality, strong emotions, as well as an endless stream of new demands, *The Dead Zone* prefers rogue actors that pursue neither fame nor glory, that is, Mencken's special sort of men.

The Dead Zone reveals the extent to which the American presidency imperializes everyday lives, or, the degree to which the concept of the presidency infiltrates and organizes the daily habits of citizens. Presidential news punctuates the plot, from George McGovern's declaration of his candidacy to Nixon's shameful resignation. King's novel prefaces updates about Johnny's medical condition with numerous asides concerning POTUS: "Four days before Nixon resigned, (Smith's father) fell . . ."; "Shortly after Gerald Ford had pardoned the ex-President, (Smith's) mother became sure . . ." (King 1979: 87). Later, when Johnny works as a tutor, he empowers his student to learn to read by asking them questions about the presidential campaign of Jerry Brown. In a word, *The Dead Zone* reveals how the stories that Americans tell about their chief magistrate orient their lives at the most basic, even unconscious level, by perpetuating an overdetermined illusion of continuity as well as coherence. The presidency comes to represent ideology itself, a regulative principle that purports to explain everything: "Whatever happens, happens according to the logic of the one 'idea'" (Arendt 1994: 469). In response, King stripped the imperial presidency—a stand-in for the widespread emphasis in the twentieth century upon ideology—of its specific content. The terror caused by King's Nixon stems not from policy proposals but from the looming threat of ideology itself, of the "one idea." King's executive represents a totalizing schema in which all points can be traced back to a single point of origin. But a crucial question remains: what, if anything, exists outside of this totalizing schema? That is, can fictional accounts of the imperial presidency inspire an escape from its clutches?

The Presidential Unconscious

As part of a symbolic shift away from mid-century presidents, late twentieth-century American authors like King moved to exorcise the presidency from the reader's everyday life. Beyond challenging centralized authority at the highest strata of society, texts like *The Dead Zone* interrogate how the concept of the presidency structures the subject's understanding of the world, his sense of history, as well as the intimate parts of himself that have been trained to accept an imposed orderliness as well as an overarching semblance of continuity. The imperial presidency thus serves as an effective *dispositif* by habituating the subject and hemming in the horizons of her imagination. Giorgio Agamben defines the concept of the *dispositif*: "I shall call an apparatus literally anything that has in some way the capacity to capture, orient, determine, intercept, model control, or secure the gestures, behaviors, opinions, or discourses of living beings . . . the pen, writing, literature, philosophy, agriculture, cigarettes, navigation, computers, cellular telephones and—why not—language itself" (Agamben 2009: 19, 14). As one can see in this quote, an increasing number of mundane objects and/or rituals have been employed by contemporary society to discipline subjects. Correspondingly, the idea of the imperial presidency has begun to mold the expectations of countless citizens. As David Greenberg argues, "Associations with the president—even the idea of the president—guide our behavior" (Greenberg 2003: xxv). Dana Nelson describes this phenomenon as "the mesmerizing power of presidentialism." For Nelson, presidentialism names "the unconscious power that the presidency works on citizens"—a power that seems almost "gravitational" (Nelson 2008: 5, 18). To give readers a feeling of emancipation from such invasive oversight, contemporary American writers have struggled to extricate the all-powerful executive and the intractable power structure for which he serves as shorthand, from the formation of individual subjectivities.

For example, Kurt Vonnegut's novel *Slapstick; Or, Lonesome No More!*, one of the earliest explorations of a post-Nixon reality, recognizes the extent to which POTUS informs the subject's desires in unanticipated ways. The text ruminates upon the presidency as a psychical structure that creates an impression of communal belonging. President Wilbur Rockefeller Swain designs a scheme to endow every American with shared middle names to foster a stronger sense of connectivity. One over-eager citizen begs Swain, "You're the president . . . you give me a name" (Vonnegut 1999: 228). But in Vonnegut's telling, the unilateral executive's grand design exposes the *ineffectiveness* of any bid to marshal the variegated desires of an entire populace in line with the "one idea." To invoke a post-imperial ecstasy, a world without a president, or, more to the point, without an overarching disciplinary structure, Vonnegut's narrative reveals how the concept of the commander in chief colonizes citizens by imposing an expansive set of emotional and intellectual coordinates. In so doing, it gestures at a compelling, if sometimes confounding, sense of anti-foundationalism.

Philip Roth's *The Plot Against America* follows the fictionalized Roth family as its members come to terms with the imagined victory of Charles

Lindbergh over Franklin Delano Roosevelt in the 1940 election. Indebted to the postmodern project at large, *Plot* recounts the perpetually unfinished work of releasing the subject from the psychic bonds that his society uses to discipline him (a theme that drives most of Roth's output). As such, the "Plot" of Roth's title resonates beyond the attempt by Nazis to undermine America by installing a populist demagogue in the nation's highest office; in truth, the novel exposes a far more intimate—that is, less allegorical— plotting that runs invasively through the internal life of the youngest Roth.

The presidency is the Roth family's Ur-plot. In effect, the mythos of the Roth family legacy depends upon the legibility and legitimacy conferred upon it by the imagined executive. For example, mother Roth conceives one of her sons in tandem with Lindbergh's electoral success, a correlation that appears to endow the boy's birth with commemorative import: "The mystery of pregnancy and the heroism of Lindbergh combined to give a distinction bordering on the divine" (Roth 2004: 5). As for the youngest son Philip, America's impressive processional of magistrates programs his developing sensorium: "Lindbergh was the first famous American whom I learned to hate—just as president Roosevelt was the first living American whom I was taught to love" (7). *The Plot Against America* renders the presidency imperial not due to geopolitical wrangling, but because the storylines associated with POTUS conscribe the innermost contours of the protagonist's private life. The *dispositif* of the presidency inspires and enrages Philip, influences how he passes his leisure time, provides his life with a chronological framework, delivers onto him a persona to worship, and enables him to gesture, however obliquely, at a world without organizing principles. In addition to its effort to expose the structural trappings of a presidential unconscious, *Plot* considers the emancipatory promise of presidential absence. (The novel was published, it should be noted, at the cusp of a resurrection of the imperial paradigm under the George W. Bush regime.)

Roth's story visualizes the tentacles of presidential influence through Philip's highly coveted stamp collection. In *The Dead Zone*, Johnny becomes "an avid politician-watcher," traveling to campaign events to shake hands with candidates and thus glimpse their future. Upon meeting Jimmy Carter, he notes: "One more politician for his collection" (King 1979: 280). He then quips, "Some people (collect) stamps" (297). In similar ways, *Plot*'s Philip emulates his hero FDR, who practices collecting stamps in the White House. The presidency alters the behavioral patterns of American youths. This particular hobby is thoroughly infused with the logic of an imperial presidency, since collecting stamps offers a method with which to organize the world, categorize its most valuable components, and instill a sense of meaning upon an otherwise random and chaotic universe. Appropriately enough, each stamp features "the lamp of knowledge," or, a tiny totem of mastery (Roth 2004: 23). When members of the Roth family visit Washington, D.C. to regain their bearings after Lindbergh's election, and to reclaim their imaged connection to Roosevelt, who bestows upon the family "a historical significance, authoritatively merging our lives with his," the family essentially engages in the real-world equivalent of stamp collection (28). In other words, they accumulate highly prized specimens by visually "taking in" prominent national relics, eagerly curating them within their family's narrative, and telling their own story through the meticulous arrangement of anecdotes concerning former presidents. Therefore, Philip's art of collecting stamps reveals the intrusion of the logic of the imperial presidency into the recesses of his private world.

In response, *Plot* critiques the fanatical exhibition of presidents that ostensibly drives the national narrative. A popular cover for *Plot* includes a stamp to highlight this connection between Philip's precious presidential stamps and the novel itself. After all, presidents are a lot like cherished stamps—FDR as a "preordained," God-like, looming figure; Lindbergh as a man with the "fortitude to shape history" (53). The symbol of the presidency marks a "deep-seated impulse to reorder things . . . (to) alter system boundaries and recast political possibilities" (Skowronek 1997: 4, author's emphasis). Like his son, who confesses that his collection represents "nine-tenths of his knowledge of the world," Philip's father clings to the erroneous belief that a different president could somehow correct everything that has gone awry. "What this country needs," he fumes desperately, "is a new president" (Roth 2004: 67, 81). This hunger for the presidential organizing principle runs at such fathoms that Philip cannot avoid using presidential reference points to comprehend even the nastiest parts of his experiences. For instance, when his family encounters an anti-semite during their trip to the Capitol, Philip's presidential unconscious bubbles to the surface. To make sense of the chaos, he relies upon internalized reference points, taking note of the offensive man's "walrus mustache of the type displayed by president Taft on the light red 1938 fifty-cent stamp" (78).

In turn, *The Plot Against America* undermines a widespread, foundational belief tied to the imperial presidency: the credence that the president arranges American life in a linear, predictable manner. As the text unfolds, the Roths loosen their perceived hold upon American history as well as their place within it. The president loses its value as the family can no longer capitalize upon the neat-and-tidy logic of the presidency to survive. The elder Roth's faith in the U.S. Postal system, a reminder of Roosevelt's hyper-managerial presidency, erodes. At a crucial moment, Philip misplaces his stamp collection—"gone and irreplaceable"—and Roth's reader recognizes that the spell of the imperial presidency has, at long last, been lifted (Roth 2004: 235). From this erosion of trust, the possibilities as well as perils of a post-imperial presidency start to emerge. Personalizing its political plight, or perhaps politicizing its personal plight, *Plot* connects a widespread disenchantment with presidential overreach to a boy who becomes disenchanted with his once-invincible parents. The novel exposes the nation's endless parade of father figures—its many Founding Fathers, often classified in this fashion *avant la lettre*—to be little more than paper men: "Never would I be able to revive that unfazed sense of security first fostered in a little child by a big, protective republic" (301). In this sense, *Plot* asks its reader: what if the imperial presidency attracts readers not because of its illusory sense of wholeness, but because it signifies a hole, an empty throne, a sense of security that has never existed (and so could never be revived)?

To critique presidentialism as a straightforward emblem of a vast disciplinary apparatus is to miss the fact that fictional presidents contain within themselves their opposite: the law as well as its limit. Roth's novel comprehends that the presidential *dispositif* does not reduce the fantasy structure of American nationhood to a moribund set of power dynamics; instead, Roth's text demonstrates how overdetermined narratives of the presidency always already depend upon a structural lack—an inarticulable surplus without which the entire fantasy would collapse. Joan Copjec argues that when citizens dwell upon positivist renderings of national leaders, they ignore the possibility that the "social surface and desire may be a negative one" (Copjec 1996: 14). That is to say, what if depictions of imperial presidents give readers pleasure not simply because they provide disciplinary guardrails, but because they mark the limit of attempts to order things? What if the fictional presidency always preserves a lack, a presidential absence, and this lack is precisely that which keeps alive the reader's desire *for something else*?

On second glance, then, presidents resemble stamps more closely when they are imperfect because imperfectly printed stamps are more coveted than their unblemished counterparts. Philip guiltily recognizes that his Lindbergh stamp will skyrocket in worth only if the "worst happens" and he is elected into office (Roth 2004: 27). However odious it may be as proof of the fascist turn in American politics, Philip cannot bring himself to part with his Lindbergh stamp. Collectors like Philip are unconsciously attracted to imperfect presidents because their oddities make them even more compelling, even more valuable. For Roth, the trope of the imperial presidency, precisely because of its flaws, should remind readers that the story of American history as a punctilious assortment of executive power struggles is only ever a false front. Beneath their highly structured surface, all-powerful chief magistrates like Lindbergh demonstrate how American history is actually comprised of ruptures, inconsistencies, and contradictions. The hugely popular genre of the alternative history to which Roth's text belongs serves a similar purpose in that it resembles misprinted presidential stamps: the stories are repulsive, without a doubt, yet they are profound reminders that American history is not a well-choreographed, pristine collection of artifacts. The election of someone like Lindbergh—or, in real-life, someone like Donald Trump— allows Philip to keep fantasizing about a world without a big Other to discipline him. He can revel, if only in his imagination, in the openness of a society that has not been scrupulously predetermined, which is to say, a society without foundations, in which human beings can persist as political animals rather than automatons.

The doubleness that this chapter has been interrogating is not merely a reversal, then—a transmission of power from tyrant to mob and then back again, *ad infinitum*. Rather, the novels in question tarry around a double negative, a refusal to align with either despot or the masses. The doubleness of the imperial president does not entail resituating or reconfiguring power; this doubleness instead reflects a desire for something beyond modern power with its totalizing logic: a loss, an absence, a hope that *things still happen here*. The Janus faces of FDR and Lindbergh gesture at a constitutional exterior that no organizational tool could ever fully encapsulate.[9] At different points, FDR and Lindbergh each vanish from the text, and the story is left to orbit around the gaping holes left in their wake. These prominent absences tell readers not to dwell upon the promise of power changing hands, but to open themselves to the possibility of a chasm in the place where power was previously thought to be centralized. Put differently, the double negations of *Plot* can be seen as proof that readers, however unconsciously, want to sustain an impossible, invisible position not yet circumscribed by the all-encompassing power grid. The presidential absences of Roth's text reveal that readers desire something that cannot be buried within existing Ur-plots.

Of course, one cannot ignore the fact that Roosevelt makes a triumphant return at the close of *Plot*: "FDR is back!" (286). Sean McCann contends that although Roth's book highlights "the allure and deception of presidential politics," its eventual restoration of Roosevelt upholds a long-standing "image of the redeemer president" (McCann 2008: 191, 196). From this vantage point, Roth's readers need not, and perhaps cannot, remove altogether the figure of the president, since it sustains the aspirational dimension of American democracy. If not quite a wholesale redemption, McCann argues that the return of FDR implies that America requires a nodal point—an avatar through which it can come to terms with its precarity. At the same time, though, Roth's readers might view the return of FDR as yet another counterfeit. Akin to the inverted stamp placed prominently upon the book's cover, the presidential icon is no longer quite right. Conjuring George Lippard's depiction of Washington discussed in Chapter 2, Roth's imperial president proves to be uncanny: familiar yet somehow unfamiliar. In the final tally, the imperial executive remains nothing more—or less— than a national "prosthesis" (362).

---

[9]In his critique of a Foucauldian system that charts power as its final principle, Jean Baudrillard notes that, "beyond power, or at the very heart of power (. . .) there is a void which gives (. . .) a last glimmer of reality" (Baudrillard 1988: 44–45).

What if America's general obsession with the president has not been a futile pursuit but the pursuit of futility? In other words, what if the imperial presidency is not a construct that unconvincingly resolves an aching need, but a vital catalyst that reminds audiences of their dissatisfaction—a fillip that motivates Philip by continually fueling his desire? For every conscious longing for an impeccable leader like FDR, Roth's narrative recalls an unconscious drive toward a Lindbergh—an imperfect figure that unsettles the status quo and thus dismantles the excessively choreographed patterns of everyday lives. That Lindbergh is an unhealthy, dangerous, and utterly untenable option should be glaringly obvious. Nevertheless, by understanding better the subject's complex desire/repulsion for imperial presidents, Roth's audience might begin to reassess the nation's primary fantasy structures.

To extend this argument a bit further, when critics catalog imperial presidents as impediments to democratic satisfaction, they risk overlooking the perverse pleasures that figures like Philip find in an inferior presidential iconography. One must recall that Roth's text is not a plotting *of*, but a plot *against*.[10] The unconscious cannot be completely colonized; there are always remainders. Like the works of Lewis, Dos Passos, and King, *Plot* guides its protagonist away from a painstakingly manicured presidential pathway. Yet, crucially, Roth charted a more constructive ending than any of his predecessors. While Lewis and his ilk exposed the fetishistic function of the imperial president by depoliticizing the American experiment, and thereby leaving disenfranchised readers with precious few options for rebuilding their political imaginations, Roth understood that to dismiss politics entirely was to throw the proverbial baby out with the bathwater. The true horror of ideology, or the "one idea," is that it persuades its followers to "escape responsibility"; to attempt to evade ideology, however, could produce a similarly dismal outcome (Arendt 1994: 9). Given the significant challenges that face its American audience, *Plot* contends that it has not been enough for literary treatments of the imperial president to accept the brokenness of a world without grand designs.[11] Indeed, Mencken's tract acknowledges the grim conclusion of its critique: "My argument goes beyond the democratic scheme and lodges against government itself" (Mencken 1926: 126). Left with neither a president nor a people, Roth's reader must consider "to what other normative injunction" citizens should form a more compelling attachment (Butler 1997: 88). In effect, Roth's text asks its reader to

---

[10]On the richness of counterfactual histories in the second half of the twentieth century, Catherine Gallagher and Stephen Greenblatt write: "The reality of unrealized possibilities become fuller and more engrossing, while deterministic and unilinear explanations become correspondingly unappealing and unsatisfying" (Gallagher and Greenblatt 2001: 54).

[11]Likewise, the fact that Agamben and theorists in a similar vein "inveigh against a collective response" can be seen as a fatal flaw in predominant theories of modern power (McGowan 2020: n.p.).

imagine herself outside of the sway of imperial presidents without becoming apolitical, that is, without forfeiting shared sites for meaningful resistance.

Tucker's novel concludes with the mantra *Sic semper tyrannis*—a line which implies that centralized power of any kind is destined to fail (Tucker 2015: 355). According to writers like Tucker, Lewis, Dos Passos, or King, alienated individuals wind up reabsorbed into the existing power structure, wandering in the wilderness, or dying a martyr's death. *Political alternatives remain utterly unimaginable.* In contrast, the concern with how to move beyond the imperial presidency in Roth's story calls to mind Judith Butler's argument that democratic reforms must instigate a stronger attachment to the "injurious name"—to the traumatic lack that characterizes citizenship. If there is no presidential parent to take care of us, we are all lonely orphans in need of communal support. *Plot* closes by retreating inward, as the Roth family cares for a displaced child with nowhere else to go: "You are rootless and you are vulnerable to everything" (Roth 2004: 358). Like Philip's cousin, who came home from the war with a prosthetic leg, Roth's characters must learn to lean upon one another—and not the imperial president—as literal as well as figurative crutches. After all, to return to Hannah Arendt's thesis, what is the worth of citizenship if it does not enforce this type of mutual support? Roth's book argues that what (unconsciously) propels American citizens is not a compensation for metaphorical missing limbs with overly inflated executives, but their mutual identification within an inherently diasporic existence. Divorcing its characters from the dictates of an imperial presidency, *Plot* privileges diasporic trauma as a generative source for new political subjectivities, which is to say, it compels its readers to imagine a form of political engagement that is no longer mired in the framework of presidential narratives. What if citizens could recognize one another's deleterious dependence upon the presidential prosthesis? Could they encounter each other as vulnerable beings, with fresh eyes and greater empathy?

Before many Americans revel in their feelings of collective release from the stagnating paradigm of Roosevelt, Nixon, or Trump, they need to consider how the double negative of imperial presidents assists them in recognizing their desire for something that lies beyond the disciplinary matrices that constrain them (or, the death drive behind the imperial presidents of American fiction). Roth's two-pronged invective against chief magistrates needs not be read as an invitation to anarchy; rather, it can be read as a provocation of a more democratic consciousness. On behalf of the displaced child who has joined his clan by the novel's end, Philip ultimately usurps the executive, a pivot that the book emphasizes with Philip's closing line: "I was the prosthesis" (Roth 2004: 362). It is not that the citizen should aim to *abolish* the logic of the prosthesis, then, because to do so would only set the stage for future imperial placeholders. Better, instead, to recognize how each citizen exists as a prosthesis for her fellow citizens. Roth's fictionalized POTUS is meant to inspire readers to rebuild their society on something other than blind submission to a disciplinary apparatus—to recycle the language of Ellison in *Invisible Man*, to speak *with* others instead of *on their behalf*.

We need not reduce the imperial presidency to an Ur-plot that cajoles witless subjects into either unproblematic conformity or apolitical release.[12] While I would concede that the power-hungry presidencies of recent memory have at times prevented citizens "from recognizing, remembering, imagining, and exercising the democratic work we can do ourselves," it is worth remembering that neither the unconscious nor depictions of the president function in a clear-cut fashion (Nelson 2008: 5). *Plot* exposes how centralized control always carries with it an accompanying drive to decentralization. The reader's position vis-à-vis the presidential icon is always-already elsewhere, dialectically shifting, interchangeably aligned with monarch as well as masses. As soon as her identification seems secure, she has already moved on. Simply put, the presidential unconscious reminds Roth's readers of what cannot be regimented. A phenomenon that was initially perceived as a repressed master-narrative—the imperial president as internalization of a big Other—reveals itself to be a phenomenon structured around its very opposite: the absence of final principle, or the "one idea." Fictional constructs of the imperial presidency offer not a stubborn obstacle to emancipatory politics, then, but a vital instrument to which readers must avail themselves in their respective journeys toward a more democratic future.

---

[12]Foucault himself resists such a static vision of the *dispositif*, a philosophical concept that he helped to insert into the public consciousness: "I do not seek to detect (. . .) the unitary spirit of an epoch, the general form of its consciousness" (Foucault 2011: 55).

Epilogue

George Saunders and Presidential Melancholia

George Saunders's acclaimed *Lincoln in the Bardo* confronts the president as a complicated figure in America's political imaginary.[1] Saunders's first novel takes place in the cemetery where Lincoln's son Willie has been recently interred. Here, Willie remains stuck in the titular bardo alongside a host of restless spirits that refuse to accept their condition and move into the proverbial light. The cemetery serves as a bardo in part because it is to this space that the historical Lincoln purportedly returned, night after night, to cradle his deceased son, unwilling to let him go. It is a space of suspended animation in which subjects remain caught between life and

---

[1]Throughout his career, Saunders has been interested in exploring how citizen-readers inscribe the unfulfilled promises of the president into their daily consciousness. Channeling the absurdity of Jonathan Swift, Saunders's earlier novel *The Brief and Frightening Reign of Phil* anticipates *Lincoln in the Bardo* by dwelling at length upon a variety of presidential figures. The first president of Outer Horner is "nostalgic" and "ineffectual"; his relentless reminiscences on the halcyon days devolve into chaos (Saunders 2005: 70). The second president, the titular Phil, reflects Carl Schmitt's account of *nomos*—the seizure of land and assets as the root of political power—an approach that mocks the lame political posturing that characterizes the novel's other presidents. The third president, Rick, defeats Phil by advocating for life's simple pleasures, such as coffee, sunsets, and walking in circles. Citing the Pleasure Index, he insists—in the vaguest sense possible—that his people "Learn to Enjoy" (120). And the final, uber-president manifests in the form of the majestic Creator, a sort of deus ex machina that clears the slate to form a New Horner. This uber-president—an entity that mirrors Saunders himself, as the author of the text—quilts together the structural pieces of the narrative and, in so doing, conjoins the story's threads concerning politics and art, power and desire. In effect, Saunders-as-president demonstrates how the fantasy structure that American society builds around the presidential figure echoes the inner logic of his narrative: it promises fulfillment, a happy ending, but it can only offer a reset—not resolution, but repetition. The first president evokes loss via ceaseless nostalgia; the second president remains driven by a bitter lack (his unrequited love); and the third president feeds upon the sheer anticipation of pleasures to come. Saunders's myriad executives thus reveal how the fantasy structure of nationhood orbits around a constitutional dissatisfaction: a melancholia that it cannot hope to cure.

death, fulfillment and dissatisfaction. When the elder Lincoln visits his son's corpse, Willie's spectral caregivers try to convince Honest Abe to release the boy from purgatory. In what follows, *Lincoln in the Bardo* explores a range of themes, including the nature of political desire, loss, and the ever-elusive concept of reconciliation.

Most significant still, the novel contemplates the presidency as an etching in the country's consciousness that promises impossible unity as well as redemptive dissolution. The stakes for Saunders's readers remain high because by coping with the complicated role of the chief magistrate, they can revive their democratic convictions and thus move beyond a relatively uncritical presidentialism (i.e., their prior reliance on executives as ideological lodestars).[2] Many Americans spend an inordinate amount of time waiting for a president to release them from their toilsome existence. Recognizing the impossibility of this deliverance, *Lincoln in the Bardo* contemplates the prospect of citizens finally addressing the futility of their interminable wait and learning to love one another without a presidential panacea.

To start, readers might ask why Saunders opted to focus on that exhausted national symbol, Abraham Lincoln, and not any of the other prominent visages with which American readers have grown familiar. Indeed, the sixteenth president has appeared frequently in the preceding chapters. A towering icon within the American consciousness, Lincoln seemingly stands alongside George Washington in rarefied air due in part to his function as a testament to the union's ability to endure a Civil War. Moreover, given Honest Abe's unusual relationship to issues of the afterlife and his family's highly publicized connection to spiritualism, Lincoln was an obvious subject with which Saunders could grapple with the questions that most concerned him. Because of these ethereal connections, Lincoln signifies an existential sense of splitting and reunification, of melancholy absence in dialogue with a stubborn faith in metaphysical Oneness. In his study of Lincoln in American memory, Merrill Peterson acknowledges "Father Abraham" as a martyred savior whose portrait hung in millions of American homes; at the same time, Peterson continues, "Lincoln was, and for some time would remain, a partial (hero). Lincoln might be a symbol of nationality, reborn and reinvigorated, but he had almost no place in the hearts of a large portion of his countrymen" (Peterson 1994: 29). While it may appear as though contemporary subjects have tamed the memory of Lincoln, *Lincoln in the Bardo* posits that the true source of Lincoln's appeal is not his status as a straightforward representative of national consensus, but his *partiality*, which is to say, his association with discord among the citizenry.

---

[2]For more on the subject of presidentialism, see Nelson (2008). Nelson contends that the unhealthy fixation of the presidency distracts citizens from engaging with one another democratically.

To borrow from contemporary parlance, for a broad array of readers, any select POTUS remains "not my president." *Lincoln in the Bardo* upholds that the presidency achieves its ends as an American symbol due neither to its coherence nor to its absolutism, but to its divisive underpinnings.

Said another way, Saunders's novel proposes that to consider the fictional president as a hagiographic constant is to miss the reality that a society populated by persons with variegated desires could never be reduced to an "indwelling network of relations of power and knowledge" (Copjec 1996: 6). Saunders's representation of the chief magistrate reveals that one's nation cannot be comprehended in a strictly positivist sense. As we have seen throughout this book, the president is a figuration that cannot be absorbed, calculated, or construed within a single articulable system; rather, the presidency marks a negative space, defined by surplus, lack, and dissatisfaction. Simply put, the commander in chief of American fiction does not reflect a totalized system that subsumes everything into itself, but an excess that endures in even the most moribund of fictions.

Yet what is to be gained by re-reading the fictional president as a sign of melancholia rather than, say, patriotic triumphalism? For one, to reinterpret the presidency along these lines empowers readers to escape from the president as a predetermination that holds citizens enthralled, and to address the myriad ways in which the imagined presidency caters to much more complex cravings. In her landmark study, Joan Copjec challenges analyses that would explain away the appeal of the executive as a static reference point for hegemonic discipline. Because, she contends, society "never stops realizing itself," and if readers can recognize the drive to negation that characterizes both poetic thought and political representation, "society ceases to be conceived as a dead structure, mappable on some flat surface" (Copjec 1996: 9). Accordingly, readers of *Lincoln in the Bardo* might revisit America's presidential obsession with a renewed focus on its attendant dissatisfactions (instead of its bald prescriptions). Saunders's reader could, in turn, keep alive her own fantasies for democratic change rather than foreclose her fantasies in compliance with the dictates of an imperial POTUS.

To address this conundrum, Saunders elected to structure his novel as a Socratic dialogue. With neither an omniscient narrator nor the absolutist qualities of free indirect discourse, Saunders's text defers a hegemonic vision and offers in its place disparate opinions on the sixteenth president. The novel places historical accounts of Lincoln into conflict; interpretations of the man as well as the myth remain hotly contested. Beyond fetishism or naïve sentimentalism, *Lincoln in the Bardo* upholds a constitutional ambivalence. Sigmund Freud argues that this sort of ambivalence is perhaps the primary symptom of melancholia: an internal struggle that eventually consumes the character of Lincoln as well as Saunders's reader. "Countless separate struggles are carried on over the object, in which hate and love contend with each other" (Freud 1957: 256). Saunders's text sustains a cult-like desire to move ever closer to the so-called real Lincoln—a national love object that will presumably envelop the reader in a state of womb-like serenity—even as Saunders's text acknowledges the hopelessness of this endeavor, or the vanity behind treating Lincoln in such an idolatrous fashion. Hardly a straightforward perpetuation of the mystique of America's original wholeness, the loathed as well as beloved Lincoln preserves America's Janus face. Lincoln exudes melancholia, and he must therefore be read in a melancholy fashion.

In short, despite America's refashioning of the rail-splitter as a granite monument to national unity, Saunders's Lincoln persists as a symptom of *democracy's incompleteness*. He reminds readers of the abiding need for civil antagonism. Put differently, even as the figure of Lincoln provides fodder for nationalist jubilation, he exists as a stranger marred by losses, personal as well as political. He can be a symbol of a nation reborn—but he can also be a lightning rod for discontented Americans. Fictional Lincoln instigates a core tension between the promise of a country congealed, that is to say, a constellation of individuals in total harmony with one another, and the gaping wound of a country forever divided. Saunders's Lincoln signals a pivot from monism to multiplicity. As the preceding chapters have demonstrated, American literature frequently plays with the presidency as a suture. These fictional portrayals do not ossify the chief magistrate into a final memorial, a fetish, or a sacred portrait denoting national synthesis.

Lincoln in the Bardo unveils how American culture has capitalized upon Lincoln's memory in knotty ways. John Bodnar remarks on the distinction between official and vernacular expressions of public memory:

> Official culture promotes a nationalistic, patriotic culture of the whole that mediates an assortment of vernacular interests. But seldom does it seek mediation at the expense of ascendancy. Vernacular culture, on the other hand, represents an array of specialized interests that are grounded in parts of the whole. They are diverse and changing and can be reformulated from time to time by the creation of new social units. (Bodnar 1993: 14)

While agents of the state frequently employ the image of Lincoln to wrangle a plurality of interest groups into something resembling a whole, other interest groups respond by poking holes in the grand narrative of these public monuments to attain their own desired outcomes—that is, to exploit time set aside for ritual for recreation, or to recycle national imagery for emergent political fights (recent examples include the Lincoln Project, a political alliance that utilizes Lincoln's image to resist Donald Trump's radical brand of conservatism). Bodnar charts the dynamic interaction of a "unitary conceptual framework" with the "inevitably multivocal" ends pursued by groups with variegated desires (16). The ceaseless friction between official and vernacular cultures manifests in the unsettled tenor of *Lincoln in the Bardo*: in one moment, the official Lincoln instigates a transcendent, albeit ill-defined, revelry based on the suppression of difference; in the very next moment, the vernacular Lincoln breaks into competing perspectives on the president's legacy. These perpetual (re)alignments maintain a distinctively political valence throughout the novel as white male ghosts move in and out of Lincoln's body, occupying his corporeal vessel as a convenient avatar through which to satisfy their longings, while marginalized groups, like the ghosts of the lower class or black specters, are excluded from the revelry and forced to maintain a distinctive relationship to the largesse of Lincoln. Against the backdrop of a presidentialism that enforces conformity, Saunders's narrative presents the chief magistrate as a source of counter-hegemonic imaginaries.

To underline this point, *Lincoln in the Bardo* muses on the rapture of presidential identification, presidential love, and the precarious promise of a cohesive national spirit. Let us briefly turn to Freud's meditation upon group psychology, in particular, his commentary on cultish reverence for "the chief." While the subject habitually indulges in exhausting fits of narcissism, the presence of a magnanimous chief allows her to project the perfection and fulfillment for which she has been internally striving outward, onto an icon—or, for Freud, an ego ideal.[3] For members of a gathering crowd, the appeal of this projection is that it loosens the intense inward scrutiny of the superego and enables the subject to escape, however tenuously, from the weight of her everyday existence. That is, the ego ideal enables the follower to suspend introspection in favor of rapturous connection with other, seemingly liberated followers of a president: "A number of individuals (. . .) put one and the same object in the place of their ego ideal and have consequently identified themselves with one another" (Freud 1999: 61). Uninhibited by the self-policing of the superego, which is now embodied in the ostensibly unblemished executive, followers shake loose the shackles of behavioral standards and stand figuratively stripped before the eyes of their all-loving leader. Freud postulated significant consequences of the abrogation of the ego experienced by members of a crowd in the presence of their charismatic leader. Most visibly, followers tend to regress to a child-like, "primitive" state (97). It remains entirely plausible that Saunders was thinking of Donald Trump's

---

[3]Lacan argues, "The point of the ego ideal is that from which the subject will see himself, as one says, as others see him . . . the Ideal point, capital I, placed somewhere in the Other, from which the Other sees me, in the form I like to be seen" (Lacan 1998: 268, author's emphasis). Much of *Lincoln in the Bardo* remains dedicated to this sort of Lacanian interaction—the desire to be seen by Lincoln and, at the same time, to see oneself *as if* Lincoln, which is to say, to project oneself into Lincoln's idealized position and then look back on the self approvingly.

Make America Great Again movement when he wrote of restless phantoms utilizing a president to achieve their own manic release from social standards.

Indeed, *Lincoln in the Bardo* remains replete with moments of manic release that stem from the satisfaction of "knowing" Lincoln (in multiple senses of the term). At the beginning of the novel, the Lincolns host a party that radiates plenitude. Standing before a veritable cornucopia at the White House, partygoers experience "transient moments of radiance" as they indulge in the presence of the larger-than-life Lincoln (Saunders 2018: 17). The first major interruption in the Lincoln's illusion of plenitude occurs when angels descend upon Willie's burial ground, with the declared mission of rescuing ghosts like Lincoln's son and hauling them up to heaven. You were denied satisfaction in life, the angels instruct the unfinished ghosts; now come with us and be satisfied. The liminal beings refer to what follows as "the matterlightblooming phenomenon" (96). Lincoln himself enters the graveyard as a sort of angel. Like the heavenly multitude sent to harvest souls, he apparently arrives to rescue his boy and release him from the bardo. Yet Lincoln quickly becomes a vehicle not just for Willie, but for all of the graveyard gatherers. They swarm into him, a "happy mob" (255). Saunders's novel reveals how the figure of the president acts as a receptacle for the masses. Lincoln embodies the "wills" and the "desires" and "raw life force" of the multiple crowd members (252). Having channeled themselves into Lincoln, and thus transformed him into their ego ideal, they are free to experience what they believe to be pure enjoyment: "What a pleasure it was, being in (Lincoln) together. United in common purpose . . . how good it felt, doing this together" (253). The previously dissatisfied ghosts achieve a degree of satisfaction as they undergo "serendipitous mass cohabitation" in the form of the president, and then emerge feeling "natural fullness" (256). By inhabiting Lincoln, the specters can "intermingle" and encounter each other in a manner that proves "intensely pleasurable" (171–72). Consequently, *Lincoln in the Bardo* confirms Freud's thesis that a group exploits a commander in chief to release its members from the agonies of the superego and thrust them into unfettered communion with their fellow followers. In the end, it appears as though Lincoln might terminate the novel's state of limbo and deliver a highly exciting sense of interconnected Oneness to individuals that have thus far gone stubbornly unfulfilled in their quotidian lives. To put an even finer point on it: the cemetery dwellers experience a presidential matterlightblooming phenomenon. Every four years, the typical American voter can "shed her attachment to her other, local identities, and (. . .) enter a new synchronic political order . . . every four years 'the people' still vote to become happy once again that a new man will try to keep the national-utopian images aligned, so that they seem inevitable and indivisible" (Berlant 1991: 216–17). The One, made indivisible through the vehicle of Lincoln.

Lincoln in the Bardo is a treatise on the seductive thrills of presidential love. Just like Willie, who awaits the return of a paternal entity that promises to give his son a purpose through deathless affections, Saunders's imagined reader (vicariously) anticipates a father figure whose devotions will offer her a magical release. Writing on Freud's theory of group psychology, Wendy Brown notes, "Individuals replace their natural rivalry toward one another with an identification achieved by loving the same object" (Brown 2005: 30). Lincoln's ghostly admirers flock to him, spellbound by the allure of eventual ecstasy: "A group becomes possible, then, when individuals put one and the same object in place of their ego ideal and consequently identify themselves with one another" (29). Lincoln provides dissatisfied phantoms with a love object that they can share by setting aside their intense rivalries. However, this elation lasts for only a limited time, because it invariably becomes clear that the love object remains remote and can never be fully integrated with the self. "We are bound to one another," Brown continues, "through our collective experience of *being in love with something that none of us can ever have*" (29, emphasis mine). Antagonism incessantly returns as the group must dissolve once more. This habitual fall of the chief—an event that American democracy attempts to systematize via scheduled election cycles, rendering the fall of the leader routine rather than unpredictable—exposes "the thinness of the membrane binding the nation" (32). Saunders's novel ultimately deflates the adoration expressed by Lincoln's fantastic flock as it exorcises members of the body politic from their mass cohabitation within the president's metaphorical body: "It had all been a flim-flam. A chimera. Mere wishful thinking" (Saunders 2018: 263).[4]

American literature proves particularly informative on this subject because it characteristically uses metaphors as devices for shaping popular attitudes toward authoritative concepts, like the presidency or, in a related register, the nation-state. A metaphor binds disparate concepts together and crafts an impression of wholeness. By compressing multiple beings as well as concepts into One, Lincoln-as-metaphor casts aside individualism at the altar of *e pluribus unum*: one God, one People. At another level, though, a metaphor creates poetic combinations without sacrificing the distinctiveness of individual components. Richard Boothby elucidates the emancipatory undercurrent of metaphors. A metaphor, he posits, holds the fixation of a singular image in tension with the power of multiple reference points, or a plenitude of associations. According to Boothby, metaphors reflect the "play of identity in difference—a conjunction that is simultaneously interpenetration and collision." Which is to say, metaphors free "previously hidden strata of meaning . . . from the domination of the primary signification . . . and awaken aspects of the terms they conjoin" (Boothby 2001: 126–27).

---

[4]Stephen Skowronek asserts, "The American presidency has proven itself most effective politically as an instrument of negation . . . clearing the way for something entirely new" (Skowronek 1997: 27).

Along these lines, the president-as-metaphor holds beings and concepts in conjunction with one another as an imperfect constellation, one that will not succumb to the urge for straightforward unity.[5] Due to its status as a metaphor, the president reminds the readers of *Lincoln in the Bardo*, however unconsciously, that they can never be corralled into complete consensus, and that they will inevitably diverge from oppressive restraints imposed by any singular presidential narrative.

Saunders's novel repeatedly exposes the presidency as a fetish, or, to borrow the metaphor employed by Philip Roth in the preceding chapter, a prosthesis. Even as Lincoln believes his dead son to be "intact and whole," he scolds himself: "It is not right to make a fetish of the thing . . . I am not stable . . . and the very buildings and monuments here are not stable . . . all alter, are altering, in every instant" (Saunders 2018: 244–46). Just as the monuments of Washington, D.C. remain partial objects—one particularly impressive monument resembles a nipple—the sixteenth president reveals his partiality, his incompleteness, as a national metaphor. He assumes the mantle of the nation's mourner in chief, thanks to a legacy defined through personal loss. In one example, the cornucopia of the opening feast at the White House contrasts sharply with the absence of joy in the Lincoln household when, during the party, Willie succumbs to illness. The figure of the president reminds Saunders's readers not of victory, then, but of loss—the loss of a bitter campaign; the loss of a vision for America that falls short; the endless losses, every day, that accumulate as a result of living in a liberal order (a model, it warrants noting, vocally championed by the historical Lincoln): "The many losses we must experience . . . (as) suffering, limited beings . . . inadequately endowed" (304). *Lincoln in the Bardo* contemplates the inadequate endowment of human beings—even the mightiest of presidents—to emphasize the dissatisfaction that truly drives American society. Ghosts enter the bardo at the cusp of pleasures that have gone unfulfilled. One phantom perishes a moment before consummating his marriage: "Our plan must be indefinitely delayed. What a frustration!" Another phantom commits suicide after resisting marriage, because he feels that marriage would "doom" him to a "dearth of fulfillment" (5, 25). Saunders's text juxtaposes this melancholy lack of satisfaction with the kind of manic release promised by an ecstatic, self-abrogating presidential love.

The unstable presence of POTUS should remind the cemetery crowd of its precarity, which is to say, a melancholic Lincoln ought to instill in members of the cemetery crowd a sense that they too exist as mere partial

---

[5] Jacques Lacan confesses: "Have you ever encountered whole beings? Perhaps it's an ideal. *I've* never seen any. *I'm* not whole. Neither are you. If we were whole, we would each be in our corners, whole, we wouldn't be here, together, trying to get ourselves into shape" (Lacan 1991: 243, author's emphasis).

beings, forever chasing what is forever absent. Like Lincoln himself, they are engaged in an unavailing search for wholeness. Saunders's presidency is not a reminder of the metaphysical glue that holds together a citizenry, but a mournful marker of what it actually means to be a citizen—namely, to compensate for one's own limitations by leaning on other citizens for support. As a result, "none were content" (82). If readers recognize Lincoln as a metaphor, a forced icon meant to hold together a loose coalition of imperfect individuals, and a compensation for something that is eternally missing (such as a fixed national essence), they will likely become a bit melancholy themselves. But, if Saunders's novel is to be believed, they will also be a bit wiser.

By disabusing the ecstatic follower of his belief in the value of self-obliteration at Lincoln's feet, Saunders's text asks its reader what it would entail to "grow up" and move beyond the confines of a self-indulgent presidentialism. Beneath its disenchantment with the presidency, *Lincoln in the Bardo* tells the tale of an intimate father–son relationship, which causes readers to contemplate the uniquely paternal dimensions of the office. In Freudian terms, the father figure interrupts a seamless impression of Oneness between child and mother. The presence of the father figure reveals that the child's treatment of the mother as a libidinous object is strictly prohibited. It nearly goes without saying that Lincoln serves as a prominent paternal metaphor in American history; many Americans consider him to be a Founding Father (*avant la lettre*, of course). For Freud, the father figure is not a sign of *uniformity* within the family. Instead, the father figure signifies a *discontinuity*: the chasm that separates the child from a state of fullness, utopia, the mother's womb.[6] Correspondingly, *Lincoln in the Bardo* contends that Americans can only mature beyond a naïve belief in presidentialism if they can first transcend the delusions of total release and conclusive contentment that accompany the Lincoln mythos. While characters in Saunders's novel wish to flee from the bardo, the narrative concludes that it is within this liminal space that American citizens must learn to bide their time. This significant paradigm shift encourages readers to dismantle fantasies of the chief magistrate as a black-and-white meeting place between the hegemonic state and the interpellated subject. Saunders, therefore, infused the presidency with the ambivalence of the bardo. Willie becomes enlightened due to his father's failure as a panacea; Saunders's reader must do the same. This melancholy state equips the reader for a future in which she might recognize her unhealthy relationship with the

---

[6]"The Name-of-the-Father is equally the No-of-the-Father. This 'no' (. . .) obliges (the child) to desire in accordance with the law of signifiers . . . abandoning the dream of complete fulfillment, and limiting oneself to objects that are accepted as possible objects of desire within the symbolic system" (Van Haute 2001: 201).

nation's executives, and learn to cope with the trials and tribulations of coexisting with her fellow wanderers.

Gazing upon this melancholy image of Lincoln, one could inquire into what Saunders's presidential fiction says about the contemporary moment, or the future of American politics. In recent memory, George W. Bush claimed to be a unilateral decider; Barack Obama postured as the meritocratic manager in whom all hope resided; Trump generally acted without sanction from the electorate. Twenty-first century presidents in particular have evoked a sense of absolutism, of wholeness, that has arguably been deleterious to the foundations of American democracy. Citizens too eagerly await the release of the presidential matterlightblooming phenomenon. In his study of Trump, Alain Badiou blames global capitalism for repressing the necessary divisions of an open society: "When there is only one path, only one strategic orientation, politics, in reality, disappears . . . the return of politics is the return to the existence of a fundamental choice . . . the return to the real Two, beyond the deceptive One" (Badiou 2019: 25). According to Badiou's logic, Americans must move away from treating the president as a fetish and reframe the figure as a metaphor, a nucleus around which distinctive subjects orbit themselves, a textual icon that loosely associates beings and ideas without melding them into a state of cult-like unity. Nothing less than the fate of democracy may be at stake in the novel's proposed passing "from One to Two" (48). Said another way, against his posthumous alignment with national reconciliation, it is Lincoln's status as the marker of a tremendous rift in the political imagination (Civil War) that his melancholy memory continues to inspire democratic sensibilities.

By privileging the Two over the One, *Lincoln in the Bardo* reveals the internally conflicted nature of the presidency. Comprised of citations from Lincoln historians both real and imagined, Saunders's text "makes a bid for the kind of democratic multivocal quality of the American novel at its finest" (Sandler n.p.). Some citizens perceive Lincoln to be "the weakest man who has ever been elected"; other spectral citizens adore him and argue that he alone can transform them into a cohesive unit (Saunders 2018: 233). Spectators are moved by their intimate encounters with Lincoln to persist in their struggles with one another: "The two might well fight on into eternity" (321). The fictional president invites restless spirits to keep disagreeing, and to avoid, in the process, the authoritarian creep that Lincoln himself could not keep at bay during his time in office (recall, for example, the historical Lincoln's infamous suspension of *habeas corpus*). Because Saunders's story leaves a host of issues unresolved, it promotes uncertainty as well as open-endedness. This lack of closure may at first seem tragic—and to some extent, it is. The novel conjures as its closing image Lincoln riding away from the cemetery in a state of abject despair at the irreversible loss of his son. While so many of the text's manic ghosts have been pursuing their own triumphant release through Lincoln, the book holds the reader's gaze at last upon what

Freud has called "the open wound" (Freud 1957: 253). As their celebrated president fades from view, Saunders's audience members, like Willie, might feel disoriented, unable to recognize precisely what it is they have lost. Watching Honest Abe's melancholy march over the horizon, readers glimpse the flip side of Lincoln's official position in American memory. Saunders's novel leaves its readers without a presidential love object, and with only their solitary ego to comfort them. In other words, it leaves its readers to confront the cold reality of their prior obsession with the president as well as a sense of nothingness—the void that had been previously concealed by over-inflated images of Lincoln. If readers are to move on, like obstinate spirits, from their earlier hang-ups on the subject of presidentialism, and discover a better-adjusted mode of citizenship, they must avoid renewing their fixation on authority figures. Saunders's text ultimately wonders if American readers could ever escape from their long-standing dependence on the presidency.

However, it would be a mistake to interpret *Lincoln in the Bardo* as a book that advocates for premature resolution. It wishes, instead, that its readers could come to grips with loss, with the "object-relationship shattered," and thereby achieve the wisdom of the melancholic subject (Freud 1957: 249). As the father figure slouches toward some distant Bethlehem, Saunders's text gestures obliquely at a different kind of presidential love. The novel invites readers to ask: what if the metaphor of the presidency could compel citizens to see the world from the point of view of Two and not One? What if the metaphor of the president promoted something like love, or perhaps just fraternity, between partisans? What if POTUS could serve as a common site within the public imagination through which partisans might imagine the world differently, together?[7]

Lincoln does not signify the end of civil strife; instead, he trumpets its enduring necessity. Coming to terms with her previous need for a presidential panacea, Saunders's reader learns invaluable lessons about herself as well as her neighbors. She could yet prove steadfast in her pursuit of a better tomorrow, in which presidential love does not involve erasing interpersonal differences in favor of a unified sense of national identity but cherishing these differences and holding them open as a genuine expression of love for—or,

---

[7]Alain Badiou adamantly segregates the field of politics from love on the grounds that love of Party, or a supreme leader, only ever affirms blind fetishism. Yet what happens when one reads the fictional president as a piece of art, or, more appropriate still, as a symbolic child? For Badiou, the arrival of a child is not the premature blending of Two back into One, or, the melting of a couple into a singular unit; rather, the child's arrival marks a reaffirmation, a redeclaration, of powerful bonds that exist between two subjects who remain different from one another and yet interlocked through constructions of their shared love. POTUS can be framed as the byproduct of a union that involves reconciliation as well as a preservation of otherness, of difference.

if one prefers, fraternity with—one's neighbors.[8] American democracy, after all, is not a story of self-dissolution, jubilant release, or utopian conformity. American democracy is a story of the difficult, melancholy work of different beings struggling to exist in concert. I would argue that many fictional presidents help to facilitate a more mature notion of love between otherwise estranged citizens.

Thankfully, most Americans still languish in the bardo. In a successful democracy, there can be no final say, since social forms are eternally under revision and individuals need not agree on everything, including who gets to be president. Mercifully so: "What differentiates democracy from other political forms of society is the legitimization of conflict and the refusal to eliminate it through the establishment of an authoritarian harmonious order" (Stavrakakis 1999: 111). In effect, the constant splitting of perspectives on Lincoln makes him a quintessentially democratic idol. Saunders's novel provokes this persistent splitting through its depiction of Lincoln as "a sculpture on the theme of Loss" (Saunders 2018: 145). The fictional Lincoln is not a nation made whole; he marks the *impossibility* of that wholeness. That is to say, Lincoln perpetually reopens holes within the political imaginary. If readers attend to how fictional presidents preserve the loss of a homogenized collective essence, they might avoid becoming "uncritically enthralled" by the executive *du jour* (Brown 2005: 28). As a textual figure that instigates divergent interpretations, POTUS provides an imaginary site at which the One unceasingly ruptures into Two. Defying the illusion of consensus proffered by global capitalists, as well as the effortless consensus advanced by fascist figureheads, *Lincoln in the Bardo* transposes the schism of Civil War into a less violent register, one that maintains disagreement without succumbing to anarchy or endless military conquest. To re-read the chief magistrate as a literary text is, therefore, to scrutinize why their elected sovereigns have long beguiled American citizens. As Saunders's work makes clear, our melancholy engagement with presidential fictions empowers us to stop trying to abscond from our liminal existence and to embrace dissatisfaction as one of democracy's greatest gifts.

---

[8]William Corlett describes a "curious doubleness" that pervades the sixteenth president's rhetoric. In his public addresses, Lincoln attempted to convey the solidity of political form without denying the "other" of that form: "flux, madness, and accident." Corlett argues that Lincoln balanced the illusion of finality in political principle with "the pleasure of pathos," or, the inherently unfinished work of fantasy (Corlett 1989: 93).

REFERENCES

Abbott, J. (2017). *Washington: American History Volume VIII*. CreateSpace Independent Publishing.

Adams, H. (2008). *Democracy: An American Novel*. Penguin Classics.

Agamben, G. (1995). *Homo Sacer: Sovereign Power and Bare Life*. Trans. Daniel Heller-Roazen. Stanford University Press.

Agamben, G. (2005). *State of Exception*. Trans. Kevin Attell. University of Chicago Press.

Agamben, G. (2009). *"What is an Apparatus?" And Other Essays*. Trans. David Kiski and Stefan Pedatella. Stanford University Press.

Alcott, L. (1875). *Eight Cousins, or, the Aunt Hill*. Sampson Low, Marston, Low, & Searle.

Alger, H. (1883). *The Backwoods Boy: Or, the Boyhood and Manhood of Abraham Lincoln*. David McKay.

Alger, H. (2018). *From Canal Boy to President: The Boyhood and Manhood of James A. Garfield*. University of Akron Press.

Altman, R. (2009). A Semantic/Syntactic Approach to Film Genre. In Leo Braudy and Marshall Cohen (Eds.), *Film Theory & Criticism: Seventh Edition* (pp. 552–564). Oxford University Press.

Altschuler, G. and Blumin, S. (2001). *Rude Republic: Americans and their Politics in the Nineteenth Century: Reprint Edition*. Princeton University Press.

Anderegg, M. (2015). *Lincoln and Shakespeare*. University of Kansas Press.

Anzaldua, G. (2012). *Borderlands La Frontera: The New Mestiza –25th Anniversary Edition*. Aunt Lute Books.

Arbuthnot, M. (1953). Books for Children. *Elementary English, 30*(5), 316–320. Retrieved August 26, 2021, from http://www.jstor.org/stable/41384090

Arendt, H. (1994). *The Origins of Totalitarianism: New Edition*. Harvest Books.

Badiou, A. (2012). *In Praise of Love*. Trans. Peter Bush. The New Press.

Badiou, A. (2019). *Trump*. Polity.

Bailey, D. (1999). *American Nightmares: The Haunted House Formula in American Popular Fiction*. University of Wisconsin Press.

Balestier, W. (2017). *James G. Blaine: A Sketch of His Life, With a Brief Record of the Life of John A. Logan*. Forgotten Books.

Barthes, R. (2010). *A Lover's Discourse – Fragments: Translated Edition*. Trans. Richard Howard. Hill and Wang.

Basler, R. (1985). Lincoln and American Writers. *Journal of the Abraham Lincoln Association, 7*(1), 6–17.

Baudrillard, J. (1988). *Forget Foucault*. Semiotext(e).

Becker, G. (1956). James Fenimore Cooper and American Democracy. *College English*, 17(6), 325-334. JSTOR. Retrieved May 7, 2021 www.jstor.org/stable /372369.

Bell, M. (1993). *The Problem of American Realism: Studies in the Cultural History of a Literary Idea*. University of Chicago Press.

Benjamin, W. (1994). Left-Wing Melancholy. In Anton Kaes and Martin Jay, et. al. (Eds.), *The Weimar Republic Sourcebook* (pp. 304-307). University of California Press.

Berlant, L. (1991). *The Anatomy of National Fantasy: Hawthorne, Utopia, and Everyday Life*. University of Chicago Press.

Berthoff, W. (1965). *The Ferment of Realism: American Literature 1884-1919*. Free Press.

Bewley, M. (1959). *The Eccentric Design: Form in the Classic American Novel*. Chatto & Windus Press.

Bloom, H. (1992). The Central Man: On Gore Vidal's *Lincoln*. In Jay Parini (Ed.), *Gore Vidal: Writer Against the Grain* (pp. 221-230). Columbia University Press.

Blouin, M. (2021). *Literary Interventions in the Campaign Biography*. Routledge.

Bodnar, J. (1993). *Remaking America: Public Memory, Commemoration, and Patriotism in the Twentieth Century*. Princeton University Press.

Bolingbroke, H. (1970). Excerpt from *The Idea of a Patriot King*. In Isaac Kramnick (Ed.), *Bolingbroke Political Writings* (pp. 43-80). Meredith Corporation.

Bonner, C. (2020). *Remaking the Republic: Black Politics and the Creation of American Citizenship*. University of Pennsylvania Press.

Boothby, R. (2001). *Freud as Philosopher: Metapsychology After Lacan*. Routledge.

Brackenridge, H. (2020). *Modern Chivalry: Abridged*. Library of Early American Literature.

Bronfen, E. (1992). *Over Her Dead Body: Death, Femininity and the Aesthetic*. Manchester University Press.

Brown, C.B. (2006). *Edgar Huntly; Or, Memoirs of a Sleepwalker with Related Texts*. Hackett Publishing.

Brown, C.B. (2009). *Wieland; Or, The Transformation with Related Texts*. Hackett Publishing.

Brown, R. (1994). *Dolley*. Bantam.

Brown, W. (2005). *Edgework: Critical Essays on Knowledge and Politics*. Princeton University Press.

Brown, W. (2002). Moralism as Antipolitics. In Russ Castronovo and Dana D. Nelson (Eds.), *Materializing Democracy: Toward a Revitalized Cultural Politics* (pp. 368-393). Duke University Press.

Brown, W. (1999). Resisting Left Melancholy. *boundary 2*, 26(3), 19-27. https://www.jstor.org/stable.303736.

Brown, W.W. (2003). *Clotel: or, The President's Daughter*. Penguin Classics.

Bruhm, S. (1994). *Gothic Bodies: The Politics of Pain in Romantic Fiction*. University of Pennsylvania Press.

Bryan, W. (1970). *George Washington in American literature, 1775-1865*. Greenwood Press.

Burke, E. (2009). *Reflections on the Revolution in France*. Oxford University Press.

Butler, J. (2002). Doubting Love. In James Harmon (Ed.), *Take My Advice: Letters to the Next Generation from People Who Know a Thing or Two* (pp. 62–66). Simon & Schuster.

Butler, J. (1997). *The Psychic Life of Power: Theories of Subjection.* Stanford University Press.

Casper, S. (1999). *Constructing American Lives: Biography and Culture in Nineteenth-Century America.* University of North Carolina Press.

Castronovo, R. (1996). *Fathering the Nation: American Genealogies of Slavery and Freedom.* University of California Press.

Castronovo, R. (2001). *Necro Citizenship: Death, Eroticism, and the Public Sphere in the Nineteenth-Century United States.* Duke University Press.

Cawelti, J. (1965). *Apostles of the Self-made Man.* University of Chicago Press.

Cawelti, J. (1961). Portrait of the Newsboy as a Young Man: Some Remarks on the Alger Stories. *The Wisconsin Magazine of History,* 45(2), 79–83. Retrieved August 26, 2021, from http://www.jstor.org/stable/4633711

Chakkalakal, T. (2012). *Novel Bondage: Slavery, Marriage, and Freedom in Nineteenth-Century America.* University of Illinois Press.

Christenson, D. and Kriner, D. (2020). *The Myth of the Imperial Presidency: How Public Opinion Checks the Unilateral Executive.* University of Chicago Press.

Clancy, T. (1997). *Executive Orders: A Jack Ryan Novel.* Berkley Books.

Clark, B. (2005). *Kiddie Lit: The Cultural Construction of Children's Literature in America.* Johns Hopkins University Press.

Clark, M. (2003). *Mount Vernon Love Story: Illustrated Edition.* Pocket Books.

Conway, M. (1889). *Omitted Chapters of History Disclosed in the Life and Papers of Edmund Randolph Governor of Virginia, First Attorney-general United States, Secretary of State.* G.P. Putnam's Sons.

Cooper, J. (1838). *Home as Found.* Lea and Blanchard Press.

Cooper, J. (1982). *The Last of the Mohicans.* Bantam Press.

Cooper, J. (1834). *A Letter to His Countrymen.* John Wiley.

Cooper, J. (1963). *Notions of the Americans: Picked Up by a Travelling Bachelor Vol. II.* Frederick Ungar Press.

Cooper, J. (1990). The Pilot. In Blake Nevin (Ed.), *James Fenimore Cooper: "The Pilot" and "The Red Rover"* (pp. 1–423). Library of America.

Cooper, J. (1988). *The Pioneers.* Penguin Classics.

Cooper, J. (1950). *The Prairie.* Rinehart.

Cooper, J. (1997). *The Spy.* Penguin Classics.

Copjec, J. (1996). *Read My Desire: Lacan Against the Historicists.* MIT Press.

Corlett, W. (1989). *Community Without Unity: A Politics of Derridian Extravagance.* Duke University Press.

Corwin, E. (1948). *The President: Office and Powers, Third Edition.* NYU Press.

Cowie, A. (1948). *The Rise of the American Novel.* American Book Company.

Crawford, T.H. (1991). Cooper's Spy and the Theater of Honor. *American Literature,* 63(3), 405–419. JSTOR. Retrieved May 5, 2021 from www.jstor.org /stable/2927240.

Crawford, T.H. (1994). Images of Authority, Strategies of Control: Cooper, Weems, and George Washington. *South Central Review,* 11(1), 61–74. JSTOR. Retrieved May 5, 2021 from www.jstor.org/stable/3190268.

Crick, B. (2002). *Democracy: A Very Short Introduction*. Oxford University Press.

Crouch, J., et al. (2020). *The Unitary Executive Theory: A Danger to Constitutional Government*. University Press of Kansas.

Curti, M. (1937). Dime Novels and the American Tradition. *Yale Review, XXVI*, 761–778. Retrieved from August 15, 2021.

Dekker, G. and McWilliams, J. (1973). Introduction. In George Dekker and John P. McWilliams (Eds.), *Fenimore Cooper: The Critical Heritage* (pp. 1–54). Routledge.

Denning, M. (1998). *Mechanic Accents: Dime Novels and Working Class Culture in America*. Verso.

Derrida, J. (2011). *The Beast and the Sovereign: Volume One*. Trans. Geoffrey Bennington. University of Chicago Press.

Derrida, J. (1997). *The Politics of Friendship*. Trans. George Collins. Verso.

De Tocqueville, A. (1840). *Democracy in America, Part the Second*. Trans. Henry Reeve. J. & H.G. Langley.

Didi-Huberman, G. (2016). To Render Sensible. In Bruno Bosteels (Ed.), *What is a People?* (pp. 65–77). Columbia University Press.

Dipple, E. (2021). *The Unresolvable Plot: Reading Contemporary Fiction – Routledge Library Edition*. Routledge.

Dorsey, P. (1995). De-authorizing Slavery: Realism in Stowe's *Uncle Tom's Cabin* and Brown's *Clotel*. *ESQ: A Journal of the American Renaissance, 41*(4), 257–288. Retrieved from May 17, 2021.

Dos Passos, J. (1949). *The Grand Design*. Houghton Mifflin.

Du Cille, A. (2000). "Where in the World is William Wells Brown?: Thomas Jefferson, Sally Hemings, and the DNA of African-American Literary History." *American Literary History, 12*(3), 443–462. Retrieved May 17, 2021, from https://academic.oup.com/alh/article-abstract/12/3/443/129852?redirectedFrom=PDF

Duffey, B. (1953). Hamlin Garland's "Decline" from Realism. *American Literature, 25*(1), 69–74. doi:10.2307/2921607

Ellis, E. (1901). *From Tent to White House: Or, How a Poor Boy Became President*. Street & Smith.

Ellis, E. (2016). *The Steam Man of the Prairies*. Dover.

Ellison, R. (1995). *Invisible Man: Second Vintage Edition*. Vintage.

Emerson, D. (2015). George Lippard's The Quaker City: Disjointed Text, Dismembered Bodies, Regenerated Democracy. *Nineteenth-Century Literature, 70*(1), 102–131. doi:10.1525/ncl.2015.70.1.102.

Emerson, R.W. (1983a). Uses of Great Men. In Joel Porte (Ed.), *Ralph Waldo Emerson: Essays and Lectures* (pp. 615–761). Library Classics.

Emerson, R.W. (1983b). Uses of Great Men. In Joel Porte (Ed.), *Ralph Waldo Emerson: Essays & Lectures* (pp. 615–632). Library of America.

Ernest, J. (2009). *Chaotic Justice: Rethinking African American Literary History*. University of North Carolina Press.

Evans, K. (2016). *Mr. President*. Katy Evans.

Feldman, E. (2003). *Lucy*. W.W. Norton & Co.

Felman, S. (1993). *What Does a Woman Want? Reading and Sexual Difference*. Johns Hopkins University Press.

Fielding, S., et. al. (2020). *The Churchill Myths*. Oxford University Press.

Fiore, J. (1953). Horatio Alger, Jr., as a Lincoln Biographer. *Journal of the Illinois State Historical Society (1908-1984)*, 46(3), 247–253. Retrieved August 26, 2021, from http://www.jstor.org/stable/40189310

Fisher, M. (2021). *Postcapitalist Desire: The Final Lectures*. Repeater.

Foucault, M. (2011). Politics and the Study of Discourse. In G. Burchell et. al. (Eds.), *The Foucault Effect: Studies in Governmentality* (pp. 53–73). University of Chicago Press.

Fletcher, D. and Feros, K. (2000). "Live from Golgotha": Gore Vidal and the Problem of Satiric Reinscription. *Mosaic: An Interdisciplinary Critical Journal*, 33(1), 133–144. Retrieved May 26, 2021, from http://www.jstor.org/stable/44030575

Frank, M. (2005). *How to Be an Intellectual in the Age of TV: The Lessons of Gore Vidal*. Duke University Press.

Freud, S. (1999). *Group Psychology and the Analysis of the Ego*. W.W. Norton & Co.

Freud, S. (1957). Mourning and Melancholia. In James Strachey (Ed.), *The Standard Edition of the Complete Psychological Works of Sigmund Freud: Vol XIV* (pp. 243–258). Hogarth Press.

Freud, S. (1925). The Uncanny. In Ernest Jones (Ed.), *Collected Papers: Volume IV* (pp. 368–408). The International Psychoanalytic Library.

Frye, K. (2009). The Case against Whiteness in William Wells Brown's "Clotel". *The Mississippi Quarterly*, 62(4), 527–540. Retrieved May 17, 2021, from http://www.jstor.org/stable/26477255

Gallagher, C. and Greenblatt, S. (2001). *Practicing New Historicism*. University of Chicago Press.

Garland, H. (1894). *Crumbling Idols: Twelve Essays on Art Dealing Chiefly with Literature, Painting and The Drama*. Stone and Kimball.

Garland, H. (1891). Up the Coulee: A Story of Wisconsin. In *Main-Travelled Roads*. (pp. 67–131). Harper & Brothers.

Garland, H. (2015). *Ulysses S. Grant, His Life and Character*. CreateSpace Independent Publishing

Gauchet, M. (2016). Toqueville, America, and Us: On the Genesis of Democratic Societies. *The Tocueville Review*, 37(2), 172–224.

Goodrich, S. (1842). *The Life of George Washington*. Thomas, Cowperthwait & Co.

Green, M. (1979). *Dreams of Adventure, Deeds of Empire*. Basic Books.

Green, M. (1991). *Seven Types of Adventure Tale: An Etiology of a Major Genre*. Penn State University Press.

Greenberg, D. (2003). *Nixon's Shadow: The History of an Image*. W.W. Norton & Co.

Haggerty, G. (1989). *Gothic Fiction/Gothic Form*. The Pennsylvania State University Press.

Hamilton, A., et al. (1987). *The Federalist Papers*. Ed. Isaac Kramnick. Penguin Classics.

Hamilton, A. and Madison, J. (2007). *The Pacificus-Helvidius Debates of 1793 - 94: Toward the Completion of the American Founding*. Ed. Morton J. Frisch. Liberty Fund.

Han, B. (2017). *The Agony of Eros*. Trans. Erik Butler. MIT Press.

Harris, W. (2005). *E Pluribus Unum: Nineteenth-Century American Literature and the Constitutional Paradox*. University of Iowa Press.

Heilbrun, C. (1981, Febuary 26). Hers. *The New York Times*. https://www.nytimes.com/1981/02/26/garden/hers-by-carolyn-gheilbrun.html

Hofstadter, R. (2008). *The Paranoid Style in American Politics: First Vintage Edition*. Vintage Books.

Horrocks, T. (2014). *Lincoln's Campaign Biographies*. Southern Illinois University Press.

Horvat, S. (2015). *The Radicality of Love*. Polity.

Howe, D. (2007). *What Hath God Wrought: The Transformation of America, 1815 – 1848*. Oxford University Press.

Hunter, M. (1978, December 14). Ford Says that Congress Hobbles President by Foreign Policy Action. *The New York Times*. Section A, Page 22.

Hurst, F. (1928). *A President is Born*. Harper & Bros.

Jackson, H. (2019). *American Radicals: How Nineteenth Century Protest Shaped the Nation*. Crown.

James, H. (2017). *The Americans*. Dover Publications.

Jameson, F. (2015). *The Antinomies of Realism*. Verso.

Jefferson, T. (1999). *Notes on the State of Virginia*. Penguin.

Johnson, L.B. (1966, June 30). Two Threats to World Peace - Remarks in Omaha on the Occasion of the Sending of the Five-Millionth Ton of Grain to India. https://www.presidency.ucsb.edu/documents/two-threats-world-peace-remarks-omaha-the-occasion-the-sending-the-five-millionth-ton.

Jordan, A. (1948). *From Rollo to Tom Sawyer and Other Papers*. Horn Books.

Kamble, J. (2012). Patriotism, Passion, and PTSD: The Critique of War in Popular Romance Fiction. In Sarah Frantz and Eric Selinger (Eds.), *New Approaches to Popular Romance Fiction* (pp. 153–163). McFarland & Co.

Kantorowicz, E. (2016). *The King's Two Bodies: A Study in Medieval Political Theology: Illustrated Edition*. Princeton University Press.

Kaplan, A. (1992). *The Social Construction of American Realism*. University of Chicago Press.

Kazin, A. (1942). *On Native Grounds: An Interpretation of Modern American Prose*. Harvest Books.

Ketcham, R. (1984). *Presidents Above Party: The First American Presidency, 1789 – 1829*. University of North Carolina Press.

King, S. (1979). *The Dead Zone*. Gallery Books.

Koerner, J. (1954, November). Hamlin Garland's "Decline from Realism." *American Literature*, 26(3), 427–432.

Kristeva, J. (1982). *Powers of Horror: An Essay on Abjection*. Columbia University Press.

Kuklick, B. (1988). *The Good Ruler: From Herbert Hoover to Richard Nixon*. Rutgers University Press.

Lacan, J. (1998). *The Seminar of Jacques Lacan: The Four Fundamental Concepts of Psychoanalysis (Book XI)*. Trans. Jacques-Alain Miller. W.W. Norton & Co.

Lacan, J. (1991). *The Seminar of Jacques Lacan: The Ego in Freud's Theory and in the Technique of Psychoanalysis, 1954–1955 (Book II)*. Trans. Sylvana Torosselli. W.W. Norton & Co.

Lapham, L. (1993). *The Wish for Kings: Democracy at Bay*. Grove Press.

Le Bon, G. (2002). *The Crowd: A Study of the Popular Mind*. Dover.

Lefort, C. (2006). The Permanence of the Theologico-Political? In Henri De Vries and Lawrence Sullivan (Eds.), *Political Theologies: Public Religions in a Post-Secular World* (pp. 148–187). Fordham University Press.

Lefort, C. (2000). *Writing: The Political Test*. Trans. David Ames Curtis. Duke University Press.

Levithan, D. (2006). *Wide Awake*. Alfred A. Knopf.

Lewis, R. (1985). Literary Conventions in the Novels of William Wells Brown. *CLA Journal, 29*(2), 129–156. Retrieved May 17, 2021, from http://www.jstor .org/stable/44322383

Lewis, S. (2014). *It Can't Happen Here: Reprint Edition*. Signet Classics.

Lhamon, W. (1976). Horatio Alger and American Modernism: The One-Dimensional Social Formula. *American Studies, 17*(2), 11–27. Retrieved August 26, 2021, from http://www.jstor.org/stable/40641216

Lippard, G. (1851). *The White Banner: Adonai, the Pilgrim of Eternity*, Vol. 1, 9–99. George Lippard.

Lippard, G. (1846). *Blanche of Brandywine: Or, September the Eleventh, 1777. A Romance, Combining the Poetry, Legend, and History of the Battle of Brandywine*. G.B. Zieber & Company.

Lippard, G. (2007). *Washington and His Generals, "1776": The Legends of the American Revolution*. Pennsylvania State University Press.

Lipsitz, G. (1998). *The Possessive Investment in Whiteness: How White People Profit from Identity Politics*. Temple University Press.

Locke, J. (1980). *Second Treatise of Government*. Ed. C.B. Macpherson. Hackett Publishing.

Longmore, P. (1999). *The Invention of George Washington*. University of Virginia Press.

Looby, C. (2015). Lippard in Part(s): Seriality and Secrecy in The Quaker City. *Nineteenth-Century Literature, 70*(1), 1–35. doi:10.1525/ncl.2015.70.1.1.

Lowi, T. (1985). *The Personal President: Power Invested, Promise Unfulfilled*. Cornell University Press.

Luck, C. (2014). *The Body of Property: Antebellum American Fiction and the Phenomenology of Possession*. Fordham University Press.

Machiavelli, N. (2007). The Prince. In Peter Constantine (Ed.), *The Essential Writings of Machiavelli* (pp. 3–101). The Modern Library.

Madera, J. (2015). *Black Atlas: Geography and Flow in Nineteenth-Century African American Literature*. Duke University Press.

Madison, J. (1836). *The Debates in the Several State Conventions on the Adoption of the Federal Constitution As Recommended by the General Convention at Philadelphia in 1787. Together with the Journal of the Federal Convention, Luther Martin's Letter, Yates's Minutes, Congressional Opinions, Virginia and Kentucky Resolutions of '98-'99, and Other Illustrations of the Constitution · Volume 2 – Second Edition*. Ed. Jonathan Elliot. Editor.

Magistrale, T. and Blouin, M.J. *Stephen King and American History*. Routledge.

Mailer, N. (2014). "When I Implied": Letter from Normal Mailer to Emile Capouya, May 26, 1962. In J. Michael Lennon (Ed.), *Selected Letters of Norman Mailer* (pp. 294–296). Random House.

Mandel, J. (1973). Dream and Imagination in Shakespeare. *Shakespeare Quarterly*, 24(1), 61–68. doi:10.2307/2868739

McCann, S. (2008). *A Pinnacle of Feeling: American Literature and Presidential Government*. Princeton University Press.

McConnell, M. (2020). *The President Who Would Not Be King: Executive Power under the Constitution*. Princeton University Press.

McCullough, J. (1978). *Hamlin Garland*. Twayne Publishers.

McGowan, T. (2009, Spring). The Exceptional Darkness of *The Dark Knight*. *Jump Cut, 51*. Retrieved May 6, 2021, from https://www.ejumpcut.org/archive/jc51 .2009/darkKnightKant/text.html

McGowan, T. (2020, April 30). State of Emergency? Bring It On!. Retrieved from http://thephilosophicalsalon.com/state-of-emergency-bring-it-on/

McLuhan, M. (1964). *Understanding Media: The Extensions of Man*. McGraw-Hill.

McWilliams, J. (1972). *Political Justice in a Republic: James Fenimore Cooper's America*. Belknap Press.

Melville, H. (1973). Authentic Anecdotes of "Old Zack." Ed. Kenneth Starosciak. Bookseller and Publisher.

Melville, H. (1892). *Moby-Dick*. Dana Estes & Co.

Mencken, H.L. (1926). *Notes on Democracy*. Jonathan Cape.

Michelet, J. (1967). *History of the French Revolution*. Trans. Charles Cocks. University of Chicago Press.

Miller, C. (1966). Hamlin Garland's Retreat from Realism. *Western American Literature*, 1(2), 119–129. Retrieved August 27, 2021, from http://www.jstor.org /stable/43017314

Milton, H. (1967). *The President is Missing!* Barner Books.

Modleski, T. (2007). *Loving with a Vengeance: Mass Produced Fantasies for Women – Second Edition*. Routledge.

Morone, J. (1998). *The Democratic Wish: Popular Participation and the Limits of American Government*. Yale University Press.

Mott, F. (1947). *Golden Multitudes: The Story of Best Sellers in the United States*. Macmillan Co.

Mouffe, C. (2013). *Agonistics: Thinking the World Politically*. Verso.

Mouffe, C. (2006). *The Return of the Political*. Verso.

Mussell, K. (1984). *Fantasy and Reconciliation: Contemporary Formulas of Women's Romance Fiction*. Greenwood Press.

Nabers, D. (2005). The Problem of Revolution in the Age of Slavery: Clotel, Fiction, and the Government of Man. *Representations*, 91(1), 84–108. doi:10.1525/rep.2005.91.1.84

Nackenoff, C. (1994). *The Fictional Republic: Horatio Alger and American Political Discourse*. Oxford University Press.

Nancy, J. (1991). *The Inoperative Community*. Trans. Peter Connor et. al. The University of Minnesota Press.

Neilson, H. (1997). Jack's Ghost: Reappearances of John F. Kennedy in the Work of Gore Vidal and Norman Mailer. *American Studies International*, 35(3), 23–41. Retrieved May 26, 2021, from http://www.jstor.org/stable/41279514

Nelson, D. (2008). *Bad for Democracy: How the Presidency Undermines the Power of the People*. University of Minnesota Press.

Newlin, K. (2008). *Hamlin Garland: A Life*. University of Nebraska Press.

Nichols, R. (1982). The Indian in the Dime Novel. *Journal of American Culture*, 5(2), 49–55.

Nye, R. (1975). *The Unembarrassed Muse: The Popular Arts in America*. Dial Books.

Oates, J. (3 June 1984). The Union Justified the Means. *New York Times Book Review*, 1, 36–37. Retrieved August 3, 2021, from https://www.nytimes.com/1984/06/03/books/the-union-justified-the-means.html.

Optic, O. (1868). *Our Standard-Bearer: Or, The Life of General Ulysses S. Grant*. Lee and Shepard.

Paredes, A. (1990). *George Washington Gomez: Second Edition*. Arte Publico Press.

Parini, J. (2015). *Empire of Self: A Life of Gore Vidal*. Doubleday.

Pearson, E. (1929). *Dime Novels: Or Following an Old Trail in Popular Literature*. Little, Brown, and Co.

Peterfy, M. (2000). Gore Vidal's "Public": Satire and Political Reality in "Visit to a Small Planet, The Best Man," and "An Evening with Richard Nixon." *Amerikastudien / American Studies*, 45(2), 201–218. Retrieved May 26, 2021, from http://www.jstor.org/stable/41157563

Peterson, M. (1994). *Lincoln in American Memory*. Oxford University Press.

Phillips, S. (2000). *First Lady: Reissue Edition*. Avon.

Pizer, D. (1967). Hamlin Garland (1860–1940). *American Literary Realism, 1870–1910*, 1(1), 45–51. Retrieved from http://www.jstor.org/stable/27747561.

Pizer, D. (1958, Winter). Romantic Individualism in Garland, Norris, and Crane. *American Quarterly*, 10(4), 463–475.

Plot, M. (2016). *The Aesthetico-Political: The Question of Democracy in Merleau-Ponty, Arendt, and Rancière*. Bloomsbury Academic.

Poe, E.A (1984a). Four Beasts in One – the Homo-Cameleopard. In Patrick Quinn (Ed.), *Edgar Allan Poe: Poetry and Tales* (pp. 181–188). Library Classics.

Poe, E.A. (1984b). The Man That Was Used Up. In Patrick Quinn (Ed.), *Edgar Allan Poe: Poetry and Tales* (pp. 307–317). Library Classics.

Poe, E. and Butterfield, R. (1955). George Lippard and His Secret Brotherhood. *The Pennsylvania Magazine of History and Biography*, 79(3), 285–309. Retrieved May 20, 2021, from http://www.jstor.org/stable/20088761.

Pudaloff, R. (1983). Cooper's Genres and American Problems. *ELH*, 50(4), 711–727. JSTOR. Retrieved May 7, 2021, from www.jstor.org/stable/2872924.

Radford, J. (1986). Introduction. In Jean Radford (Ed.), *The Progress of Romance: The Politics of Popular Fiction* (pp. 1–20). Routledge.

Radway, J. (1991). *Reading the Romance: Women, Patriarchy, and Popular Literature*. University of North Carolina Press.

Rancière, J. (2014). *Hatred of Democracy: Reprint Edition*. Verso.

Reyes, X.A. (2014). *Body Gothic: Corporeal Transgressions in Contemporary Literature and Horror Film*. University of Wales Press.

Reynolds, D. (2011). *Beneath the American Renaissance: The Subversive Imagination in the Age of Emerson and Melville*. Oxford University Press.

Reynolds, D. (2015). Deformance, Performativity, Posthumanism: The Subversive Style and Radical Politics of George Lippard's The Quaker City. *Nineteenth-Century Literature*, 70(1), 36–64. doi:10.1525/ncl.2015.70.1.36.

Ridgley, J.V. (1974). George Lippard's *Quaker City*: The World of the American Porno Gothic. *Studies in the Literary Imagination, 7*(1), 77–94.

Ringe, D. (1988). *James Fenimore Cooper: Updated Edition*. Twayne Publishers.

Rodgers, D. (2014). *The Work Ethic in Industrial America 1850–1920*. University of Chicago Press.

Rosanvallon, P. (2018). *Good Government: Democracy Beyond Elections*. Trans. Malcolm DeBevoise. Harvard University Press.

Roth, P. (2004). *The Plot Against America*. Vintage.

Rudalevige, A. (2006). *The New Imperial Presidency: Renewing Presidential Power after Watergate*. University of Michigan Press.

Sandler, M. (2017). Presidential Purgatories: George Saunders's *Lincoln in the Bardo*. *L.A. Review of Books*. Retrieved April 5, 2021, from https://lareviewofbooks.org/article/presidential-purgatories-george-saunderss-lincoln-in-the-bardo/.

Saum, L. (1972). *Hamlin Garland* and Reform. *South Dakota Review, 10*(4), 36–62.

Saunders, G. (2005). *The Brief and Frightening Reign of Phil*. Berkley Publishing.

Saunders, G. (2018). *Lincoln in the Bardo*. Random House.

Schatz, T. (2009). Film Genre and the Genre Film. In Leo Braudy and Marshall Cohen (Eds.), *Film Theory and Criticism: Seventh Edition* (564–576). Oxford University Press.

Schlesinger Jr., A. (2004). *The Imperial Presidency: Reprint Edition*. Mariner Books.

Schmitt, C. (2014). *Dictatorship*. Trans. Michael Hoelzl and Graham Ward. Polity.

Schmitt, C. (2003). *The "Nomos" of the Earth in the International Law of the "Jus Publicum Europaeum."* Telos Press.

Schmitt, C. (2020). *Political Theology*. Trans. C.J. Miller. Antelope Hill Originals.

Schorer, M. (1962). Afterword. In Mark Schorer (Ed.), *Main-Travelled Roads* (pp. 259–269). Signet Classic.

Schwartz, B. (1987). *George Washington: The Making of an American Symbol*. Free Press.

Senchyne, J. (2012). Bottles of Ink and Reams of Paper: Clotel, Racialization, and the Material Culture of Print. In Cohen L. and Stein J. (Eds.), *Early African American Print Culture* (pp. 140–158). University of Pennsylvania Press. Retrieved May 17, 2021, from http://www.jstor.org.milligan.idm.oclc.org/stable/j.ctt3fhdr3.11

Shaffer, A. (2018). *Hope Never Dies: An Obama Biden Mystery*. Quirk Books.

Shakespeare, W. (2004a). *Julius Caesar: Updated Edition*. Simon & Schuster.

Shakespeare, W. (2004b). *King Lear: Updated Edition*. Simon & Schuster.

Shakespeare, W. (2003). *Macbeth: Updated Edition*. Simon & Schuster.

Shakespeare, W. (2004c). *A Midsummer Night's Dream: Updated Edition*. Simon & Schuster.

Shapira, Y. (2018). *Inventing the Gothic Corpse: The Thrill of Human Remains in the Eighteenth-Century Novel*. Palgrave Macmillan.

Simpson, C. (1941). Hamlin Garland's Decline. *Southwest Review, 26*(2), 223–234. Retrieved August 27, 2021, from http://www.jstor.org/stable/43462626

Skowronek, S. (1997). *The Politics Presidents Make: Leadership from John Adams to Bill Clinton, Revised Edition*. Belknap Press.

Smith, H.N. (2007). *Virgin Land: The American West as Symbol and Myth: Reissued Edition*. Harvard University Press.

Smith, J. (2009). *The Presidents We Imagine: Two Centuries of White House Fictions on the Page, on the Stage, Onscreen, and Online*. University of Wisconsin Press.

Smith, N. (1980). Mexican Stereotypes on Fictional Battlefields: Or Dime Novel Romances of the Mexican War. *Journal of Popular Culture, 13*(3), 526–541.

Snee, B. (2016). *Lincoln Before Lincoln: Early Cinematic Adaptations of the Life of America's Greatest President*. University of Kentucky Press.

Snow, S. (2018). *Commander: Politics of Love*. Sienna Snow.

Spencer, H. (1860). *First Principles*. D. Appleton.

Stavrakakis, Y. (1999). *Lacan and the Political*. Routledge.

Stein, D. (2017). Serial Politics in Antebellum America: On the Cultural Work of the City-Mystery Genre. In Kelleter F. (Ed.), *Media of Serial Narrative* (pp. 53–73). Ohio State University Press. doi:10.2307/j.ctv10crd8x.7.

Stolberg, S. (2006, December 24). The Decider. *The New York Times*.

Stone, I. (1954). *Love Is Eternal*. Doubleday.

Stone, I. (1951). *The President's Lady: A Novel about Rachel and Andrew Jackson*. Rutledge Hill Press.

Stone, I. (1965). *Those Who Love: A Biographical Novel about Abigail and John Adams*. Doubleday.

Stout, R. (1934). *The President Vanishes*. Jove Books.

Streeby, S. (2002). *American Sensations: Class, Empire, and the Production of Popular Culture*. University of California Press. Retrieved May 20, 2021, from http://www.jstor.org/stable/10.1525/j.ctt1ppppr.

Streeby, S. (1996). Haunted Houses: George Lippard, Nathaniel Hawthorne, and Middle-Class America. *Criticism, 38*(3), 443–472. Retrieved May 20, 2021, from http://www.jstor.org/stable/23118109.

Suskind, R. (2004, October 17). Faith, Certainty and the Presidency of George W. Bush. *The New York Times*.

Talaraich-Vielmas, L. (2013). Sensation Fiction and the Gothic. In Andrew Mangham (Ed.), *The Cambridge Companion to Sensation Fiction* (pp. 21–33). Cambridge University Press.

Tatum, J. (1992). The *Romanitas* of Gore Vidal. In Jay Parini (Ed.), *Gore Vidal: Writer Against the Grain* (pp. 199–221). Columbia University Press.

Taylor, W. (1985). Comment on "Hamlin Garland's Decline from Realism." In Charles L.P. Silet et al. (Eds.), *The Critical reception of Hamlin Garland, 1891–1978* (pp. 171–178). Whitston Publishers.

Thayer, W. (1882). *From Pioneer Home to the White House*. Hurst.

Trachtenberg, A. (2007). *The Incorporation of America: Culture and Society in the Gilded Age*. Hill and Wang.

Trites, R. (2000). *Disturbing the Universe: Power and Repression in Adolescent Literature*. University of Iowa Press.

Tucker, N. (2015). *The Partisan Leader: A Tale of the Future*. CreateSpace Independent Publishing.

Tyler, M. (1899). *Patrick Henry*. Houghton Mifflin.

Van Haute, P. (2001). *Against Adaptation: Lacan's Subversion of the Subject*. Other Press.

Vidal, G. (2002). *The American Presidency.* Odonian Press.

Vidal, G. (1998). *The Best Man: Revised Edition.* Dramatists Play Service.

Vidal, G. (1972). *An Evening with Richard Nixon.* Random House.

Vidal, G. (2004). *Inventing a Nation: Washington, Adams, Jefferson.* Yale University Press.

Vidal, G. (1984). *Lincoln: A Novel.* Random House.

Vidal, G. (2019). *Myra Breckenridge: Vintage International Edition.* Vintage.

Vidal, G. (1977a). President and Mrs. U.S. Grant. In Gore Vidal (Ed.), *Matters of Fact and Fiction (Essays 1973 - 1976): Second Edition* (pp. 175–191). Random House.

Vidal, G. (1977b). The State of the Union. In Gore Vidal (Ed.), *Matters of Fact and Fiction (Essays 1973 - 1976): Second Edition* (pp. 265–285). Random House.

Vidal, G. (1992). *Screening History.* Harvard University Press.

Vidal, G. (1993). Theodore Roosevelt: An American Sissy. In Gore Vidal (Ed.), *United States: Essays 1952 - 1992* (pp. 723–738). Random House.

Vivanco, L. (2016). *Pursuing Happiness: Reading American Romance as Political Fiction.* Humanities-Ebooks.

Vonnegut, K. (1999). *Slapstick; Or, Lonesome No More!* Dial Press.

Weber, M. (1994). Parliament and Government in Germany under a New Political Order. In Peter Lassman and Ronald Speirs (Eds.), *Weber: Political Writings* (pp. 130–272). Cambridge University Press.

West, E. (2012). The Enigmatic "Clear Black" in William Wells Brown's "Clotel." *CLA Journal, 56*(2), 170–183. Retrieved May 17, 2021, from http://www.jstor .org/stable/44325821

White, R. (1968). *Gore Vidal.* Twayne Publishers.

Williams, L. (2009). Film Bodies: Gender, Genre, and Excess. In Leo Braudy and Marshall Cohen (Eds.), *Film Theory and Criticism: Seventh Edition* (pp. 602–616). Oxford University Press.

Williams, N. (2013). George Lippard's Fragile Utopian Future and 1840s American Economic Turmoil. *Utopian Studies, 24*(2), 166–183.

Williams, R. (2001). *The Long Revolution.* Broadview Press.

Woodworth, F. (1856). *The Young American's Life of Fremont.* Miller, Orton & Mulligan.

Ziff, L. (1981). *Literary Democracy: The Declaration of Cultural Independence in America.* Viking.

Žižek, S. (2009). *The Sublime Object of Ideology: Second Edition.* Verso.

Zoellner, R. (1960). Conceptual Ambivalence in Cooper's Leatherstocking. *American Literature, 31*(4), 397–420. JSTOR. Retrieved May 5, 2021, from www.jstor.org/stable/2922434.

INDEX

Page numbers followed with "n" refer footnotes

11/22/63 (King)   13, 172 n.6

Abbott, Jacob   82–3
Adams, Abigail   117–19
Adams, Henry   8–9
Adams, John   56, 117–19
Adams, William T. *See* Optic, Oliver
ad nauseam 55
Adonai, The Pilgrim of Eternity
    (Lippard)   56
The Adventures of Huckleberry Finn
    (Twain)   124
Agamben, Giorgio   23, 31, 39, 176
    state of exception   28, 28 n.12
Alcott, Louisa May   90
Alger, Horatio   85, 90–5, 100
Altman, Rick   45
ambivalent fiction   100
ambivalent president   89–91
American imperialism   88, 98
American realism   8–9, 121, 122,
    135–6, 138
    covert romance of   124–9
The Americans (James)   128 n.7
Anzaldua, Gloria   10 n.11
Arbuthnot, May Hill   83
Arendt, Hannah   65
Article II of the Constitution   22,
    140, 153

*The Backwoods Boy: Or, the Boyhood
    and Manhood of Abraham
    Lincoln* (Alger)   91–2
Badiou, Alain   106, 112, 194, 195 n.7
Bailey, Dale   47 n.8

Balestier, Wolcott   125, 125 n.6, 136
Baruth, Philip   13–14
Basler, Roy   142
Baudrillard, Jean   152
Beccaria, Cesare   27
Benjamin, Walter   107
Berthoff, Warner   126, 127
The Best Man (Vidal)   150–1, 155–6
Blaine, James G.   125, 125 n.6
Blanche (Lippard)   48–50, 53, 55, 56
Bloom, Harold   142
blue moods of melancholy
    marriage   104–9
bodiless presidents   69–74
Bodnar, John   188
Bolingbroke, Henry St. John, Patriot
    King concept   22–3,
    22 n.7, 33–4
Bonner, Christopher James   64
Boothby, Richard   191
border culture   10 n.11
bourgeois marriage   105–6
Brackenridge, Hugh Henry   5, 6 n.7
Bronfen, Elisabeth   51
Brown, Charles Brockden   5, 47, 49
Brown, Jerry   175
Brown, Rita Mae   104–7
Brown, Wendy   191
Brown, William Wells   9, 16, 61–5
    and Jefferson, Thomas
        bodiless presidents and somatic
            slaves   69–73
        metaphysical musings   65–8
        president, interrupted   76–9
        president without politics   73–6

Bryce, James   7
Bumppo, Natty (character)   24–33, 36, 38
Burke, Edmund   65, 77
Bush, George W.   22, 40, 99, 159, 172 n.6, 177, 194
Bush, H. W.   150, 151
Butler, Judith   182

Carter, Jimmy   177
Castronovo, Russ   55, 64, 69
Cawelti, John   93
Char, René   120
Chase, Kate   145, 148
Chase, Salmon P.   143
Clancy, Tom   13, 14
Clark, Mary Higgins   113
Clay, Henry   63, 68, 75, 104–9, 114
Clinton, Bill   12, 13, 107, 112
Clotel; Or, the President's Daughter (Brown)   61–79, 68 n.3
commander in chief   1–5, 11, 13–15, 23, 24, 41, 46, 62, 65, 67, 79, 84, 92, 94, 100
Commander: The Politics of Love (Snow)   110–11
Cooper, James Fenimore   6, 19–40
Copjec, Joan   15–16, 179, 187
Corlett, William   196 n.8
Crawford, T. Hugh   23
criminality   37
Crumbling Idols (Garland)   130
curious doubleness   196 n.8

The Dark Knight (Nolan)   36–8
The Dead Zone (King)   172–7
democracy   8–9, 14–17, 42, 43, 57–9, 114, 114 n.10, 118, 124, 126, 128, 154–6, 161–2, 165, 171, 191, 194, 196
Denning, Michael   46 n.6, 94
Derrida, Jacques   30
Didi-Huberman, Georges   112
disembodiment   63, 70–1
dispositif concept   176, 177, 179
Dolley (Brown)   104–9
Duncan, King (character)   144

Eisenhower, Dwight D.   151, 152
Ellis, Edward S.   98–9
Ellison, Ralph   159–62
embeddedness   67
Emerson, Ralph Waldo   7–8, 24, 62
entailed inheritance   77
Ernest, John   67
erratic portrait of Grant, Ulysses S.   129–34
Evans, Katy   103–4
An Evening with Richard Nixon (Vidal)   151–4
Executive Orders (Clancy)   13

Fairfax, Sally   113
fascists   166–72
FDR. *See* Roosevelt, Franklin Delano
federalism   64, 65, 68, 69, 77–9
Feldman, Ellen   108–9, 111, 112
feminization, of Washington's body   50–4
fiction   2–3, 113
   of a modern democracy   16–17
Fiore, Jordan D.   91
First Lady (Elizabeth)   111, 112
Ford, Gerald   172–3, 175
Franklin, Benjamin   164
Fremont, John Charles   85–8
Freud, Sigmund   42–3, 45, 187, 189–91, 193, 195
From Canal Boy to President (Alger)   92–5
From Pioneer Home to the White House (Thayer)   96–8
From Tent to White House: Or, How a Poor Boy Became President (Ellis)   98
Frye, Katie   78 n.10

Garfield, James A.   92–5
Garland, Hamlin   121–4, 127–8, 132, 134–8
   American realism   124–9
   depiction of Grant   134
   erratic portrait of Grant, Ulysses S.   129–34, 137 n.14
   literary criticism on   122 n.1, 130

realism 130–2, 134
romance 130–2
Spencerian approach 130
Veritism 130 n.12
Gauchet, Maurice 65
George Washington Gomez
(Americo) 10–11
global capitalism 194
Goodrich, Samuel G. 82, 83
Gothic 52 n.13
body and soul 45–50
Gothicism 46, 49, 52, 56
The Grand Design (Passos) 170–1
Grant, Ulysses S. 89–90, 121–3, 125,
127–8, 131–8
Greenberg, David 152, 176

Haggerty, George E. 45
Hamilton, Alexander 2, 3, 22 n.5
Hamlet (Shakespeare) 144, 148, 155
Hamlet, Prince 143–4
Han, Byung-Chul 113
Harrison, William Henry 42, 62,
75, 115
Harvey Birch 33–6, 38, 39
Hawthorne, Nathaniel 7, 131, 137
Hayes, Rutherford B. 125
Henry, Patrick 164
heroism 37
Heyward, Duncan 29–32
Hofstadter, Richard 160
Honest Abe. *See* Lincoln, Abraham
Hoover, Herbert 99
Hope Never Dies (Shaffer) 81
Horvat, Srecko 105, 109
Howells, William Dean 122, 124–6,
136, 137

Illouz, Eva 102
imperial presidents/presidency 159–
66, 168–79, 181–3
"imperiled" presidency 173
interpersonal romance 114
Invisible Man (Ellison) 159–62
Irving, Washington 5, 22 n.6
It Can't Happen Here (Lewis) 167–
9, 173

Jackson, Andrew 5–8, 14, 62, 67,
115–17, 164, 165
Jackson, Rachel 115–17
James, Henry 128 n.7
Jameson, Fredric 90
Jefferson, Thomas 5, 22, 61–5,
69–73, 169
bodiless presidents and somatic
slaves 69–73
liberalism 77
meta-executive 65–8
president, interrupted 76–9
president without politics 73–6
Jessup, Doremus 167–71
Johnson, Lyndon B. 159, 172, 173
Julius Caesar (Shakespeare) 143

Kamble, Jayashree 106 n.5
Kantorowicz, Ernst 57
Kaplan, Amy 126–7
Kazin, Alfred 124
Kennedy, John F. 12, 13, 151–2, 174
King, Stephen 13, 14, 172–3,
172 n.6, 175, 181, 182
King Lear (Shakespeare) 143

lasting love 109–13
The Last of the Mohicans
(Cooper) 27, 29–31
Leatherstocking tales 25–7, 31
Le Bon, Gustave 170
Lefort, Claude 16, 59
left-wing melancholia 107, 110, 111,
114, 119
Lewinsky, Monica 112
Lewis, Richard O. 78
Lewis, Sinclair 167–70, 173,
181, 182
liberalism 27, 28, 76, 77
liberal universalism 63, 66–8, 74
Life of Fremont (Woodworth) 85
The Life of Washington
(Goodrich) 82
Lincoln (Vidal) 141–9, 145 n.3, 156
Lincoln, Abraham 12, 91–2, 96–8,
115, 121, 125, 134, 135,
142–50, 156, 164

fictional 188, 196
historical 187, 194
melancholia 185–96
as metaphor 191–3
official and vernacular
culture 188–9
symbol of nationality 186
Lincoln, Mary 145
Lincoln in the Bardo
(Saunders) 185–96
Lindbergh, Charles 176–81
Lippard, George
democracy 59
and Washington, George
feminization of 50–4
Gothic depictions of 41–51,
55, 58
reincarnation of 54–9
Lipsitz, George 74
Locke, John, prerogative concept
21–2, 22 n.5
Looby, Christopher 43–4
love
lasting 109–13
and politics 111–12, 116
presidential 109–20
Love is Eternal (Stone) 114–15
Lucy (Feldman) 108–9
lasting love 109–10, 112

Macbeth (Shakespeare) 144–5,
145 n.3
Macbeth, King 144–5
Macbeth, Lady 145, 146
McCann, Sean 5, 180
McConnell, Michael 164
McGovern, George 175
McGowan, Todd 36–7
Machiavelli, Niccolo 148–9
McKinley, William 98, 99
McLane, Howard 127, 128
McWilliams, John 19–20, 37
Madera, Judith 70
Madison, Dolley 104–6
Madison, James 2, 22 n.5,
104–7
Magua (character) 29–32, 38
Mailer, Norman 156

Main-Travelled Roads
(Garland) 127–8
Manifest Destiny 131–2, 135
Marmaduke Temple 25–9
melancholy marriage, blue moods
of 104–9
Melville, Herman 7, 7 n.10, 8
Mencken, H.L. 102, 156, 170,
175, 181
Mercer, Lucy 108–10
metaphors 68, 78, 191–5
Mexican War 131, 134, 135
A Midsummer Night's Dream
(Shakespeare) 142, 146–7
Miller, Charles 122
Milton, Henry 12
Modern Chivalry
(Brackenridge) 5, 5 n.7
Morone, James A. 162
Mount Vernon Love Story
(Clark) 113
Mr. President (Evans) 103–4
Mussell, Kay 102
Myra, Ovidian 141
Myra Breckenridge (Vidal) 141

Nackenoff, Carol 91
Nancy, Jean-Luc 111
Napoleonic president 87–8
Neilson, Heather 153
Nelson, Dana 3, 176
Neutrality Proclamation in
1793 22 n.5
Newlin, Keith 122
Nichols, Roger L. 95
Nixon, Richard 22, 151–3, 157, 159,
167, 172–5, 182
Nolan, Christopher 36
nomos 26, 27
Norton (imperial president) 159,
160, 162
*Notions of the Americans: Picked
Up by a Travelling Bachelor
Volume II* (Cooper) 34 n.14
Nye, Russell 85

Obama, Barack 40, 81, 107,
111, 194

Optic, Oliver 85, 89–91, 95
organizational politics 111, 115
Orwell, George 170
Our Standard-Bearer: Or, The Life of General Ulysses S. Grant (Adams) 89

Paredes, Americo 9–11
The Partisan Leader: A Tale of the Future (Tucker) 163–6
Passos, Dos 170–1, 173, 181, 182
patriotic triumphalism 187
Patriot King 22–3, 22 n.7, 29, 30, 33–4, 39, 40
permanent democracy 114
Peterson, Merrill 186
Pierce, Franklin 7, 131
The Pilot (Cooper) 32 n.13
The Pioneers (Cooper) 25–8
Pizer, Donald 130
The Plot Against America (Roth) 176–83
Poe, Edgar Allan 6, 51, 147
popular romance 102–4, 106 n.5, 112–20
   seminal critics of 103 n.3
post-imperial presidency prophets 172–5
POTUS. *See* President of the United States (POTUS)
presidentialism 3–4, 15, 114, 176, 179, 193, 195
presidential love 109–20
presidential melancholia of Lincoln, Abraham 185–96
presidential prerogative 21–2, 22 n.5, 37 n.16
presidential reincarnation of Washington, George 54–9
presidential unconscious 175–83
The President is Missing! (Milton) 12
President of the United States (POTUS) 2–4, 7, 62, 65, 68, 76, 79, 81–3, 88, 91, 95, 99, 126, 147, 163, 168, 196
   democracy and 14–17
   fictional 3–4, 11–17, 39, 43, 44, 63, 77, 79, 92, 99, 100, 119

staging 148–52
presidents in American fiction 17
   history of 4–9
The President's Lady (Stone) 115–17
The President Vanishes (Stout) 11–12
The Prince (Machiavelli) 149
prison-house of genre 95–9
prophylactic remoteness 156
pseudo-biographies 89–95, 98–9, 121, 123, 127, 129

The Quaker City (Lippard) 47

radical democracy 42, 43
Ragged Dick (Alger) 91
Rancière, Jacques 112, 155, 161
Randolph, Edmund 168
Reagan, Ronald 140
realism 91, 129–34, 168
   American 8–9, 121, 122, 135–6, 138
   covert romance 124–9
Reynolds, David S. 44, 44 nn.3–4
Richard III (Shakespeare) 143
Ridgley, J. V. 46 n.7
Ringe, Donald 31
Rodgers, Daniel T. 84
romance 102, 136
   misreading of 113–14
   popular (*see* popular romance)
   realism and 129–31, 134, 138
romanticism 122 n.3, 124, 130–1
Roosevelt, Eleanor 108, 110
Roosevelt, Franklin Delano 12, 108–10, 164, 166–7, 169–71, 177, 178, 180–2
Rosanvallon, Pierre 3, 113–14, 114 n.10
Roth, Philip 176–83, 192
Royal Christology 57–8
royal phantasmagoria 59
Russell, William 151, 155

Sartre, Jean-Paul 71
Saunders, George 185 n.1
   and Lincoln's melancholy 185–96
Schlesinger, Arthur Jr. 164
Schmitt, Carl 25, 27, 28

Schwartz, Barry   20
Seth Jones; Or, The Captives of the Frontier (Ellis)   98
Seward, William H.   143, 148
Shaffer, Andrew   81
Shakespeare, William   141–50, 155
Simpson, Claude   129
Slapstick; Or, Lonesome No More! (Vonnegut)   176
slavery   70, 75, 97
Smith, Henry Nash   24 n.9, 97
Smith, Jeff   2, 3
Smith, John   174
Smith, John A. B. C.   6
Snow, Sienna   110–11
somatic slaves   69–73
sovereignty   6 n.8, 22–8, 30–3
Spencer, Herbert   130 n.11
The Spy (Cooper)   19–21, 27, 32–9
state of exception   25–32, 36–9
Stillson, Greg   173–5
Stone, Irving   114–19
Stout, Rex   11–12
sui generis   29, 113, 134
Swain, Wilbur Rockefeller   176

Thayer, William Makepeace   96
Theodore Tinker. *See* Woodworth, Francis C.
Those Who Love (Stone)   117–19
Tocqueville, Alexis de   162
Todd, Mary   114–15, 145, 146
Tonkin Golf Resolution   172 n.5
Trachtenberg, Alan   125–6
transcendentalism   85–7
Trump, Donald   111–12, 151, 157, 159, 167, 179, 182, 188–90, 194
Tucker, Nathaniel Beverley   163–6, 182
    imperial president   165
    paradoxical construct of the presidency   166

Ulysses S. Grant: His Life and Character (Garland)   121–5, 127, 129, 131–8

"Up the Coulee: A Story of Wisconsin"   127, 128, 132

Van Buren, Martin   12, 42, 75, 163, 165–6
Vidal, Gore   139–42, 148–50, 167
    democracy   154
    Lincoln as Shakespearean president   142–9
    presidents   153–4, 156
    staging the President of the United States   148–52
    study of lonely decomposition   157
Vivanco, Laura   102
Vonnegut, Kurt   176

Walker, Daniel   6 n.8
War of 1812   105, 107
Washington, George   19–24, 26, 31–9, 62, 82, 83, 105, 113, 151–4, 186
    feminization of the body   50–4
    incarnation of   54–9
    Lippard's Gothic depictions of   41–50
    Neutrality Proclamation in 1793   22 n.5
Watergate scandal   174
Webster, Daniel   72
Weems, Parson   10
West, Elizabeth   78
Wheatley, Phillis   71
whiteness   66, 67, 74
Wieland; Or, The Transformation: An American Tale (Brown)   47
Williams, Raymond   121, 134
Wilson, Woodrow   108
Windrip, Buzz   167–9, 173
Woodworth, Francis C.   84–7, 100
    and Napoleonic president   87–8

The X-President (Baruth)   13–14

The Young American's Life of Fremont (Woodworth)   85–7